ZONES OF ENCUENTRO

Global Latin/o Americas

FREDERICK LUIS ALDAMA AND LOURDES TORRES, SERIES EDITORS

ZONES OF ENCUENTRO

LANGUAGE AND IDENTITIES IN NORTHERN NEW MEXICO

Lillian Gorman

THE OHIO STATE UNIVERSITY PRESS
COLUMBUS

Copyright © 2024 by The Ohio State University.
All rights reserved.

Library of Congress Cataloging-in-Publication Data
Names: Gorman, Lillian, 1979– author.
Title: Zones of encuentro : language and identities in northern New Mexico / Lillian Gorman.
Other titles: Global Latin/o Americas.
Description: Columbus : The Ohio State University Press, [2024] | Series: Global Latin/o Americas | Includes bibliographical references and index. | Summary: "Examines articles, historical memoirs, interviews, surveys, and ethnographic data and applies theories of Latinidad to the study of heterogenous linguistic practices, ideologies, and identities among Nuevomexicano-Mexicano families to understand how different New Mexican Latinx groups theorize language and identity"—Provided by publisher.
Identifiers: LCCN 2024024716 | ISBN 9780814215739 (hardback) | ISBN 0814215734 (hardback) | ISBN 9780814283707 (ebook) | ISBN 0814283705 (ebook)
Subjects: LCSH: Mexican Americans—New Mexico—Social conditions. | Hispanic Americans—New Mexico—Social conditions. | Spanish language—Social aspects—New Mexico. | Language acquisition. | Sociolinguistics—New Mexico. | Language and culture—New Mexico.
Classification: LCC F805.M5 G67 2024 | DDC 305.868/720789—dc23/eng/20240805
LC record available at https://lccn.loc.gov/2024024716

Other identifiers: ISBN 9780814259238 (paperback) | ISBN 0814259235 (paperback)

Cover design by adam bohannon
Text composition by Stuart Rodriguez
Type set in Minion Pro

♾ The paper used in this publication meets the minimum requirements of the American National Standard for Information Sciences—Permanence of Paper for Printed Library Materials. ANSI Z39.48-1992.

For Nani and Papa (Ruth and Gilbert Sánchez) and Nani and Papa (Virginia and Robert Gorman Sr.). I am forever proud to be your granddaughter.

CONTENTS

List of Illustrations   ix

Agradecimientos   xi

INTRODUCTION   Encuentros, Desencuentros, and Northern New Mexico Shared Homeplaces   1

CHAPTER 1   Recontact Zones: Generational Complications, Language Recovery, and Transculturations   53

CHAPTER 2   From Language Shift to Language Shaping   86

CHAPTER 3   The Weight of Words: Spanish Language Ideologies, Lexical Choices, and Authenticity in Mexicano/a/x-Nuevomexicano/a/x Families   112

CHAPTER 4   Disjunctures and Difference: Theorizing the Mixed Identities of Mexicano/a/x-Nuevomexicanos/as/xs   139

CHAPTER 5   "The Spanglish Lives We Live": Reframing New Mexican Spanish through Spanglish and Contemplating Ethnolinguistic Futures   165

CONCLUSION   Herencia, Heritage, and Latino/a/x Homes   188

Appendix 1	Interview Guide—English Version	193
Appendix 2	Interview Guide—Spanish Version	205
Bibliography		215
Index		229

ILLUSTRATIONS

FIGURES

FIGURE 1	Map of northern New Mexico	32
FIGURE 2	Family language use patterns of directionality in Guzmán and Molina families	94
FIGURE 3	Family language use patterns of directionality in Quintana, Medina, Maestas, and Jurado families	95
FIGURE 4	Family language use patterns of directionality in Loredo and Navarro families	95
FIGURE 5	Family language use patterns of directionality in Fierro and Santos families	96

TABLES

TABLE 1	US Census 2020 population figures for northern New Mexico cities and towns	34
TABLE 2	Family names and demographics	49

AGRADECIMIENTOS

Zones of Encuentro is a project nearly thirteen years in the making, and I am deeply grateful for the many levels of support I have received over these years. This project is largely about home (homemaking, homework, and homeplaces), and I want to thank the ten participating families for welcoming me into their homes, for the feeling of home created in our conversations, and for challenging me to see home from new viewpoints. I thank you for sharing your time, for trusting me to share your stories, and for your vulnerability. I want to acknowledge that two participants have passed away since their participation in this research. I hope your family members hear your voices and feel your presence through these pages.

Through various stages of this research, Las Vegas, New Mexico, has served as a homebase and a homeplace. I want to thank my colleagues and friends with the Programa de Inmersión para Maestros Bilingües at New Mexico Highlands University: Loretta Salazar, Sara Harris, Merryl Kravitz, and Alice Menzor. Thank you for your encouragement and for the opportunity to stay connected to the Las Vegas community. I thank my cousins Frank and Cathy Aragón for always providing a home for me in Las Vegas (especially when I was no longer living there!) and to close friends Tina Tapia, Carolina Martínez, Eric and Renee Romero, and María Montoya. I also thank my elder cousin Dolores "Lola" Alire (1908–2008) for sharing so many family stories of our antepasados and forever connecting me to Las Vegas.

I am indebted to a few amazing northern New Mexican educators who shared important insights and allowed me to talk through my ideas for this project, including María Cristina García, Dabi García, Elena Valdez, Rena Stone, Carla Pacheco, and Brenda Ortega. Additionally, the insights, friendship, and mentorship of John LeDoux (1970–2022) have been invaluable both to this project and to my career in academia—que en paz descanses, amigo querido. I still turn to your words for encouragement.

Also, I want to thank Kim Potowski, Richard Cameron, and Alejandro Madrid for their guidance in the initial stages of this project. Additionally, I am grateful to Sandra Nielson, Edith Tovar, Jessica Amashta, and Nancy Domínguez-Fret for their assistance in the tedious task of transcription.

The community of the Linguistic Ethnography Forum (LEF) and the sixth Explorations in Ethnography, Language and Communication conference at Södertörn University in 2016 played a key role in encouraging me to think of my research in new ways. A portion of the content in chapter 4 appeared in the article "(Dis)Connecting U.S. Latina/o Cultural Identities and Language: The Case of Mexican-Nuevomexicano Families in Northern New Mexico," published as part of the seventh issue of the Södertörn Discourse Studies series, *Explorations in Ethnography, Language and Communication: Capturing Linguistic and Cultural Diversities*. I am grateful for the opportunity to draw attention to US Latino/a/x linguistic realities within the field of linguistic ethnography through my article's inclusion in the series.

I give a special thanks to Gabriel Meléndez for his generous support as director of the Center for Regional Studies at the University of New Mexico and for the Center for Regional Studies Scholar in Residence award during the semester of spring 2020. Despite the shutdowns due to the first months of the COVID-19 pandemic, the CRS fellowship allowed for protected time to reconnect with my writing and research for *Zones of Encuentro*. I also thank Shari Montoya for the use of her casita during this period.

Over the past ten years, Michelle Boyd has provided precious writing support through the UIC Write Out! Program, one-on-one coaching, and virtual writing retreats through her InkWell Writing Retreats program. I thank Michelle for creating a platform designed with scholars of color in mind, as well as Roxanne Donovan's Well Academic. Both have been crucial to the development of *Zones of Encuentro*.

I want to express my sincerest thanks to my editor at the Ohio State University Press, Kristen Elias Rowley, for her relentless support. Your flexibility, patience, and commitment to Latinx scholarship is rare and truly appreciated. I am also extremely thankful to Global Latin/o Americas series editor Lourdes Torres—thank you for your belief in this project, and in me! I also thank the reviewers of this book for their generous time commitment and comments.

Thank you to my colleagues at the University of Arizona who have provided guidance and mentorship: Santa Arias, Ana M. Carvalho, Javier Durán, Faith Harden, Sonia Colina, Carmen King de Ramirez, Leah Durán, and Kaitlin Murphy. Also, I am thankful to Jina Yoon and the Minority Women's Faculty Group at the University of Arizona for creating a space for femtorship and much-needed writing retreats in the desert and the mountains.

I have worked in what I call "the HSI world" for more than twenty years, both with the federal government and within Hispanic Serving Institutions. The commitment that Marla Franco, Andrea Romero, and Judy Márquez-Kiyama have shown to truly creating an environment of "servingness" for Hispanic/Latina faculty at the University of Arizona is unparalleled. Thank you for crafting a space for a Chicana professor to thrive. I am especially grateful for the UA HSI Fellows Program and my fellow fellows Melissa Dye, Lyn Durán, Desiree Vega, Karina Rodríguez, and Adrián Arroyo. I am also thankful for the Adalberto and Ana Guerrero Center at the University of Arizona and its leadership with Elizabeth Soltero, Dominique Calza, and Índira Arce for creating a Latinx homeplace on campus for my students and me. I want to give a special note of thanks to Sr. Adalberto Guerrero for his mentorship and friendship. Also, within the larger Tucson community, I thank the Hispanic Leadership Institute (HLI) and my HLI Tucson class of 2016 for welcoming a New Mexico Chicana recién llegada de Chicago to Tucson.

I am fortunate to have a special group of long-time mentors/friends who have stayed present with me through many stages of my academic journey. Thank you to Enrique Lamadrid, Richard Pineda, Glenn Martínez, and John Nieto-Phillips. Also, to Frances R. Aparicio—I am deeply grateful for your unwavering support, friendship, and enthusiastic belief in me and my work. Your extraordinarily generous mentorship provides a model I strive to embody, and your vision of Latino/a/x studies and the politics of language has forever impacted my scholarly trajectory. De todo corazón, thank you.

I have also been blessed with a trifecta of chingonas en Arizona who have made it possible for me to survive and thrive en este pedacito del desierto—thank you, Anita Huizar-Hernández, Martiza Cárdenas, and Michelle Téllez. I also thank my amazing network of academic comadres y compadres for your friendship: MaryAnn Parada, Jessica Rodríguez, José Quintana, Martín Ponti, Vanessa Fonseca-Chávez, and Xavier Medina.

I am grateful for the opportunity to have taught hundreds of students in Spanish as a Heritage Language classes and Latina/o/x studies classes in New Mexico, Chicago, and Tucson over the past twenty years. I thank my students at UNM, NMHU, UIC, Daley College, and the University of Arizona for sharing your knowledge and inspiring my research. In particular, I thank former students Xochilt Montaño and Gabrielle Yocupicio for their tireless commitment to nurturing cultural and linguistic pride in Latinx students in the borderlands. I am also extremely grateful for my academic comadre, hermanamiga, and former student Myrriah Gómez as we have navigated academia together un día a la vez.

My familia of friends in Chicago have sustained a support network for me during my graduate studies and beyond. Thank you to mis hermanas del alma en Chicago Juanita del Toro, Jennie Rosas, and Nancy Domínguez-Fret for your friendship and love. Juanita, thank you for always making sure I have a Chicago home in which to live, work, and write. I also thank Julio Puentes, Luvia Moreno, Tom Howard, Theresa Christenson Caballero, Amanda Cortés, and fellow Nuevomexicano Eric García for your consistent friendship and support during this journey. Additionally, I thank my comadres, the ladies of Puntadas del alma quilting group with the National Museum of Mexican Art, Dolores Mercado, María Tortolero, Mary Herrera, Christina Carlos, Socorro Carlos, Carina Yepez, Lucy Campos, and Martha Domínguez.

Also, thank you to Our Lady of the Most Holy Rosary parish in Albuquerque, Immaculate Conception parish in Las Vegas, Good Shepherd parish in Little Village, Chicago, the UIC Newman Center, and Abbot Joel and the Santa María de la Vid Norbertine Abbey in Albuquerque for providing nurturing community and spiritual spaces for my work.

My family has laid a precious foundation of love, support, and inspiration for this book. I am endlessly grateful for this foundation that has sustained me through this yearslong process. Thank you to my aunts, uncles, and cousins, who support me through your sincere interest in my work. Thank you to my aunt Peggy Martínez and Aunt Shea Gorman for taking special care to walk with me through the ups and downs of my scholarly life while also serving as caregivers in our familia. Thank you to my uncle Richard Gorman (1953–2014) for your special words of encouragement—and tough love! I miss our long chats about northern New Mexico. I am fortunate to have my primas Bernadette Cornelison and Marissa Sánchez in Tucson—thank you for the prima love!

Thank you to my partner, Baltazar Campos, for walking with me through every challenge and joy of this book-writing process. Thank you for your patience, for listening when I needed to talk out my ideas, for listening when I needed to vent, and for sharing your insights about my research. Gracias por tu amor. También, les doy mis más sinceras gracias a mis suegros la Señora Teresa Campos y el Señor Baltazar Campos Sr. por el apoyo constante y un hogar en Chicago. And a special thanks to three special canine babies who provided much-needed emotional support during this process. Thank you to Dusty and Carnittas for opening my heart. And thank you to my Chuy for six years of love.

Thank you to my sisters Sarah and Stephanie for your genuine interest and consistent love and support. My parents, Robert and Cathy Gorman, have been the number one champions of my research and scholarly journey. This book would most certainly never have come to fruition without my mom's daily words of encouragement, her passionate words of defense when perceiving any academic slights, and her steady presence. And at every turn, my dad has provided advice, countered my insecurities, offered suggestions, and was the first to read the draft of *Zones of Encuentro*. My dad has always been a caretaker of our Nuevomexicano/Chicano culture, and I am grateful for his lessons and example.

I am blessed beyond words to still be able to sit down at the kitchen table and visit with Nani, my ninety-three-year-old grandma Virginia (Montoya) Gorman. Full of spirit and wisdom, she provides an unconditional abuelita love, and her insights about "our raza" continue to guide my work. I am eternally grateful for Papa, my grandpa Gilbert Sánchez (1924–2015), his belief in me, and our daily conversations during the initial stages of *Zones of Encuentro*. My grandma, my Nani, Ruth (Aragón) Sánchez (1929–2009) fiercely supported me in every way, and I am thankful to still feel her guidance while I navigate this academic life. My grandparents are my first reference points for what it is to be Nuevomexicano/a. Their everyday lived language experiences in Santa Fe, Taos, Albuquerque's South Valley, and Belén continuously inform *Zones of Encuentro* and orient my scholarly and personal life.

INTRODUCTION

Encuentros, Desencuentros, and Northern New Mexico Shared Homeplaces

> We were raised in a bicultural home with subtle differences in the Mexican and Spanish subcultures in our house. ... Dad was the only native Mexican in town for many years, so there was lots of finger pointing at us for being "different." Yet, owing to Mom's heritage, we knew we belonged.
>
> —Mari Luci Jaramillo, *Madam Ambassador*

On November 5, 2005, the front page of the *Albuquerque Journal* reported "Tensions among Hispanic Groups Erupt in Schools." The article described a lunchtime cafeteria fight at Capital High School in Santa Fe and explained that "school district officials [were] interpreting the clash as part of long-brewing tensions between 'Hispanics'—northern New Mexico natives—and 'Mexicans' that exist in Santa Fe and other parts of New Mexico."[1] It further reported on efforts to resolve a feud "brewing between 25 girls whose families were native to Santa Fe and others whose families were from Mexico" at a Santa Fe middle school. The article discussed statewide opinions regarding immigration and reported on focus groups in which "native Hispanics express concern about Spanish-speaking immigrants taxing the resources of the school system with their special needs and requirements, particularly language-barrier issues." Given the context of conflict depicted in the article, Mari Luci Jaramillo's "bicultural home" described in the epigraph above stands in contrast to these contentious encounters. Nevertheless, Jaramillo's experience speaks to a history of Mexican immigrant and New Mexican Hispanic interactions from more than sixty years ago and represents an understudied archive of Mexicano-Nuevomexicano relationships in northern New Mexico.

---

1. Guzmán, "Tensions among Hispanic Groups."

Discussions around internal differences within the New Mexico Hispanic or Latino/a/x population have been largely absent in previous research and in demographic accounts of the state's population. Both the 2010 and 2020 US Census[2] numbers reflect a majority Hispanic or Latino/a/x population in the state of New Mexico. The *Albuquerque Journal*'s August 12, 2021, headline reports that "At Nearly Half the Population, New Mexico Still Most Latino State."[3] With 47.7 percent of the state's population claiming Latino/a/x or Hispanic ethnicity, Latinos/as/xs or Hispanics in the state outnumber all other ethnic groups. These demographics have remained relatively constant throughout New Mexico's existence as a state. Yet, these numbers do not highlight the specificities within the Latino/a/x population of New Mexico. Very little research on New Mexico has acknowledged the heterogeneity within the state's Latino/a/x communities, and no research has addressed mixed Latino/a/x families and their children in northern New Mexico. *Zones of Encuentro* takes an in-depth look at the cultural and linguistic interactions between two distinct Latino/a/x communities in northern New Mexico: Nuevomexicanos/as/xs and first-generation Mexicano/a/x immigrants. The *Albuquerque Journal* article refers to these two groups as "Hispanics" or "native Hispanics" and "Mexicans," while Mari Luci Jaramillo describes these groups as "Spanish" and "Mexican."[4] In *Zones of Encuentro*, I denote these populations by employing the terms "Mexicano/a/x" to describe first-generation immigrant populations from Mexico and "Nuevomexicano/a/x" for the Hispanic population in northern New Mexico who traces its presence in northern New Mexico back to Spanish colonial times, before Mexican independence.[5] My use of the "o/a/x" accounts for gender inclusivity and nonbinary gender identities.[6] I also use the term "Mexicano-Nuevomexicano" to describe the mixed family units that are the focus of this study and to refer to the context of these interactions in general.

---

2. See United States Census 2020. http://quickfacts.census.gov/qfd/states/35000.html.
3. Lee, "Nearly Half."
4. Guzmán, "Tensions among Hispanic Groups"; M. L. Jaramillo, *Madam Ambassador*, 18.
5. A more in-depth context for the term "Nuevomexicano" is provided in a later section of this introductory chapter.
6. I use "o/a/x" rather than "x" in the spirit of the discussion in de Onís, "'What's in an X?,'" 90, in which Pérez explains that the term Latinx "brings new, diverse, politically resistant subjects into existence against imperialist containment," and that we're asked to stand alongside each other. The o/a/x embodies this solidarity. I also acknowledge, as Alan Pelaez López's article "The X in Latinx" reminds us, that the "X" is not meant to be for everyone. The "X" is not to be normalized as a term for all or to neutralize the struggles, wounds, and identities within the X. In short, *Zones of Encuentro* does not employ Latinx, Nuevomexicanx, or Mexicanx as umbrella terms so as to homogenize identities or take the power away from the "X."

PART 1: ETHNOGRAPHIC STARTING POINTS AND NECESSARY CONTEXTS

Contemplating Shared Cultural and Linguistic Homeplaces

When the 2005 *Albuquerque Journal* article came out, I was living and working in Las Vegas, New Mexico. The article underscored realities that my family in Santa Fe had previously expressed to me and debunked my own assumptions that a sizeable Mexicano/a/x immigrant population did not exist in northern New Mexico. Several years later, my family was part of a newsworthy event in Santa Fe that further piqued my interest in the relationships between Nuevomexicanos/as/xs and Mexicanos/as/xs in northern New Mexico. On July 22, 2008, the pastor of Our Lady of Guadalupe parish in Santa Fe was notified that the long-awaited four-thousand-pound, twelve-foot statue of Our Lady of Guadalupe, commissioned by the parish from artist Georgina Farias in Mexico City, was not allowed to continue her journey to Santa Fe. The truck carrying the statue was not able to cross with the sculpture across the Cd. Juárez/El Paso border due improper paperwork for the statue. The *Santa Fe New Mexican* reported on the incident and the "rescue mission"[7] that ensued to secure the detained Virgen de Guadalupe. Yet, the Mexicano-Nuevomexicano solidarity that made the statue's completed journey possible remains untold. It was actually a team of Mexicano/a/x and Nuevomexicano/a/x parishioners that led the effort to recover the statue. After the pastor received the initial phone call alerting him to the problem, my uncle Richard Gorman (a lifelong parishioner of Our Lady of Guadalupe, a Nuevomexicano, and the architect of the space that was to hold the statue) declared, "Let's just go down and get her, Father! And we won't leave until we have her."[8] Hours later, he and two Mexicano staff members from the parish piled into a large pickup truck, hooked a flatbed trailer to the vehicle, and set out to retrieve the undocumented Virgen. The next day, the truck returned with the statue in tow having journeyed along the historical Camino Real to end at the Virgen's new home in Santa Fe. Arriving to welcome her, and assist with the installation, were generations of lifelong Our Lady of Guadalupe Nuevomexicano/a/x parishioners and newer first-generation immigrant Mexicano/a/x parishioners. As in the pickup truck, Nuevomexicanos/as/xs and Mexicanos/as/xs conversed, interacted, and worked side by side to welcome the detained statue. The communicative spaces created in the pickup truck, and during the installation,

---

7. Constable, "Our Lady, Almost Home."
8. Richard Gorman, personal communication.

are part of the understudied Mexicano-Nuevomexicano archive and served as starting points for this book project.

I witnessed these communicative spaces from within my own Nuevomexicana family. I observed my Nuevomexicana grandmother with fellow Mexicano/a/x parishioners conversing in Spanish as they readied the church for the welcoming reception. I listened as my Nuevomexicano uncles spoke more Spanish than I had ever heard them speak as they problem-solved the transport and final bolting down of the statue with Spanish monolingual Mexicano volunteers. I heard discussions in which Nuevomexicanos contemplated the experience of being undocumented and the realities of the border through both the lens of the statue's detainment and the experiences of so many recently arrived Mexicano immigrant parishioners. Just as Mari Luci Jaramillo's memoir provides a counternarrative to the notion of constant conflict between Mexicanos/as/xs and Nuevomexicanos/as/xs, the events surrounding the Virgen's homecoming to Santa Fe underscore the multidimensional nature of these relationships. However, these unifying encounters do not erase the very real tensions that exist within Mexicano/a/x and Nuevomexicano/a/x interactions. There are struggles around belonging in these shared spaces and meeting places.

Jaramillo's narrative addresses a feeling of "belonging" within her northern New Mexico town. Similarly, notions of (un)belonging are at play at Our Lady of Guadalupe parish. Former parishioner and Nuevomexicana Ana Quintana[9] explains, "It doesn't belong to the old people that used to be there, you know. It's all Mexican now, and, you know, I left the parish for that reason. It wasn't home anymore." For Quintana, there is an experience of a home disrupted rather than the unifying experience of a homecoming with the arrival of the statue. She continues, "I remember what the religious celebrations were like as a kid . . . for the Feast of Our Lady of Guadalupe, it was so different than it is now, you know. They definitely brought their culture here and their ideas and, I don't know, . . . it feels foreign." Cristina Durán's research in Albuquerque echoes the ways in which Mexicano/a/x immigrants' "elaborate shrines of the Virgen de Guadalupe could be seen [as] going beyond the simple statue or tile design of the Virgen found in the yards of native-born residents"[10] and perpetuate a sense of unfamiliarity for Nuevomexicanos/as/xs. For some former Our Lady of Guadalupe parishioners who "don't want to go there because it's the Mexican church now" (Rose Jurado,[11] personal interview), there is a foreignness to the once familiar home of the parish.

---

9. Ana Quintana is a participant in this study. The name is a pseudonym.
10. Durán, "Panaderias, peluquerias, y carnicerias," 69.
11. Rose Jurado is a participant in this study. The name is a pseudonym.

Chicana anthropologist Aimee Villarreal reminds us that "home is never as comfortable or settled as it seems. . . . Home embodies multiple tensions, desires, disaffections, and dislocations."[12] This book explores the shifting nature of home among Mexicano/a/x immigrants and Nuevomexicanos/as/xs in northern New Mexico. The parish of Our Lady of Guadalupe serves as a site for starting a conversation around these unsettled Mexicano/a/x and Nuevomexicano/a/x homeplaces. In her essay on Latina immigrant homemaking practices, Verónica Montes asks, "In the context of migration, what does home mean to immigrants? And how do immigrants feel at home?"[13] My project extends Montes's questions and asks, How do Mexicanos/as/xs (Mexican immigrants) and Nuevomexicanos/as/xs feel at home together? I situate *Zones of Encuentro* as "homework" in the spirit of Villarreal's decolonial practice of homeplace ethnography, in which she explains that "homework" not only unsettles home but is also "about the relations that compose a shared homeplace."[14] *Zones of Encuentro* is homework because it documents the unsettled Mexicano/a/x and Nuevomexicano/a/x encounters that shape this homeplace and because, as a Chicana and Nuevomexicana, I am interrogating my home. Additionally, quite literally, this project serves as homework because I am exploring encounters from within the same household while being welcomed into actual Mexicano-Nuevomexicano family homes. Thus, *Zones of Encuentro* contemplates what a shared cultural and linguistic homeplace looks like for Mexicanos/as/xs and Nuevomexicanos/as/xs in northern New Mexico.

Recall that Mari Luci Jaramillo describes her sense of belonging in northern New Mexico as grounded in both her mother's claim to place as a Nuevomexicana and her father's claim to the Spanish language as a Mexicano. Jaramillo's experience underscores the interconnectedness of place, language, and culture. *Zones of Encuentro* undertakes the necessary work of examining the everyday lived language experiences of Mexicanos/as/xs and Nuevomexicanos/as/xs together, specifically through the case of mixed Mexicano-Nuevomexicano families like Jaramillo's family. Glenn Martínez and Richard Train describe "language experience" as

> the multiple layered, positioned and particular language experiences of Latinxs in relation and in tension with group experiences. . . . Language experience is a complex of dynamic, tension-filled sites of locally embodied particularities, relationalities, positionalities and subjectivities that are

---

12. Villarreal, "Anthropolocura as Homeplace Ethnography," 198.
13. Montes, "Mujeres luchadoras," 97.
14. Villarreal, "Anthropolocura as Homeplace Ethnography," 199, 197.

woven into our human experiencing, languaging and translanguaging, as we live in the world.[15]

Martínez and Train stress that the two concepts (language and experience) are interconnected and that there is no divorcing language from context. They elaborate, "We reject reducing language experience to either 'language' or 'experience' or 'languages' and 'experiences.'"[16] I position *Zones of Encuentro* as an interdisciplinary ethnographic study of mixed Mexicano-Nuevomexicano families that centers on their language experiences and ethnolinguistic identities. Michael Silverstein explains ethnolinguistic identity as

> a fact of a psychosocial sort that has emerged where people ascribe a certain primordiality to language and a certain consequentiality to language difference. They consider it for one or another cultural reason to be a guide to socially meaningful differences among people and to people's socially effective membership in groups.[17]

Silverstein highlights the central roles of language and language difference in the formation of cultural identities. *Zones of Encuentro* highlights the ways in which Mexicanos/as/xs and Nuevomexicanos/as/xs conceptualize these differences within the context of their language experiences. Accordingly, *Zones of Encuentro* takes an in-depth look at the cultural and linguistic interactions between Nuevomexicanos/as/xs and first-generation Mexicano/a/x immigrants residing in northern New Mexico by looking at the intersecting language experiences and ethnolinguistic identities of mixed Mexicano-Nuevomexicano families. Specifically, I explore family units with one Mexicano/a/x parent, one Nuevomexicano/a/x parent, and at least one adult or teen mixed Mexicano/a/x-Nuevomexicano/a/x child. Amidst current debates around histories and heritage in New Mexico,[18] I contend that these families' language experiences diversify the narratives that comprise New Mexico Hispanic and/or Latino/a/x histories and allow for new ways of thinking about home. Through a critical reading of semistructured sociolinguistic interviews, pláticas, and linguistic ethnography with ten mixed Mexicano-Nuevomexicano families in northern New Mexico, I first ask, How do

---

15. Martínez and Train, *Tension and Contention*, 17–18.
16. Martínez and Train, *Tension and Contention*, 18.
17. Silverstein, "Whens and Wheres," 532.
18. See Villarreal, "Coming to Terms"; Valdez, "Ownership and Order"; Fonseca-Chávez, "Contested Querencia"; Contreras, "Spanish Colonial Monuments"; and Montoya and Nieto-Phillips, "Conversation about Oñate."

Mexicanos/as/xs and Nuevomexicanos/as/xs in northern New Mexico define and view themselves and each other, and what role does language experience play in these conceptualizations? Second, I contemplate what factors shape the ethnolinguistic identities of mixed Mexicano/a/x-Nuevomexicano/a/x adult children. To understand how *Zones of Encuentro* addresses these questions, it is critical to understand historical and contemporary claims to identity terms.

Contextualizing the Historical Dimensions of Claiming (Nuevo)Mexicanidad

Chicano/a/x Studies scholar Michael Trujillo makes note in his ethnography of Española, New Mexico that "no term fully captures New Mexican Latino identity and nonidentity,"[19] and in this spirit I acknowledge that my use of identity terms in *Zones of Encuentro* cannot fully encompass the complexities of identity in northern New Mexico. Indeed, one objective of this introduction is to tease out the histories of these imperfect terms. Trujillo also explains that in Española alone he has heard people use the terms "Chicana/o, Spanish, Latina/o, Mexican, Mexicano, *raza,* and *la plebe.* In formal situations, most northern New Mexicans self-identify as Hispanic, Chicano, or Spanish/Spanish American. In contrast, when speaking Spanish, many use terms such as *mexicanos de aquí* (Mexicanos from here)."[20] Trujillo's ethnographic work draws attention to the highly contextual and relational use of identity terms in northern New Mexico. *Zones of Encuentro* makes intentional use of specific identity terms to describe the communities that are the focus of this study, namely, Mexicano/a/x and Nuevomexicano/a/x. Below I outline important historical context around claims to Mexican identity among the communities of northern New Mexico and why, ultimately, Nuevomexicano/a/x is my term of choice.

In an extensive study of the history of Chicano families in the Southwest from 1848 to the present day, Richard Griswold del Castillo notes that "in the nineteenth century a third-generation Mexican-heritage population hardly existed, except among the Hispanos of New Mexico, a group which did not consider itself of Mexican nationality or culture."[21] This group of Hispanos in New Mexico was comprised of more than half (60,000) of the 100,000 inhabitants of the Mexican territory ceded to the US in 1848. According to David Gutiérrez, "Most communities of Mexican origin in the United States

---

19. Trujillo, *Land of Disenchantment,* xv.
20. Trujillo, *Land of Disenchantment,* xv.
21. Griswold del Castillo, *Familia,* 122.

trace their roots to waves of immigration that have occurred throughout the twentieth century. Only a proportionally small number identify with the first group of Mexican-Americans."[22] A majority of the Hispanic population in New Mexico does, in fact, identify with this first group of Mexican Americans. And, as Griswold del Castillo points out, this New Mexican population does not identify with a Mexican nationality.

John Nieto-Phillips elaborates on the historical context of this disassociation from a Mexican national identity: "Mexican independence from Spain in 1821 did not significantly alter the ethnic consciousness of northern New Mexicans, nor did it instill a profound and pervasive Mexican consciousness rooted in national sentiment."[23] There is no doubt that this disassociation was politically motivated in the nineteenth century, as "both Anglo and Nuevomexicano statehood proponents made congressional approval of statehood possible by recasting New Mexico's 'Mexicans' as Spanish in race, culture, and history, and American in citizenship and national loyalty."[24] Most certainly this move in self-representation among Nuevomexicanos/as/xs was also in reaction to the growing national "rhetoric surrounding the 'Mexican problem'" and the fact that "some treaty citizen families sought to distance themselves from Mexican immigrants."[25] This distancing was not necessarily unidirectional. Rosina Lozano explains, "Ethnic Mexican citizens of long standing increasingly distanced themselves from Mexican immigrants and Spanish. This was a defensive move intended to protect their waning political power and way of life. Mexican immigrants often distanced themselves from ethnic Mexican citizens, too, because of cultural differences."[26] Casandra Salgado's recent research reiterates the identification patterns found in Lozano and Nieto-Phillips's historical analysis. After conducting seventy-eight interviews in Albuquerque, Salgado concludes that Nuevomexicanos/as/xs "generally prioritized their roots in the original Spanish settlement of New Mexico to emphasize distinctions in ancestry, nationality, and regionality from Mexican immigrants. . . . Thus, I argue that Nuevomexicanos' enduring claims to Spanish ancestry represent a defensive strategy to enact dissociation from stigmatized Mexican immigrants."[27] Beyond disassociation from Mexican immigrants, Nieto-Phillips highlights that New Mexicans' Spanish identity also served as "the source of collective identification with the land and

---

22. Gutiérrez, "Globalization," 44.
23. Nieto-Phillips, *Language of Blood*, 37–38.
24. Nieto-Phillips, "Spanish American Ethnic Identity," 99.
25. Lozano, *American Language*, 146.
26. Lozano, *American Language*, 147.
27. Salgado, "Mexican American Identity," 179.

with a historical discourse of conquest, settlement, and occupation . . . and a source of ethnic agency as Nuevomexicanos (of various echelons) struggled to reclaim some degree of control over their political destiny and cultural assets."[28] This place-based and historically inflected identity stands in contrast to the post-1848 Mexican national sense of identity developing in Mexico and has historically manifested itself in the use of terms such as Spanish, Spanish American, Hispano, and Hispanic.[29] Scholars of and from these communities also deploy the term "Nuevomexicano," and, as previously mentioned, this is also my term of choice for *Zones of Encuentro*.

As editors of *The Contested Homeland: A Chicano History of New Mexico*, Erlinda Gonzales-Berry and David Maciel explain their use of the term "Nuevomexicano." They state, "When all is said and done this is the label that best identifies a culture and a people whose roots reach deep into the brown earth of their homeland and across its cultural borderlands."[30] Like Gonzales-Berry and Maciel, I believe that the identifier "Nuevomexicano" provides a useful term that captures the deep roots and profound sense of a land-based, place-based identity among this population. This place-based identity predates Mexican rule and extends beyond the moment of US annexation into the present day.[31] Take, for example, Shelly Roberts's 2001 ethnographic study[32] of a small northern New Mexico town. Roberts examines issues of cultural identity among school-age children (K–12). Her students state, "Somos de la tierra," and emphasize that this connection to land is an integral part of their identity. Juan Estevan Arellano has termed this connection as "querencia,"[33] and Rudolfo Anaya extends this deep sense of place in New Mexico toward the notion of a local homeland. He explains, "If we pinpoint all our querencias on a map of New Mexico, they form a grid—millions of querencias connected to each other. This grid is our patria chica, our community, our village. This querencia grid identifies and describes our knowledge and cultura, and it is a great source of power."[34] It is this very real connection to land that motivates the deployment of a regional term such as "Nuevomexicano" and a disassociation

---

28. Nieto-Phillips, *Language of Blood*, 8.
29. The *Albuquerque Journal* article by Guzmán utilizes "native Hispanics" to refer to the Hispanic population in New Mexico who traces its roots back to Spanish colonial times. "Native New Mexicans" is also a commonly used term.
30. Gonzales-Berry and Maciel, "Introduction," 7.
31. See Meléndez, *So All Is Not Lost*; Gonzales-Berry and Maciel, *Contested Homeland*; Lomelí, Sorell, and Padilla, *Nuevomexicano Cultural Legacy*; and Otero, Meléndez, and Lamadrid, *Santa Fe Nativa*.
32. Roberts, *Remaining and Becoming*.
33. Arellano, *Enduring Acequias*.
34. Anaya, "Foreword," xx.

from the term "Mexican" or "Mexicano." This does not imply that those who identify as Mexican or Mexicano/a/x do not have a connection to land. In fact, Pablo Vila emphasizes the regional and land-based identities within Mexico.[35] However, in the context of New Mexico, "Nuevomexicano" refers to a specific connection to a history of land possession and dispossession. Because of this particular connection, *Zones of Encuentro* utilizes "Nuevomexicano/a/x" as the identifier for the Hispanic population in northern New Mexico who traces its presence in northern New Mexico to before Mexican independence.

Scholars such as Laura Gómez and Anthony Mora discourage an isolated analysis of New Mexico that emphasizes regional identities at the expense of drawing larger cultural connections between New Mexico and Mexico. For example, Gómez takes care to deconstruct what she terms "the exceptionalism thesis" among New Mexicans that designates the state's inhabitants as regionally distinctive with an intense, long-standing claim to Spanish, rather than Mexican heritage.[36] Similarly, Mora actively works to reinsert a Mexican identity into New Mexico. Mora uses southern New Mexico (Las Cruces) to complicate the meaning of "Mexican" in New Mexico.[37] He recovers the reality that many New Mexicans, in fact, did actively claim a Mexican national identity. He also troubles the notion that northern Mexico and the southwestern United States developed in isolation from other areas in Mexico. I acknowledge the importance of emphasizing these connections; however, I do not believe that their arguments form the basis for discrediting Hispanic New Mexicans' rejection of the term "Mexican" in favor of labels such as "Spanish," "Hispano," and "Nuevomexicano." The desire among some scholars to "correct" New Mexicans' Spanish or regional identity in favor of the "correct" Mexican identity actually erases Nuevomexicano/a/x agency and imposes an anachronistic historical and political simplicity on their cultural experience. That being said, it is worth noting that even though Nuevomexicanos/as/xs may disassociate themselves from a contemporary Mexican national identity, this does not necessarily mean that they never use the term "Mexican" to self-identify.

Similar to Vila's 2006 study[38] regarding the polysemy of the term "Mexican" on the El Paso/Juárez border, María Dolores Gonzales's study[39] on the construction of identity labels indicates this fluidity in the use of the terms "Mexican" and "mexicano" in New Mexico. Gonzales finds that "all terms

---

35. Vila, *Crossing Borders, Reinforcing Borders*.
36. Gómez, *Manifest Destinies*, 8.
37. A. Mora, *Border Dilemmas*.
38. Vila, "Polysemy of the Label."
39. Gonzales, "Todavía decimos 'Nosotros [los] mexicanos.'"

exist simultaneously; sometimes they are used interchangeably, others in contestation."[40] Gonzales analyzes the simultaneous rejections and uses of the term "Mexican." She documents one participant's opinion: "Semos mexicanos, pero nunca dicíamos Mexican in English because it was bad!"[41] Gonzales finds that some participants reject both the English and Spanish term; however, other participants use the term in Spanish, "mexicano," to describe themselves and to refer to the Spanish language. These findings are similar to Julie Dowling's 2005 study[42] of ethnic labels in Texas. Dowling states, "Although US born interviewees denied that they were Mexican (at times adamantly) the use of the term mexicano/a was acceptable to them in Spanish conversation with co-ethnics in their community."[43] Both Dowling and Gonzales's studies indicate the importance of context and interlocutors when employing the terms "Mexican" and "mexicano." For the purposes of this book, especially given these nuanced uses of the terms "Mexican" and "mexicano," I would like to be clear that when I use the term "Mexicano/a/x" I am referring to the first-generation immigrant population from Mexico in New Mexico.

I would also like to make clear that the Mexican immigrant experience in northern New Mexico has received very little scholarly attention. The significant multigenerational Mexicano/a/x population that does identify with an immigration history from Mexico in New Mexico is oftentimes neglected in academic literature on New Mexico, in favor of scholarship focusing on Nuevomexicanos/as/xs. María Rosa García Acevedo emphasizes that "the flow of population from Mexico to the 'Land of Enchantment' has been constant, even when these immigrants encountered a less than welcoming border. . . . In a state where the Spanish roots of the native Nuevomexicanos have been stressed, the historical role of the Mexican immigrants has been deemphasized and all but forgotten."[44] Cristina Durán's dissertation provides much-needed research around the emergence of Mexican businesses in Albuquerque. She states that through their businesses "Mexicanos are re-creating 'home' as they simultaneously change the landscape. At the same time, Mexican immigrants are making 'home' unrecognizable to native residents through the establishment of shops and storefronts that stand out for their perceived foreignness and even un-American-ness."[45] Her work "breaks an extended silence in

---

40. Gonzales, "Todavía decimos 'Nosotros [los] mexicanos,'" 75.
41. Gonzales, "Todavía decimos 'Nosotros [los] mexicanos,'" 72.
42. Dowling, "'I'm not Mexican.'"
43. Dowling, "'I'm not Mexican,'" 61.
44. García Acevedo, "Forgotten Diaspora," 217, 232.
45. Durán, "Panaderias, peluquerias, y carnicerias," 3.

scholarship on Mexican immigration in New Mexico"[46] and acknowledges García Acevedo's designation of the Mexican immigrant population and their descendants as "the forgotten diaspora" in New Mexico. Many times, this segment of the population of New Mexico is conceptualized as belonging only to the southern region of the state due to its proximity to the border, while northern New Mexico has historically been associated with geographic isolation from Mexico.[47]

Chicano/a/x studies scholar Norma Valenzuela provides an interesting and relevant perspective regarding the presence of Mexicanos/as/xs in New Mexico. Drawing from her personal experience and connecting to her querencia, she reveals, "Mapping the journey of myself and my family allowed me to anchor my querencia and embrace both my Mexicanidad and Chicanidad."[48] Valenzuela theorizes her migration story and her relationship to New Mexico as a Mexicana who has grown into a Chicana identity. She draws parallels between northern Mexicans and northern New Mexicans. She explains, "The Mexican norteños (Northerners) had to learn to survive in a hostile environment far away from Mexico City, and where food and water were as precious as gold. Like the Nuevomexicanos from up north, all we had was the land, our family, community, and traditions."[49] Valenzuela's insights provide a unique perspective regarding Mexicano-Nuevomexicano interactions. Valenzuela challenges static notions of being Mexicana or being Chicana and presents a self-portrait of a Mexicana contextualizing her evolving identity through northern New Mexico. Valenzuela states, "Historically, Chicanas have looked south to make sense of who they are as subjects existing in this region. I, on the other hand, look to northern Nuevo México to provide me with ways to legitimize my positionality within contemporary Albuquerque society."[50] Valenzuela's experience speaks to the understudied ways that northern Mexicanos/as/xs may contextualize their experience and identities in northern New Mexico. Like Valenzuela's account, *Zones of Encuentro* complicates the north/south geographic dichotomy[51] by focusing on the inevitable contemporary cultural and linguistic associations between first-generation Mexicano/a/x immigrants and Nuevomexicanos/as/xs in northern New Mexico.

---

46. Durán, "Panaderias, peluquerias, y carnicerias," 10.
47. Gonzales-Berry and Maciel, "Introduction," 3.
48. Valenzuela, "Mestiza Consciousness a la MeXicana," 182.
49. Valenzuela, "Mestiza Consciousness a la MeXicana," 183.
50. Valenzuela, "Mestiza Consciousness a la MeXicana," 194.
51. This dichotomy is also challenged from a sociolinguistic point of view in Waltermire, "Mexican Immigration," and Del Angel Guevara, "Returning to Northern New Mexico."

Contextualizing Hidden Historical Mexicano-Nuevomexicano Portraits

> Evidence indicates that the native New Mexican Hispanos and the Mexican immigrants seemed to be the most at odds. There was a more deeply seated prejudice between the Spanish Americans and the Old Mexicano Mexicans (immigrants) than . . . between Anglos and Spanish Americans.[52]
>
> —Richard Griswold del Castillo

Griswold del Castillo's words historically situate the tensions between Mexicanos/as/xs and Nuevomexicanos/as/xs as extending back to the nineteenth century. The account offers a point of departure for considering the unique opportunity that the Mexicano-Nuevomexicano families provide in examining the everyday lived dynamics of negotiation within a historically charged zone of encuentro. Despite the lack of formal research on these interactions, I focus here on several overlooked historical Mexicano-Nuevomexicano encounters that challenge the erroneous assumptions that Mexicano-Nuevomexicano relationships are not part of northern New Mexico's history. Elena Valdez[53] documents one Mexican travel writer's bewilderment upon encountering Nuevomexicanos/as/xs over a hundred years after US annexation of the Southwest. Valdez describes Amalia Millán's reaction to Nuevomexicanos/as/xs in Millán's 1949 article, "Viaje por Nuevo Mexico." Valdez notes that the article "demonstrates one way in which people of Mexican descent were introduced to localized ways of being Mexican in the United States that did not necessarily cohere to nationalist ideologies but were engendered by histories embedded in distinct landscapes throughout the US West and Southwest."[54] Millán seems to be puzzled by Nuevomexicanos/as/xs' sense of identity. She writes,

> No me explicaba porque ahí, en Nuevo México, existía tal conciencia racial, ya que en esencia toda aquella gente que mal hablaba el español y aún el inglés, era mexicana por los cuatro costados. Pero ellos han pugnado, en su gran mayoría, por que se les llame españoles y en su tono y maneras parecen indicar que pertenecen a una raza diferente a la americana y a la llamada mexicana.[55]

---

52. Griswold del Castillo, *Familia*, 104.
53. Valdez, "Chicana/o Literature."
54. Valdez, "Chicana/o Literature," 66.
55. Millán, "Viaje," 33.

[I couldn't understand why there, in New Mexico, there existed such a racial consciousness, given that in their essence all of the people there who spoke bad Spanish, and English, were clearly Mexican. But the majority have insisted that they be called Spanish and in their way of being they seem to a different race from both the American race and the Mexican race.]

Millán not only critiques Nuevomexicanos/as/xs' understanding of their identity, but also their Spanish (and English) language use. In her report, Millán comments on the conversation with the individual who was driving her. She adds, "Aquel neomexicano estaba firmemente convencido de que hablaba un correcto español y yo lo dejaba en su ingenua convicción"[56] [That Nuevomexicano was firmly convinced that he spoke correct Spanish and I left him in his mistaken belief]. Millán's article is part of a historical conversation around historical Mexicano/a/x and Nuevomexicano/a/x encounters that has not been told. The article contributes to an understanding of the ways in which Mexicanos/as/xs and Nuevomexicanos/as/xs historically disidentify from each other.

Another "hidden" Mexicano-Nuevomexicano moment of interest revolves around one of the earliest caretakers and preservers of northern New Mexican traditions, Cleofas Jaramillo. Born into one of the original families of Arroyo Hondo, the founder of La Sociedad Folklórica in 1939, and author of four books including her memoir *Romance of a Little Village Girl*, Jaramillo is regarded as a guardian of Nuevomexicano/a/x culture, particularly during a time of increasing Anglo presence in northern New Mexico. Yet, Jaramillo's family also has connections to Mexico. In the chapter of her memoir entitled "An Enchanting Trip," Jaramillo tells of a time when she joins her family on a trip to Mexico. She explains, "With my father and little sister, we started in November for El Paso, rested a day there, and went on to Chihuahua, the city my mother had always desired to visit, as it was connected with a romantic incident of her mother's and father's marriage."[57] She recounts that her maternal grandparents were married at the Chihuahua Cathedral. Jaramillo explains that "during the picturesque days of the caravan, her father, Jesús María Lucero, while traveling in a caravan led by his brother-in-law, Don Gaspar Ortiz, met his bride at a hacienda, well on the outskirts of the city of Chihuahua."[58] Jaramillo's account does not elaborate on a specific lineage tied to Chihuahua, and she explains that, shortly after the wedding, the couple continue with the caravan north. However, the fact that Jaramillo's mother resided outside of Chihuahua and was married at the cathedral there, points

---

56. Millán, "Viaje," 33.
57. C. Jaramillo, *Romance*, 100.
58. C. Jaramillo, *Romance*, 100.

to a relationship with Mexico in its early years as a nation. Jaramillo's narrative indicates movement and connection between northern Nuevomexicanos/as/xs and Mexicanos/as/xs at a time when these exchanges were being downplayed as a means for Nuevomexicanos/as/xs' political survival. Nevertheless, these obscured encounters speak to the ways in which Mexicano/a/x voices may often be assimilated into Nuevomexicano/a/x narratives. Catherine Ramírez discusses the importance of "absence" and drawing attention to what (or who) is missing in conversations about assimilation and how that absence produces meaning.[59] Instances of Mexicano/a/x assimilation into Nuevomexicano/a/x culture are important elements explored within *Zones of Encuentro*.

An additional example of a lesser known historical Mexicano-Nuevomexicano profile is that of Dr. Mari Luci Jaramillo. The first Latina to hold a United States ambassadorship, Jaramillo was a native of Las Vegas, New Mexico, and often spoke and wrote about her northern New Mexican upbringing. Her collection of stories *Sacred Seeds: A Girl, Her Abuelos, and the Heart of Northern New Mexico* centers on her maternal grandparents, life on their ranch in Las Manuelitas, New Mexico, and lessons learned about community, traditions, and education. In *Sacred Seeds* and her memoir *Madame Ambassador: The Shoemaker's Daughter,* Jaramillo is clear that her mother is Nuevomexicana from Las Vegas and that her father is Mexicano from Mexico. Although Jaramillo references her father's background in her writings, Jaramillo is known in New Mexico as a scholar of bilingual education, for her fierce advocacy for Hispanic students and Spanish language maintenance, and for her pride in her northern New Mexican (Las Vegas) roots. Yet, there has been no exploration of the implications of Jaramillo's Mexicana-Nuevomexicana profile beyond her own personal reflections in her writings. In the introduction to *Sacred Seeds,* Jaramillo explains, "I write in English, the language of my formal education, but also use my grandparents' and Mamita's archaic Spanish, as well as Papito's standard Mexican Spanish."[60] Jaramillo's emphasis on her language experience points to another underexplored Mexicano-Nuevomexicano zone of encuentro in northern New Mexico, and her experience and ethnolinguistic identity serves as a reference point throughout this book.

Last, the public information campaign titled Somos Primos, launched in 2009 by Somos un Pueblo Unido, an immigrants' rights group based out of Santa Fe, represents a more contemporary moment in Mexicano-Nuevomexicano encounters. The campaign worked to dispel what the organization's founder

---

59. Ramírez, *Assimilation*, 17.
60. M. L. Jaramillo, *Sacred Seeds*, 4.

called "the myths that are perpetuated to divide las comunidades Nuevo Mexicanas y Mexicanas"[61] in northern New Mexico. The campaign worked particularly hard to disprove the notion that the two communities do not interact, get along, or support each other. The role of language took center stage in the public dialogues, and the campaign encouraged honest questions and an open conversation about tensions surrounding Spanish, English, and language loss. A public service announcement broadcast on YouTube with multigenerational representatives from both communities explained that "Nuevomexicanos grew up not knowing the deep roots they shared with their primos on the other side. Mexican textbooks do not mention the over 60,000 Mexicans that remained in the conquered territory. What happened to those primos? Why did they lose their lands and why were they punished for speaking Spanish?"[62] Somos un Pueblo Unido's short-lived campaign illustrates a skillful decolonial attempt to create inter-Latino/a/x knowledge production and encapsulates the complex histories and encounters that inform *Zones of Encuentro*.

Important Inter-Mexican and Inter-Latino/a/x Starting Points

One approach to contextualizing *Zones of Encuentro* in previous studies is to turn to research that documents interactions between distinct generations of Mexicans and Mexican Americans in other regions of the US. I refer to these as "inter-Mexican" interactions. Though diverse in setting and approach, the studies from Menchaca, Vila, Ochoa, Vázquez, and Telles and Sue explore some similar sociocultural processes that are relevant to the Mexicano-Nuevomexicano context.[63] These processes primarily center around association and disassociation as they relate to the articulation of identities. Menchaca and Vila's participants engage in an active categorization of different types of Mexicans. Similarly, Ochoa's participants seem to constantly negotiate their position along the continuum of conflict and solidarity with Mexican immigrants, and these positions are mediated by differing degrees of distinction and disassociation. Additionally, within the linguistic studies of Galindo, Rivera-Mills, and Mendoza-Denton, participants actively disassociate from recent arrivals and form groups that represent different regional

---

61. María Cristina García, personal communication.
62. Somos un Pueblo Unido, "Somos Primos."
63. Menchaca, *Mexican Outsiders*; Vila, *Crossing Borders, Reinforcing Borders*; Ochoa, *Becoming Neighbors*; Vázquez, *Mexican Americans across Generations*; and Telles and Sue, *Durable Ethnicity*.

ideologies.[64] These examples reveal the central role of language (Spanish) in producing these (dis)associations. Additionally, Schecter and Bayley's extensive 2002 research[65] provides an important and relevant model for the exploration of family language socialization patterns through four intensive case studies of family units of Mexican descent in California and Texas. Over a series of years, Schecter and Bayley map out each family's thoughts about cultural identity, language use patterns, and language attitudes. At the heart of these ethnolinguistic negotiations seems to be the notion of cultural and linguistic authenticity.

Zones of Encuentro is also informed by the increasing number of studies that focus on inter-Latino/a/x interactions.[66] These interactions refer to encounters between different Latino/a/x groups. Gina Pérez's 2003 study, for example, examines the interactions between Puerto Rican and Mexican women in Chicago and discovers that sites of food, music, and language are politicized activities that many times are defined in contrast to Mexican culture. Pérez explains that these activities are important for second- and third-generation migrants, who often worry that they are not "Puerto Rican enough."[67] These are important concerns to keep in mind when I address attitudes of cultural dominance between Nuevomexicanos/as/xs and Mexicanos/as/xs. Also, the increasing amount of research regarding mixed Latino/a/x identities (intra-Latino/a/x scholarship) and these individuals' linguistic profiles[68] provides a useful point of departure from which to examine the Mexicano-Nuevomexicano family unit and mixed Mexicano/a/x-Nuevomexicano/a/x individuals. With the exception of Steven Osuna's work in Los Angeles in the Salvadoran-Mexican context,[69] these studies highlight the mixed Latino/a/x subjects of Latino/a/x groups in Chicago. Mérida Rúa[70] examines the daily identity negotiations of mixed Mexican and Puerto Rican young people in the city, and she employs the metaphor of "colar" to illustrate the ways in which

---

64. Galindo, "Language Attitudes"; Rivera-Mills, "Intraethnic Attitudes among Hispanics"; and Mendoza-Denton, *Homegirls*.

65. Schecter and Bayley, *Language as Cultural Practice*.

66. See Pérez, "Puertorriqueñas rencorosas y mejicanas sufridas"; De Genova and Ramos-Zayas, *Latino Crossings*; García and Rúa, "Processing Latinidad"; and Hernández, "Language, Contact, and the Negotiation."

67. Pérez, "Puertorriqueñas rencorosas y mejicanas sufridas," 113.

68. See Rúa, "Colao Subjectivities"; Potowski and Matts, "Interethnic Language and Identity"; Potowski, "'I Was Raised Talking'"; Aparicio, "Chicago Latinidad"; Potowski, "Intrafamilial Dialect Contact"; Osuna, "Intra-Latina/Latino Encounters"; Potowski, *IntraLatino Language and Identity*; Aparicio, *Negotiating Latinidad*; and Rosa, *Looking like a Language*.

69. Osuna, "Intra-Latina/Latino Encounters."

70. Rúa, "Colao Subjectivities."

her informants highlight and downplay certain aspects of their Mexican and Puerto Rican identities in different contexts in daily social practice. Also in the Chicago context, Kim Potowski's extensive work[71] with mixed Mexican and Puerto Rican individuals reveals that, even though most participants possessed highly identifiable dialect features of either Puerto Rican or Mexican Spanish, they did not feel pressure to "pass" or elevate one culture over the other. In contrast, Frances Aparicio's in-depth interviews with twenty mixed Latino/a/x individuals (i.e., Mexican-Guatemalan, Colombian-Mexican, Mexican-Puerto Rican) in Chicago[72] discovers narratives of contextual downplaying, highlighting, and accommodating of certain identities in favor of others. These explorations of the daily identity negotiations of mixed Latinos/as/xs in Chicago serve as useful conceptual and methodological models for the Mexicano-Nuevomexicano context.

Contextualizing the Study of Spanish in New Mexico

An additional (and necessary) approach to contextualizing my study is to situate it among previous research on Spanish in New Mexico. Northern New Mexico has the distinction of being the home to the "oldest continually spoken variety of Spanish anywhere in the Americas that has not been updated by more recent immigration," as well as the oldest variety of a European language spoken in the US and the oldest surviving variety of New World Spanish (NWS) in North America.[73] Additionally, Traditional New Mexican Spanish is the most extensively researched variety of Spanish currently spoken in the US, beginning with Espinosa's work in 1911.[74] Garland Bills and Neddie Vigil's foundational research in the 1990s with the New Mexico Colorado Spanish Survey (NMCOSS) was the first comprehensive, systematic study of New Mexican Spanish across the entire state[75] and represents over three years of data collection. The New Mexico and Colorado Spanish Survey (NMCOSS) details the speech of 357 Spanish speakers in New Mexico and southern Colorado, and the editors' 2008 volume[76] brings together all of the data from this

---

71. Potowski, "Intrafamilial Dialect Contact"; Potowski, "Ethnolinguistic Identities and Ideologies"; and Potowski, *IntraLatino Language and Identity*.
72. Aparicio, "Chicago Latinidad"; Aparicio, "Intimate (Trans)Nationals"; and Aparicio, *Negotiating Latinidad*.
73. Lipski, *Varieties of Spanish*, 193; Bills and Vigil, "Ashes to Ashes," 43; Bills, "New Mexican Spanish."
74. Sanz and Villa, "Genesis," provides an excellent outline of this history.
75. Vigil and Bills, "New Mexico and Colorado Spanish," 3.
76. Bills and Vigil, *Spanish Language of New Mexico*.

comprehensive survey project. It is also the main source of Bills and Vigil's research that I will be citing throughout *Zones of Encuentro*.

Bills and Vigil differentiate between two primary varieties of New Mexican Spanish: "Border Spanish," or the Spanish generally spoken in southern New Mexico near the Mexican border and a few other areas with substantial immigration,[77] and "Traditional Spanish." This second variety was previously referred to by Lope Blanch as "Traditional Southwest Spanish" and dominates in the remainder of the region that is "the traditional heartland of the Spanish-speaking population that traces its presence in New Mexico to the arrival of Oñate's colonists in 1598 or de Vargas's recolonizers at the end of the seventeenth century."[78] The "Traditional Spanish" variety or "Traditional New Mexican Spanish" is generally what my participants and I refer to when using the phrase "New Mexican Spanish."

Israel Sanz and Daniel Villa underscore Traditional New Mexican Spanish's local roots and explain that TNMS developed as a distinct dialect during the colonial period through two rounds of dialect mixture and leveling, one in the early seventeenth century, and the other following the resettlement of the region in 1693.[79] Sanz and Villa's research provides important context for the development of northern New Mexico's historical variety of Spanish. This context informs claims around difference and distinction to be seen in later chapters of *Zones of Encuentro*. Villa and Sanz-Sánchez's research and Villa and Clegg[80] also provide important insights toward establishing a broader picture of Traditional New Mexican Spanish as pertaining to the macrodialect of US Mexican Spanish (USMS). Villa and Sanz-Sánchez emphasize the historical presence of Spanish in the western United States that predates English as well as the various waves of immigration from Mexico beginning in the early twentieth century. For this reason, they declare, "it is not a foreign language, but rather a national one and must be analyzed as such."[81] Villa and Sanz-Sánchez's assertions regarding Traditional New Mexican Spanish and US Mexican Spanish align nicely with land-based and querencia-informed ideas around Nuevomexicanos/as/xs' histories and identities. An additional, more recent resource for the study of Spanish in New Mexico is Rena Torres Cacoullos and Catherine Travis's New Mexico Spanish–English Bilingual Corpus (NMSEB). The corpus consists of thirty hours of spontaneous speech interactions from forty-one bilingual Nuevomexicanos/as/xs, and the authors

---

77. Bills and Vigil, *Spanish Language of New Mexico*, 5.
78. Lope Blanch, "El estudio del español"; Bills and Vigil, *Spanish Language of New Mexico*, 5.
79. Sanz and Villa, "Genesis," 437.
80. Villa and Sanz-Sánchez, "U.S. Mexican Spanish"; Villa and Clegg, *U.S. Mexican Spanish*.
81. Villa and Sanz-Sánchez, "U.S. Mexican Spanish," 130.

make clear that they advocate for "community-based fieldwork for the collection of speech data by community members."[82] I hope to have modeled this approach on a smaller scale with *Zones of Encuentro*.[83]

My research in the Mexicano-Nuevomexicano family context allows me to carefully review Bills and Vigil's extensive and trailblazing research and flesh out many of the trends and tendencies documented in their findings, as well as to rethink these trends, tendencies, and findings. A central concern of *Zones of Encuentro* is how the Mexicano-Nuevomexicano families contribute to a richer understanding of language maintenance and language shift in northern New Mexico from within the same household. One way that I reconsider these issues is through applying an exceptionally relevant sociolinguistic model for the study of Spanish language maintenance and shift in New Mexico proposed by Villa and Rivera-Mills.[84] The authors outline a revision to the traditional three-generation model of language shift through what they term the "contact generation." The contact generation "consists of a generation monolingual in Spanish that comes into contact with English speakers after the critical period ... either through its own migration or the arrival of English speakers into its territories."[85] *Zones of Encuentro* applies this underused model to characterize Nuevomexicano/a/x generations in the context of Mexicano/o/x immigrant generations.[86] This specific application, as well as this book as a whole, allows for reflection on the predictions made by Bills regarding the "demise" of Traditional New Mexican Spanish in northern New Mexico.[87]

Colleagues such as Travis and Villa, Waltermire, and Arnold and Martínez-García[88] also reflect on these predictions. Travis and Villa explain that the two largest Spanish-speaking communities in New Mexico are on different trajectories. Mexican Spanish continues to benefit from ongoing migration, leading to maintenance, particularly in the southern and border region, while Traditional New Mexican Spanish experiences increased loss.[89] Arnold and Martínez-García emphasize the urgent need to document Traditional New

---

82. Travis and Torres Cacoullos, "Making Voices Count," 171.

83. I discuss my multifaceted positionality as community member and academic later in this introductory chapter.

84. Villa and Rivera-Mills, "Integrated Multi-Generational Model."

85. Villa and Rivera-Mills, "Integrated Multi-Generational Model," 32.

86. See chapter 1 for an in-depth application of Villa and Rivera-Mills's "contact generation" model.

87. The "demise" is referenced in the title of Bills's 1997 article: "New Mexican Spanish: Demise of the Earliest European Variety in the United States."

88. Travis and Villa, "Language Policy and Language Contact"; Waltermire, "Mexican Immigration"; and Arnold and Martínez-García, "Traditional New Mexican Spanish."

89. Travis and Villa, "Language Policy and Language Contact," 137.

Mexican Spanish while speakers still exist and advocate for resources to preserve the sounds and features of this "linguistic treasure of the American Southwest" before it is too late.[90] In the following section I briefly summarize some key features of this linguistic treasure of Traditional New Mexican Spanish in order to better understand the Mexicano-Nuevomexicano families' discourse around the variety. *Zones of Encuentro* adds a new dimension to the preservation called for by Arnold and García-Martínez by creating space for the documentation of Mexicano-Nuevomexicano language experiences and ethnolinguistic identities in northern New Mexico.

Key Features of Traditional New Mexican Spanish

When the twentieth-anniversary edition of Rubén Cobos's *A Dictionary of New Mexico and Southern Colorado Spanish* was released in 2003, I was present at the reception honoring Cobos at the National Hispanic Cultural Center in Albuquerque, along with hundreds of community members. The dictionary's impact on everyday Nuevomexicanos/as/xs cannot be understated. It sits upon the bookshelves of many Nuevomexicano families (mine included), and its popularity speaks to the book's accessibility regardless of a background in linguistics. *A Dictionary of New Mexico and Southern Colorado Spanish* makes visible one of the features that the Mexicano-Nuevomexicano families in *Zones of Encuentro* discuss the most regarding New Mexican Spanish: the lexicon.

Unlike the salient differences between Mexican and Puerto Rican Spanish noted by Potowski's 2016 research and Potowski and Torres,[91] Mexican and New Mexican Spanish dialects depart from each other in more subtle ways. Traditional New Mexican Spanish has distinguishing features in its phonology and phonetics, morphosyntax, and lexicon.[92] Damián Vergara Wilson's overview outlines four major themes that characterize Traditional New Mexican Spanish from Bills and Vigil's data: (1) the perseverance of archaisms in the lexicon, grammatical forms, and pronunciation; (2) internal linguistic developments; (3) language contact with English; and (4) dialectal contact with both

---

90. Arnold and Martínez-García, "Traditional New Mexican Spanish," 175–76, 175.

91. Potowski, *IntraLatino Language and Identity*; and Potowski and Torres, *Spanish in Chicago*.

92. For detailed accounts of these features, Bills and Vigil, *Spanish Language of New Mexico*, and Lipski, *Varieties of Spanish*, provide comprehensive descriptions. Additionally, Arnold and García-Martínez, "Traditional New Mexican Spanish," and Vergara Wilson, "Panorama of Traditional New Mexican Spanish," provide excellent overviews of the features found in Bills and Vigil's corpus.

Mexican and standard Spanish.[93] The most distinctive features discussed by my participants regarding New Mexican Spanish are primarily lexical. In terms of lexical items, the persistence of archaisms is an often-discussed feature of Traditional New Mexican Spanish. Vergara Wilson provides a useful explanation of the two general types of archaism in the New Mexico setting. He explains that "conventional archaisms are linguistic forms that have endured in a specific speech community but have been rendered obsolete or have become altered in standardized varieties of Spanish."[94] He clarifies that the second type of archaism is seen in the New World and comes from terms that emerged to describe new concepts, plants, animals, and other objects encountered by Spanish explorers and colonizers.[95] Discussions around these types of archaic retentions surface within the Mexicano-Nuevomexicano family conversations.

Additionally, regarding lexical features, John Lipski documents that many Mexicanisms (usually of Nahuatl origin) are found in all varieties of New Mexican Spanish, yet "most if not all appear to be early borrowings that entered New Mexico with the original settlers."[96] He continues to delineate the completely different lexical items that exist in New Mexican Spanish versus contemporary Mexican Spanish. Lipski states, "New Mexicans who have had contact with Mexican-born Spanish speakers may use 'Mexican' words, but they do so while being conscious of incorporating elements from another dialect."[97] He emphasizes that English has had a greater effect on New Mexican Spanish than modern Mexican Spanish, "which has little or no effect on the Spanish spoken by native New Mexicans."[98] Lipski underscores a lack of dialect contact between New Mexican Spanish and Mexican Spanish. Yet, more recent research from Mark Waltermire and Mario Esteban Del Angel Guevara[99] provides new insights regarding Traditional New Mexican Spanish and the increased use of Mexican lexicon in northern New Mexico.

Waltermire finds that the use of Mexicanisms in Northern New Mexican Spanish "far outnumbers that of archaisms and Anglicisms."[100] He suggests that this fact calls for a rethinking of the characterization of Northern New Mexican Spanish. Relevant to the Mexicano-Nuevomexicano family context,

---

93. Vergara Wilson, "Panorama of Traditional New Mexican Spanish," 2.
94. Vergara Wilson, "Panorama of Traditional New Mexican Spanish," 2.
95. Vergara Wilson, "Panorama of Traditional New Mexican Spanish," 2.
96. Lipski, *Varieties of Spanish*, 207.
97. Lipski, *Varieties of Spanish*, 208.
98. Lipski, *Varieties of Spanish*, 207–8.
99. Waltermire, "Mexican Immigration"; and Del Angel Guevara, "Returning to Northern New Mexico."
100. Waltermire, "Mexican Immigration," 149.

Waltermire explains that "the use of Mexicanisms in Northern New Mexican Spanish starts with younger speakers, likely those who were raised with at least one Mexican-born parent."[101] He elaborates that most of these speakers were raised in northern New Mexico over the course of decades of increased Mexican immigration to the region and that this accounts for the increased use of Mexicanisms in this area.[102] Similarly, Del Angel Guevara's dissertation observes the adoption of Mexican variants in typical TNMS speech in the Nuevomexicano/a/x participants he interviewed, particularly among younger speakers. Both of these studies provide important updates to the earlier work of Bills and Vigil and Lipski and are exceptionally relevant when considering the Mexicano-Nuevomexicano interactions, families, and general zones of encuentro.

PART 2: THEORIES, FRAMEWORKS, AND METHODS

Theoretical Frameworks: Contact Zones, Zones of Encuentro, and Latinidad

I propose "zones of encuentro" as a concept through which to consider the language experiences of mixed Mexicano-Nuevomexicano families, like those of Mari Luci Jaramillo, by examining the intersections of language, culture, and society. This is what Mary Bucholtz and Kira Hall designate a "sociocultural linguistics perspective on identity" or an approach "that focuses on both the details of language and the workings of culture and society."[103] Similarly, Alastair Pennycook conceptualizes these ideas through a critical applied linguistics framework. Critical applied linguistics focuses on finding "ways of thinking about the micro contexts of everyday language use and macro concerns of society, culture, politics, and power."[104] These perspectives already appreciate the interconnected nature of language and context that is expressed through language experience. The framework of "zones of encuentro" is a starting point from which to explore intersecting language experiences from both a sociocultural linguistics perspective and a critical applied linguistics approach. I utilize this framework throughout the entirety of this book.

---

101. Waltermire, "Mexican Immigration," 160.
102. Waltermire, "Mexican Immigration," 160.
103. Bucholtz and Hall, "Identity and Interaction," 586.
104. Pennycook, *Critical Applied Linguistics*, 172.

From Contact Zone to Encuentro

My use of the term "zone" in "zones of encuentro" recalls Mary Louis Pratt's foundational notion of "contact zones."[105] Pratt designates "contact zones" as "social spaces where disparate cultures meet, clash, and grapple with each other, often in highly asymmetrical relations of domination and subordination—such as colonialism and slavery, or their aftermaths as they are lived out across the globe today."[106] Utilizing the model of contact zones in the Mexicano-Nuevomexicano context allows for the consideration of power differentials in cultural and linguistic meeting places between Latino/a/x groups (i.e., Mexicanos/as/xs and Nuevomexicanos/as/xs) specifically from within the same household. In Schecter and Bayley's 2002 research on language socialization patterns in Mexican American families, they emphasize that "there is no necessary opposition between a focus on the contact zone and a focus on the home front because, in many cases, the home front, whether conceived as the immediate community or as the individual household, is also a contact zone."[107] This study suggests the use of the concept of contact zones for inter-Latino/a/x spaces and inter-Latino/a/x households. I am interested in the struggles that emerge when language experiences collide and ethnolinguistic identities are shaped.

In revisiting her 1992 work, Pratt explains that she is often asked to determine whether a particular context represents a contact zone. She emphasizes that the point is not if certain contexts are contact zones or not, but rather "what insights emerged from thinking about them that way,"[108] rather than a focus on what is and what is not a contact zone. Additionally, Pratt cautions against a misguided use of the contact zone concept. She explains,

> Sometimes, in liberal thought, the contact zone gets articulated not as a device for imagining situations of heterogeneity, inequality, and conflict but as the name of a solution for these challenges. It becomes an ideal to be aspired to—an Edenic, harmonious place where people separated by deep historical differences successfully collaborate, cooperate, and resolve their differences, each side responsive to the others' needs and interests.... Contact becomes the alternative to conflict. Such a normative use of the contact zone is ideologically coherent; that is, it makes sense. But it denies the

---

105. Pratt, *Imperial Eyes*.
106. Pratt, *Imperial Eyes*, 7.
107. Schecter and Bayley, *Language as Cultural Practice*, 178–79.
108. Pratt, *Planetary Longings*, 126.

concept's critical force, jumps over the necessary step of thinking through the chaotic, uncontrollable energies that are in play.[109]

My focus on the Mexicano-Nuevomexicano encounters does not intend to minimize difference, conflict, and the chaos of the contact zone, although I recognize that contact zones can also bring forth moments of solidarity. My intent is to unpack the heterogeneity in these zones and to identify the insights we can gain by thinking through the intersecting language experiences within the contact zones.

I am also interested in extending the contact zone to denote long-term interactions and experiences. For me, looking at the contact zone of Mexicano-Nuevomexicano language experiences calls for a conceptual framework that addresses the intertwined, shared, and contested histories between Mexicanos/as/xs and Nuevomexicanos/as/xs. I propose the notion of "zones of encuentro" as a term that heeds Pratt's call to contemplate the insights that emerge from thinking through and beyond the contact zones. "Zones of encuentro" both recalls and extends the contact zone toward an explicit focus on long-term encounters between participants whose experiences are grounded in "analogous sociopolitical conditions and colonial and neocolonial legacies."[110] More than simply a Spanish translation of the English word "encounter," I draw my definition of "encuentro" from the Latin American and Caribbean regional feminist meetings termed "Encuentros."[111] These encuentros enabled long-term conversations focused on "refashioned and renegotiated identities, discourses, and practices."[112] Zones of encuentro allow me to highlight the analogous colonial and neocolonial long-term cultural and linguistic legacies of Mexicanos/as/xs and Nuevomexicanos/as/xs and the ways in which their language experiences and ethnolinguistic identities mutually influence each other.

In the Zones of Latinidad

In a similar fashion, Aparicio's proposal around the concept of Latinidad also opens discussions that search for "the analogous (post)colonial conditions and experiences"[113] among Latino/a/x groups. Aparicio thinks through Lati-

---

109. Pratt, *Planetary Longings*, 130.
110. Álvarez et al., "Encountering Latin American," 539.
111. Álvarez et al., "Encountering Latin American."
112. Álvarez et al., "Encountering Latin American," 537.
113. Aparicio, "Jennifer as Selena," 94.

nidad as a theory that allows us "to explore moments of convergences and divergences in the formation of Latino/a (post)colonial subjectivities."[114] A central aspect of this proposal focuses on the decolonial move to construct "interlatino knowledge that allows Latino/as from various national groups to understand their Latino counterparts, a knowledge that itself represents an alternative discourse given the silenced knowledge about each other that has been our educational legacy."[115] This notion of Latinidad provides a space for agency and self-affirmation in which differences and similarities among Latinos/as/xs are simultaneously activated and deactivated. Alberto Sandoval-Sánchez observes that this process can even result in "an increasing consciousness and affinity among U.S. Latinos/as (and other Latin Americans)."[116] This idea is nicely complemented by Rúa and García as they conceptualize Latinidad as an "ethnoracial configuration and sociocultural practice in placemaking, where a shared sense of being Latino transpires within diverse social settings and associations," while not ignoring the existence of Aparicio's concept of "competing authenticities" among Latino/a/x groups.[117] Additionally, Aparicio offers the plural term "Latinidades" as an additional layer to Latinidad that "allows us to document, analyze, and theorize the processes by which diverse Latina/os interact, subordinate, and transculturate each other while reaffirming the plural and heterogeneous sites that constitute Latinidad."[118] In this spirit, I draw on Latinidad as a multidimensional theoretical framework that is exceptionally useful for interrogating zones of encuentro. In this book, Latinidad functions as an active process, a placemaking practice, and a useful theoretical tool for unpacking the unity and diversity of Latino/a/x lives.

Yet, Latinidad has not always been viewed as the dynamic theoretical space that Aparicio, García and Rúa, and Sandoval-Sánchez conceptualize. It has often been criticized for its homogenizing tendencies. Even scholars who intend to confront the tensions between homogenization and difference, as in Juan Flores's notion of the "Latino Imaginary,"[119] often end up reproducing essentializations. Ana Aparicio and colleagues coin the phrase "unruly Latinidades" to refer to "the way the very notion of Latinidad can often be narrow and constraining."[120] Through their ethnographic work, Aparicio and colleagues emphasize "the complexities and possibilities of Latinx difference,

---

114. Aparicio, "Jennifer as Selena," 93.
115. Aparicio, "Jennifer as Selena," 94.
116. Sandoval-Sánchez, *José, Can You See?*, 15.
117. García and Rúa, "Processing Latinidad," 318; and Aparicio, "Reading the 'Latino.'"
118. Aparicio, *Negotiating Latinidad*, 31.
119. J. Flores, "Latino Imaginary."
120. A. Aparicio et al., "Introduction," xxxi.

signaling toward Latinidad as always socially contingent, contextual, and framed by both erasures and violences from without and within, in a word, unruly."[121] In the spirit of reclaiming[122] the complexity, utility, and dynamicity of Latinidad, I locate my approach to Latinidad within this unruliness. Informed by the work of my colleagues cited above, *Zones of Encuentro* actively weaves Latinidad within the consideration of new contexts, spaces, and places in northern New Mexico. The multifaceted framework of Latinidad provides a necessary tool for putting Latino/a/x language experiences into dialogue with one another.

Moreover, Ana Celia Zentella directly links theories of Latinidad with language practices. She explains,

> Understanding the crucial yet contradictory role of Spanish in Latina/o identity and its repercussions for Latina/o unity requires an anthropological linguistic perspective, incorporating socioeconomic and political realities that determine how and why Latinas/os speak as members of different groups at different times, and even at the same time, and how they evaluate those differences.[123]

Zentella's anthropolitical linguistics links the moments of convergence and divergence among Latinos/as/xs to the evaluation of linguistic sameness and difference, and it calls attention to the utility of what I term "linguistic Latinidad," or the application of theories of Latinidad to linguistic situations to highlight language ideologies and linguistic hierarchies. An additional productive pairing between linguistics and Latinidad exists in a focus on competing linguistic authenticities. Bucholtz highlights the need to separate out authenticity as an ideology from authentication as a social practice.[124] Bucholtz explains the idea of "authenticating practices":

> In place of the unexamined notion of authenticity, I offer the alternative concept of authentication. Where authenticity presupposes that identity is primordial, authentication views it as the outcome of constantly negotiated social practices. . . . Thus sociolinguists should speak not of authenticity but more accurately of authenticity effects, achieved through the authenticating practices of those who use and evaluate language. This perspective does not

---

121. Aparicio et al., "Introduction," xx.
122. Frances Aparicio's *Negotiating Latinidad* has discussed this reclamation, and I locate García and Rúa and Sandoval-Sánchez as also being located on this trajectory.
123. Zentella, "'Dime con quién hablas,'" 25.
124. Bucholtz, "Sociolinguistic Nostalgia," 410.

deny the cultural force of authenticity as an ideology but emphasizes that authenticity is always achieved rather than given in social life, although this achievement is often rendered invisible.[125]

Utilizing Bucholtz's framework of "authenticating practices" provides a complementary tool for examining the competing authenticities present within Latinidad. Authenticity, or notions of "real" Spanish or being "really" Mexican, surface within the inter-Mexican and inter-Latino/a/x studies that inform *Zones of Encuentro*. They also circulate throughout the narratives of the Mexicano-Nuevomexicano families in my study. I underscore the importance of Bucholtz's theories because I think they represent a useful analytical tool and a method for combining theoretical frameworks within Latino/a/x cultural studies and sociolinguistics to effectively explore the zones of encuentro within the Mexicano-Nuevomexicano family by activating discourse on Latinidad in the context of language. In summary, theories of Latinidad are useful in studying the heterogeneity among US Latinos/as/xs in relation to language use, maintenance, ideologies, ethnolinguistic identities, and linguistic hierarchies.

Latinidad in New Mexico

Latinidad's approach to unpacking power dynamics within and between Latino/a/x groups is helpful in studying the unaddressed heterogeneity among US Latinos/as/xs in New Mexico and has not previously been applied to this context. I contend that Latinidad allows me to conceptualize Mexicanos/as/xs and Nuevomexicanos/as/xs as distinct Latino/a/x groups, rather than simply different generational groups of the same Mexican national origin. Due to a shared Mexican nationality of less than thirty years, Nuevomexicanos/as/xs and Mexicanos/as/xs represent, in a sense, different national origins. In fact, recognizing Nuevomexicanos/as/xs' homeland as New Mexico indexes the US as an always already Latino/a/x homeland. My emphasis on the long history of disidentification from a Mexican national identity, the deep attachment to place, the absence of an immigration history, and the reality that New Mexico is, indeed, the homeland of Nuevomexicanos/as/xs aligns well with theories of Latinidad that push back against rigid national categories and homogenizing forces.[126] Latinidad provides a framework for placemaking, understanding

---

125. Bucholtz, "Sociolinguistic Nostalgia," 408.
126. See Griswold del Castillo, *Familia*; Nieto-Phillips, "Spanish American Ethnic Identity"; Nieto-Phillips, *Language of Blood*; and Lozano, *American Language*, as well as Gonzales-Berry and Maciel, "Introduction"; Arellano, *Enduring Acequias*; and Anaya, "Foreword."

simultaneous moments of conflict and solidarity, and conceptualizing new ways of being Latino/a/x that are not limited by national categories within the Mexicano-Nuevomexicano context. For this reason, I propose theories of Latinidad as useful, applicable, and underused for examining linguistic and cultural realities in New Mexico.

Before moving forward, I would like to clarify my use of the term Latino/a/x in the northern New Mexico context. Despite its use in local publications such as the *Albuquerque Journal,* the panethnic term "Latino/a/x" or "Latinx" is not generally a term with which communities in my study identify. However, I do deploy this term (and already have) throughout *Zones of Encuentro.* It is not my intention to impose the use of this term on communities that clearly do not use it. However, I do think it is useful in the spirit of Dávila as a term of entry. Dávila explains, "It is a term to open up conversations on all the different Latinx stories, backgrounds, and identities that have seldom been given the necessary attention."[127] Therefore, when I am intentionally connecting New Mexico to broader conversations around Latinos/as/xs in the US or when I highlight the power dynamics or knowledge that is produced between Mexicanos/as/xs and Nuevomexicanos/as/xs, I use the term strategically throughout this book. Thus, my use of Latino/a/x is necessarily relational and is useful in teasing out "the power differentials and the historical, social and cultural dilemmas that these terms evoke as we identify the interactions between and among peoples of various Latin American national identities,"[128] and, in the case of *Zones of Encuentro,* distinct and emerging regional and national identities.

Disciplinary Encounters

Importantly, the "zones of encuentro" framework signals a space for encounters between disciplines and methodologies. Jonathan Rosa elaborates that the goal of his ethnographic work is to open up "an alternative conceptual space" in order to "understand the everyday practices through which Latinxs creatively contest, reimagine, and redefine ethnoracial, geopolitical, and linguistic borders."[129] I intentionally situate *Zones of Encuentro* as an intervention within this type of alternative conceptual space at the intersection of US Latino/a/x cultural studies and critical studies of Latinos/as/xs and language, including models from sociolinguistics, linguistic anthropology, linguistic ethnography,

---

127. Dávila, *Latinx Art,* 9.
128. Aparicio, "Cultural Twins and National Others," 625.
129. Rosa, *Looking like a Language,* 8.

and critical applied linguistics. Indeed, I have already centered Bucholtz and Hall's sociocultural linguistics and Pennycook's critical applied linguistics as key perspectives within the contact zones and zones of encuentro of my study. Bucholtz's proposal for approaching authenticity, as well as Zentella's reframing of linguistic anthropology as anthropolitical linguistics pair effectively with the theories of Latinidad that emerge from Latino/a/x cultural studies.

Because the focus of *Zones of Encuentro* is on lived Latino/a/x language experiences, the study is already grounded in cultural studies and its emphasis on "the cultures of everyday life."[130] Ann Gray explains, "One of the key characteristics of cultural studies is that of understanding culture as constitutive of and constituted by 'the lived,' that is the material, social and symbolic practices of everyday life,"[131] and, by extension, the lived social and symbolic practices of Latinos/as/xs constitute US Latino/a/x cultural studies. It is important to note that, in line with Aparicio's theories,[132] I frame US Latino/a/x cultural studies as a field, rather than a discipline, due to its multi- and interdisciplinary approaches and its foundational methodological practices "through which storytelling, personal narratives, and testimonios are critical interventions in reclaiming historical agency and acquiring a public voice and a collective visibility within the dominant US culture."[133] US Latino/a/x cultural studies both crosses and resists disciplinary boundaries. Likewise, Rúa and Ramos-Zayas emphasize the inherently dialogical nature of the field and the constructive "blurring of conventional distinctions between the humanities and the social sciences."[134] *Zones of Encuentro* models this approach. I want to emphasize that my analysis of the Mexicano-Nuevomexicano context seeks to make use of the "alternative and multiple methodologies that challenge traditional disciplinary approaches to understanding our communities,"[135] rather than simply situating US Latino/a/x communities as the object of study within a specific discipline. Thus, *Zones of Encuentro* addresses the Mexicano-Nuevomexicano context through an interdisciplinary approach that draws from Latino/a/x cultural studies and its theories of (unruly) Latinidades, as well as sociolinguistics, linguistic ethnography, anthropology, critical applied linguistics, and Chicana feminist studies. This blurring of disciplinary boundaries allows for a productive engagement with ethnolinguistic identities and language experiences, while reframing notions of home and enabling more effective study of

---

130. Gray, *Research Practice for Cultural Studies*, 12.
131. Gray, *Research Practice for Cultural Studies*, 1.
132. Aparicio, *Negotiating Latinidad*, 10.
133. Aparicio, *Negotiating Latinidad*, 4.
134. Rúa and Ramos Zayas, "Introduction," 3.
135. Aparicio, "Latinx Studies."

what I term "linguistic Latinidad" in the Mexicano-Nuevomexicano context. Uniting these approaches and disciplines allows for language to take a more central role in Latinidad and for Latinidad to be utilized as a critical tool for analysis of language. The zones of encuentro framework allows me to work at this intersection of disciplines and methodologies and within the *field* of US Latino/a/x cultural studies.

In the Zones: Setting, Participants, Methods, and Analysis

Setting

The setting of northern New Mexico itself serves as a sort of macrolevel ethnolinguistic zone of encuentro. The region embodies the sociohistorical linguistic legacies of both Nuevomexicanos/as/xs and Mexicanos/as/xs. Additionally, the use of the Spanish language in the region extends back to approximately 250 years of Spanish colonial rule and twenty-four years of Mexican rule.[136] This heritage established Spanish as the native language among most of New Mexico's inhabitants until the Americanization efforts in the 1930s and 1940s solidified an eventual shift to English.[137] Lozano emphasizes that "Spanish-language rights persisted longer in New Mexico than anywhere else in the Southwest. Beyond demography, more nuevomexicanos were involved in public life in New Mexico than in any of the other former Mexican territories."[138] Also, New Mexico's century-long record of developing, maintaining, and innovating models for bilingual education in the state[139] (particularly in northern New Mexico) contributes to a unique profile within the Southwest and the Latino/a/x US more generally. This history contextualizes the varying degrees of bilingualism that have survived within the Nuevomexicano/a/x population and serves as the backdrop for more recent generations of Mexicanos/as/xs who have experienced their own encounters with language shift. These multilayered language experiences in northern New Mexico are crucial to understanding the zones of encuentro that I explore.

Before delving into the rich Mexicano-Nuevomexicano family narratives that run throughout my chapters, I would like to acquaint readers with the northern New Mexico setting for *Zones of Encuentro*. The families in my study

---

136. Lozano, *American Language*.
137. Gonzales-Berry, "Which Language?"
138. Lozano, *American Language*, 148.
139. See R. B. Martínez and Habermann López's extensive edited volume *The Shoulders We Stand On: A History of Bilingual Education in New Mexico*.

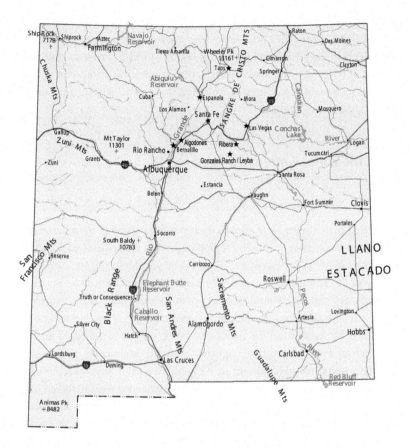

FIGURE 1. Map of northern New Mexico. Adapted from GISGeography.

reside in eight cities and towns in northern New Mexico: Taos, Española, Las Vegas, Santa Fe, Gonzales Ranch / Leyba, Ribera, Bernalillo, and Algodones (see figure 1). Each town included in my research is denoted with a star in the partial map of northern New Mexico.[140]

In studying Spanish in New Mexico and southern Colorado, Bills and Vigil[141] divide the region into twelve sectors, taking into account historical settlement patterns. They specifically describe two sectors: "The initial Hispanic colonization in the sixteenth and seventeenth centuries took place along the Río Grande in sectors 5 and 6, with most of the population located between

---

140. Unless otherwise noted, when referring to these (and several other) cities and towns throughout *Zones of Encuentro*, it is assumed they are in New Mexico and the state specification is omitted.

141. Bills and Vigil, *Spanish Language of New Mexico*.

the present-day town of Socorro and the Río Grande's confluence with the Chama River just north of Santa Fe, although there were some ranchos (small farms) as far north as Taos."[142] This is the region in which the Mexicano-Nuevomexicano families that form *Zones of Encuentro* reside and is generally the same area Rubén Cobos describes as the region for his dictionary, as "the towns and villages of the upper Rio Grande in northern New Mexico."[143] In line with Bills and Vigil and Cobos, I define northern New Mexico in *Zones of Encuentro* as any town north of Albuquerque along the Upper Río Grande Valley, including the Río Arriba region, as well as communities to the northeast of the Río Grande Valley along the Pecos River Valley. I am aware that the designation of northern New Mexico is somewhat contested. All of the towns included in my study are geographically situated in the northern half of the state; however, many northern New Mexico residents do not consider anything south of Santa Fe to be included in northern New Mexico. Even some northern New Mexico residents do not consider Santa Fe as northern New Mexico. For the purposes of my study, I do include Santa Fe as part of northern New Mexico. I also include Algodones and Bernalillo primarily because the characteristics of these small towns (population, history, sociolinguistic history) have more in common with small towns in northern New Mexico than with Albuquerque or other central New Mexico towns. The inclusion of Algodones and Bernalillo also allowed for the addition of two more families, as it was difficult to identify more than one Mexicano-Nuevomexicano family unit in each town. All of the towns in this study have a majority Hispanic population with a foreign-born population of 15 percent or less. In table 1, I have included the population numbers, the percent of the population that is Hispanic, and the percent of foreign-born individuals taken from the US Census 2020.

Clearly, "foreign-born" is not synonymous with Mexican-born, but it gives us a ballpark idea of how many residents of these towns could potentially have been born in Mexico. For the state of New Mexico as a whole, 9.2 percent of the population is foreign-born, and this represents an increase from 2010. The American Immigration Council denotes that, of New Mexico's immigrant community, more than 70 percent are from Mexico.[144] However, it is important to keep in mind the significant limitations of census data, particularly regarding the categorization of Latinos/as/xs.[145] I mentioned one such limita-

---

142. Bills and Vigil, *Spanish Language of New Mexico*, 22.
143. Cobos, *Dictionary of New Mexico*, vii.
144. American Immigration Council, "Immigrants in New Mexico."
145. See Leeman, "Categorizing Latinos"; Dowling, *Mexican Americans*; and Leeman, "Becoming Hispanic."

TABLE 1. US Census 2020 population figures for northern New Mexico cities and towns

NAME OF TOWN	POPULATION	POPULATION THAT IS HISPANIC (%)	POPULATION THAT IS FOREIGN-BORN (%)
Algodones	976	68.5	1.23
Bernalillo	10,077	63.5	11.9
Española	10,071	84.3	8.1
Las Vegas	13,855	81	3
Ribera	501	65.7	1.2
El Pueblo*	125	87	No information available
Santa Fe	84,418	54.7	14.2
Taos	5,950	45.4	5.76

*The neighboring places of Gonzales Ranch and Leyba had no population data available through the US Census. El Pueblo is the closest place with population data and is also where one of the family participants lives.

tion at the beginning of this introduction, in that the Census does not distinguish between Mexicanos/as/xs and Nuevomexicanos/as/xs. Additionally, these numbers may be undercounting the Mexican foreign-born population in New Mexico due to inaccurate figures regarding undocumented individuals. However, the numbers make it clear that all of these towns have Hispanic-designated populations of over 50 percent[146] and that the majority of these individuals are US-born.

Returning to the setting of the parish of Our Lady of Guadalupe in Santa Fe, the changing demographics and increased Mexicano/a/x presence in the parish were the driving factors for the pastor to commission the statue. After all, the devotion to Our Lady of Guadalupe at the parish spans generations. The original adobe structure was built between 1776 and 1795, and the parish describes itself as the oldest church still standing dedicated to Our Lady of Guadalupe in the United States.[147] Many old-timer parishioners are proud to call themselves lifelong Guadalupanos and Guadalupanas (my grandparents included). Pairing this history with the image of la Virgen de Guadalupe as a centuries-old symbol of faith and national pride for Mexicano/a/x immigrants in a city that was historically part of the same Spanish and then Mexican territory seemed like an ideal scenario for creating a shared faith homeplace that would be legible to both groups. Yet, despite the analogous histories with la Virgen de Guadalupe, moments of unity and discord emerged. In what follows, I outline the methods utilized in *Zones of Encuentro* that allow me to

---

146. With the exception of Taos.
147. See The Shrine of Our Lady of Guadalupe website.

work at the intersection of Latino/a/x cultural studies and sociocultural linguistics to theorize these unsettled homeplaces.

Participants

In *Zones of Encuentro*, I conceptualize multiple zones of contact that stem from the primary zone of encuentro in this study: the Mexicano-Nuevomexicano family unit. Not only are we able to consider the home front as a contact zone[148] through this unit, but we are also able to explore how larger cultural, historical, and linguistic conflicts are mapped onto the romantic relationships, marriages, and (adult) children within this home. Like peeling the layers of an onion, the consideration of one zone of encuentro reveals the presence of additional zones below it. In essence, the more we look, the more we see. My "looking" at these zones of encuentro is guided by two primary research questions: (1) How do Mexicanos/as/xs and Nuevomexicanos/as/xs in northern New Mexico define and view themselves and each other, and what role does language experience play in these conceptualizations? (2) What factors shape the ethnolinguistic identities of mixed Mexicano-Nuevomexicano Latino/a/x subjects? The answers to these questions emerge from forty-five interviews and pláticas with ten Mexicano-Nuevomexicano families from eight northern New Mexico towns.

The Mexicano-Nuevomexicano families consist of one Nuevomexicano/a parent, one Mexicano/a first-generation parent, and one or two adult or teenage Mexicano/a-Nuevomexicano/a children.[149] In denoting "first-generation," I adhere to Silva-Corvalán's[150] established generational distinctions, in which first-generation (G1) denotes an individual born abroad who came to the US after the age of twelve. However, as noted in Villa and Rivera-Mills,[151] and as I explore in chapter 1, these generational designations do not match the historical sociolinguistic situation of the Nuevomexicano/a participants in my study. For this reason, I do not refer to the Nuevomexicano/a participants with the first-generation (G1), second-generation (G2), or third-generation (G3) categories.

All participants chose a pseudonym through which to be identified, and these pseudonyms are the names I use to identify the participants throughout

---

148. Schecter and Bayley, *Language as Cultural Practice*, 178–79.
149. When referring to individual Mexicano/a and Nuevomexicano/a partners and the Mexicano-Nuevomexicano participants in this study, I do not employ the "x" due to the fact that none of the participants identified as nonbinary or gender fluid.
150. Silva-Corvalán, *Language Contact and Change*.
151. Villa and Rivera-Mills, "Integrated Multi-Generational Model."

this book.[152] I provide detailed participant portraits with the circumstances around how I came to know each family in a later section of this introduction. However, my identification of potential participants began in the classroom. As faculty in a summer institute designed for K–12 teachers in New Mexico to prepare for the state bilingual certification exam (La Prueba) to earn their state bilingual endorsement at New Mexico Highlands University in Las Vegas, New Mexico, I came to know two participants as my students first. My involvement with colleagues and students at the dual-language immersion elementary school in Las Vegas led me to identify two more participants. Between the former students and educators at the dual-language immersion school, I was connected with three more families. The remaining three families were identified through friend and familial connections. One family was identified to me through my cousin; one was identified by a close friend; and the last participant was my first close friend when I moved to Las Vegas to work at the university in 2005. Clearly my role as professor and community member in Las Vegas, as well as having credibility through my family's presence in northern New Mexico, were instrumental in gaining trust and access to this group of Mexicano-Nuevomexicano families.[153] Over an eighteen-month period from 2012 to 2013, ten families welcomed me into their homes, kitchens, backyards, birthday parties, places of work, and places of worship. We shared conversations over meals into the late hours of the night, at church fiestas, and even over beers. I also reconnected with three of the families for follow-up pláticas in 2022.

Methods

Drawing on methodologies and analytical tools from Chicana feminist studies, anthropology, linguistic ethnography, sociolinguistics, critical applied linguistics, and cultural studies, the core methods for data collection in my study of the Mexicano-Nuevomexicano family unit consist of participant observation, semistructured interviews, pláticas, and a short lexical elicitation activity. My approach to participant observation within the interdisciplinarity of linguistic ethnography and under the larger framework of hometown

---

152. Written informed consent was obtained from all participants per IRB consent forms in English and Spanish, and all participants were informed that participation in this IRB-approved research was voluntary and that they could withdraw at any time.

153. I provide more detailed reflections regarding my positionality in a later section of this introductory chapter.

ethnography reveals multiple, overlapping, and intersecting language experiences.[154] My methods were informed by the qualitative case study approaches of Schecter and Bayley and Yin.[155] The methods used in gathering the Chicago MXPR interview corpus documented in Potowski's 2016 research and Potowski and Torres (2023), as well as the interview methods utilized in the New Mexico Colorado Spanish Survey, played a central role in forming the outlines for the semistructured questions I formulated.[156] I based these questions on a modified version of the sociolinguistic interview used for the Chicago MXPR corpus, guided by some elements from the New Mexico Colorado Spanish Survey interview.[157] The questions touched on the following themes: family background, language use patterns, language attitudes, family relationships, traditions, identity, and community.

The semistructured interviews and pláticas lasted in length from forty minutes to three hours, with the average conversation lasting ninety minutes. For each family unit, I met with every family member separately and then engaged in a follow-up group family plática. Each interview and plática was conducted in the language preference of the participant.[158] In my time with the families, it was my goal through the plática to create a conversational partnership[159] through in-depth qualitative interviewing. Rubin and Rubin characterize responsive interviewing as "a dynamic and iterative process" and remind us that "qualitative research is not simply learning about a topic, but also learning what is important to those being studied."[160] Pláticas serve as a tool or a "disruptive methodology" that "in turn produces different posibilidades for understanding or seeing a particular nuanced experience that may not be captured through other methods."[161] These co-constructed conversations allowed for the Mexicano-Nuevomexicano families to guide our talks. Therefore, my sets of structured and semistructured questions were not necessarily "set." In most of my meetings with the participants, I began with structured and semistructured questions to open the conversation and

---

154. Creese and Copland, *Linguistic Ethnography*, 13; and Villarreal, "Anthropolocura as Homeplace Ethnography."

155. Schecter and Bayley, *Language as Cultural Practice*; Yin, *Case Study Research*.

156. Potowski, *IntraLatino Language and Identity*; Potowski and Torres, *Spanish in Chicago*; and Bills and Vigil, *Spanish Language of New Mexico*.

157. See appendix 1 with question sets in English and appendix 2 with question sets in Spanish.

158. When quoting participants' interviews/pláticas in Spanish, all translations to English appearing after the quotation are my own.

159. Rubin and Rubin, *Qualitative Interviewing*, 79.

160. Rubin and Rubin, *Qualitative Interviewing*, 15.

161. Saavedra and Esquierdo, "Pláticas on Disrupting Language," 39.

establish a rapport. However, I only loosely followed the order of interview questions and allowed stories, memories, and narratives to emerge organically without interruption. It was always preferable that the participants bring up a topic of interest to me on their own without prompting. Our conversations generally evolved into free-flowing back-and-forth under the framework of the five principles of plática methodology. Fierros and Delgado-Bernal outline these principles as the following: the research draws upon Chicana/Latina feminist theory; there is a relational principle that honors participants as co-constructors of knowledge; a plática methodology makes connections between everyday lived experiences and the research; a plática methodology provides a potential space for healing; and the methodology relies on reciprocity, vulnerability, and researcher reflexivity.[162] The follow-up group/family meetings and my conversations with the three participants in 2022 followed a clear plática approach because there was an already-established trust and confianza.

Every individual interview and/or plática consisted of a minimum of two sections conducted in Spanish. One of these sections consisted of three questions about the participants' childhood, and the other section consisted of questions regarding the legend of la Llorona and asked the interviewees to retell the version of the story that they knew. These sections allowed for potential narratives in Spanish or in a mix of Spanish and English for participants who had conducted most of our conversation in English. However, simply because I initiated these topics in Spanish and maintained my portion of the conversation in Spanish, this did not ensure that participants would follow suit. The retelling of the legend of La Llorona is also a component of the NMCOSS. The retelling of this legend in the Mexicano-Nuevomexicano context opens a space for different discourses regarding ownership of the legend, as well as potential Spanish or translanguaging discourse among participants who had primarily spoken English in our interview and/or plática. Kelly Medina López explains that, "as New Mexicans, we claim La Llorona as our story. She is part of the common experience of growing up New Mexican, and she shapes our understanding of what New Mexico means. Claiming her story is complicated because it is not only a shared story, but also an individual story."[163] I contend that the retelling of this story among my participants allows for differing accounts and another site in which to explore authenticating practices and competing authenticities of Latinidad. Lastly, at the conclusion of the individual conversation, the participants engaged in a short lexical elicitation activity with ten items modeled after the NMCOSS

---

162. Fierros and Delgado-Bernal, "Vamos a platicar," 109–14.
163. Medina-López, "La Llorona as Querencia," 279.

lexical elicitation task. The participants were asked to provide the word that they used the most for the pictures of the given lexical variables that I showed them from a color printout of a document that I put together with the following items: strawberry, nurse, postage stamps, dress, pea, green beans, apricot, turkey, bat, and light bulb. In summary, by adopting an ethnographic mode of cultural studies and utilizing qualitative ethnographic research methods and Chicana feminist pláticas, I was able to gather rich narratives emphasizing cultural identities, language maintenance and shift, and language ideologies. Gray notes that a flexible approach to research methods in cultural studies "acknowledges the dynamic nature of cultural and social processes and of meaning production, and has the potential to respond to the complex ways in which individuals or agents, or subjects, inhabit their specific formations, identities, and subjectivities."[164] *Zones of Encuentro* implements this flexible approach in order to unpack the multilayered ethnolinguistic identities of Mexicano-Nuevomexicano families.

Critical Approaches to Analysis

I would like to call attention to the concept of "narratives" and to the process of self-narration and self-reporting within my project. Keeping in mind that participants' self-reports about their own attitudes, language use, and language ideologies have their limitations, my main objective in conducting the interviews and pláticas with the families was to document the family members' stories, voices, and experiences through their own self-narration. I wanted the participants to tell me about their lives in their own words. This method is consistent with an approach to Latinidad that allows these Latinos/as/xs to theorize about their daily lived experiences in their own words.[165] It is also consistent with pláticas. Saavedra and Esquierdo explain, "Pláticas as a methodology stem from and honor the rich cultural tradition of communicating and transferring cultural knowledge, wisdom and consejos (advice) in our familias. Important to acknowledge is that pláticas are not only good for collecting data or as a method, but pláticas are also intimately tied to meaning making."[166] Part of this meaning-making manifests itself in theorizing together our language experiences. Gray explains the importance of theorizing experience. She states,

---

164. Gray, *Research Practice for Cultural Studies*.
165. This approach is consistent with the methods in Rúa, "Colao Subjectivities."
166. Saavedra and Esquierdo, "Pláticas on Disrupting Language," 39.

> We need to theorise "experience." . . . Experience can be understood as a discursive "site of articulation" upon and through which subjectivities and identities are shaped and constructed. . . . Experience is not an authentic and original source of our being, but part of the process through which we articulate a sense of identity. . . . Thus, attention to the lived, to how individuals account for their lives and how they position themselves in relation to their experience can produce new knowledges. . . . This work is essential if cultural studies is to remain a dynamic field of inquiry.[167]

Accordingly, giving voice to the narratives of the lived experiences of my participants, and using this experience as the basis for the production of theory, is a key element to cultural studies methodologies and, specifically, Latino/a/x cultural studies methodologies. Ana Aparicio and colleagues highlight their ethnographic approach to centering community knowledge production through the idea of "refusals." They explain, "Refusals, too, push against the discipline in capturing how marginalized populations are never just objects of research but are engaging in their own analytics: they are intellectuals in their own right: they want to tell stories of love, pleasure, as well as—or perhaps beyond—struggle and pain."[168] I invoke this notion of ethnographic refusal in the intentional creation of a space within my data collection methods for the Mexicano-Nuevomexicano participants to engage in meaning-making processes through a safe and respectful conversational partnership and plática.

Aparicio cites Daiute and Lightfoot[169] in emphasizing that "narratives serve as a genre that offers 'culturally developed ways of organizing experience and knowledge.'"[170] My methods of analysis approach this organizing of personal knowledge and experience as a space from which the themes for my study, and the organization of my chapters, emerge. This is consistent with Rúa's approach to her data.

> In analyzing the data, I used a grounded theory approach, the researcher actively suspending her preconceived assumptions about what the data would reveal, inductively, developing arguments and theories from material collected. This requires the researcher to rely on data as a guide to sense-making, to detect meanings and associations within the data, and to generate theory.[171]

---

167. Gray, *Research Practice for Cultural Studies*, 25.
168. Aparicio et al., "Introduction," xxxix.
169. Daiute and Lightfoot, *Narrative Analysis*.
170. Aparicio, "Intimate (Trans)Nationals," 274.
171. Rúa, *Grounded Identidad*.

Rúa highlights two key steps in the data analysis procedures that I follow. First I allow the different linguistic and cultural themes to emerge from the data, and then I generate theory from these themes. This is the structure I follow throughout this book. Each chapter is organized around the themes that emerged. These themes include identity, language practices, opinions and evaluations about language varieties, language loss, and mentions of the term Spanglish. These themes then allowed me to structure the chapters around the topics of cultural and linguistic influence (recontact), language maintenance and shift, language ideologies and authenticating practices, ethnolinguistic identities, and translanguaging practices. For each chapter, I present the data, describe it, connect it to previous work, and theorize about it. In the production of this theory, I seek to highlight the theorizations produced by my participants while also drawing attention to the cultural processes and contradictions that surround these theorizations. Integrating a performance studies lens allows me to do this. Alejandro Madrid explains, "Performance studies does not seek to describe actions so they could be faithfully reproduced later; instead, it attempts to understand what these actions do in the cultural field where they happen and what they allow people to do in their everyday life."[172] In the chapters that follow, I analyze cultural processes and ask questions about these processes that focus on what a particular cultural text or linguistic practice does rather than adopt a solely descriptive focus on what it is.

Auto-Encuentro Zone: Position as a Chicana Researcher

> For Chicana feminists, the recuperation of history happens through the recuperation of language—mainly Spanish. They use the Spanish language as a tie to the past, as a link to the memory of colonization as they cross the border, and as a recuperation of a culture and a self that is not defined by oppression alone.[173]
>
> —Aída Hurtado

I approach *Zones of Encuentro* not only as decolonial homeplace ethnography but also as a Chicana feminist project. For me, it is a site for self-encuentro (auto-encuentro zone?) that allows me to achieve a process of conocimiento[174] about my intergenerational ethnolinguistic histories and the language experi-

---

172. Madrid, "Why Music and Performance Studies?," para. 4.
173. Hurtado, *Intersectional Chicana Feminisms*, 74.
174. In Anzaldúa, "Now, Let Us Shift," 577, she defines "conocimiento" as a deep awareness and "the aspect of consciousness urging you to act on knowledge gained."

ences in my family. Delgado Bernal[175] explains that a Chicana feminist epistemology approach utilizes a Chicana perspective that uniquely and usefully informs every aspect of the research and analysis process. Delgado Bernal's notion of "cultural intuition"[176] allows me to put my viewpoint as a Chicana, my personal experience, and the collective experiences of my community into dialogue with my research. Through the co-construction of conversations and the opportunity for participants (including myself) "to assess or theorize about their own lived experiences,"[177] Chicana feminist epistemology allows for a deeper exploration of the recuperation of history and language referenced by Hurtado.

I am a Chicana, Nuevomexicana, heritage learner of Spanish, and professor of Spanish who has been on this complex recuperation journey of my familia's language and ethnolinguistic history for almost as long as I can remember. Growing up hearing all four of my grandparents speak Spanish to each other, their friends, and their siblings, but rarely to my parents or the grandchildren illustrates a reality of linguistic colonization that was part of their language experiences and was passed on intergenerationally. The colonized educational sites that contributed to my grandparents' linguistic oppression, and deprived later generations of the whys and hows of our familia's linguistic dispossession, still impact us today. All four of my Nuevomexicano/a grandparents grew up with Spanish as a primary language. Whether it be in Taos (my paternal grandmother's homeland), Santa Fe (my paternal grandfather's homeland), or Belén (my maternal grandparents' homeland), the geographies of their language experiences were similar. Putting together the pieces of their experiences with my own language recovery work has been a decolonial project. Lugones explains that "'decolonial' marks or forms sites and methods of resistance to the colonization that dehumanized most of the people in the world."[178] Centering Latino/a/x language experiences in the US is a site of resistance to linguistic colonization and manifests itself in the decolonial vision of *Zones of Encuentro*.

Additional pieces of my journey of familial language recuperation include the letter that my paternal grandpa's older brother wrote to him as a teenager from World War II, one week before he would die in the war, encouraging my grandpa to stay in school, leave Spanish behind, and get rid of his accent. Having already experienced punishment and placement in "special ed" classes in Santa Fe for speaking Spanish during his early school years, my grandpa

---

175. Delgado-Bernal, "Using a Chicana Feminist Epistemology."
176. Delgado-Bernal, "Using a Chicana Feminist Epistemology," 563.
177. Fierros and Delgado-Bernal, "Vamos a platicar," 109.
178. Lugones, "Decolonial," 43.

Robert Gorman Sr. was surrounded by ideologies of one-language, one-nation normative monolingualism. These pieces also include memories of my maternal grandparents watching Mexican telenovelas and frequently pulling out a large dictionary that they kept on the side of the couch to look up unfamiliar words. My grandma explained to me it was so that they could learn "the right way" to say things. These intergenerational language experiences also include my dad, a proud Chicano from Santa Fe who always served as a caretaker of our linguistic and cultural querencias, expressing insecurities about his own Spanish after having interacted with monolingual Mexicanos/as/xs or other Latin Americans.

I contend that we cannot learn about our own encuentros with linguistic oppression without contextualizing them with other Latino/a/x groups, namely, Mexicanos/as/xs. How do we learn about our own linguistic dispossession without studying these zones of encuentro? These zones of encuentro are sprinkled throughout my and my families' language experiences. There seems to have always been a subtle sense of defining ourselves "against" Mexicanos/as/xs and Mexicano/a/x Spanish varieties among my abuelitos and my parents. And part of my linguistic revitalization was located in Mexico. The only reason I was able to sit down at the dining room table and feel confident conversing in Spanish with my grandparents in my twenties and thirties was because of Mexicanos/as/xs who increased my linguistic security throughout my journey. Hurtado reminds us that the recuperation of culture and self "is not defined by oppression alone,"[179] and being able to relate to my grandparents in the sweet translanguaging spaces of our living rooms and kitchen tables provided access to a linguistic dimension of our relationship and a linguistic homemaking or querencia that would not have been possible without my personal zones of encuentro and recovery. Aimee Carrillo-Rowe's notion of differential belonging references these types of connections. Differential belonging calls "attention to the ways in which we are already constituted in and through often overlooked modes of belonging."[180] I suggest that my own decolonial process of recovery of language and ethnolinguistic history must always be characterized by locating ourselves within the context of belonging with Mexicanos/as/xs in New Mexico. I learn about the colonial traces in my own familial language experience by reconstructing, recovering, y encontrando los pedazos in the "productive spaces of transformation" between "local/national struggles and regional processes,"[181] embodied in the encuentros of differential belonging.

---

179. Hurtado, *Intersectional Chicana Feminisms*, 74.
180. Carrillo-Rowe, "Be Longing," 32.
181. Álvarez et al., "Encountering Latin American," 540.

García and Sánchez's explicit focus on centering the work of "pioneering studies of Latina scholars" such as Anzaldúa, Valdés, and Zentella "to affirm the complex bilingualism of Latinx communities"[182] is a model I follow in *Zones of Encuentro*. I explicitly elevate this work not only because this research is important and has greatly influenced me, but also because it is decolonizing work to center Latina language scholars. It is also a move that embodies Chicana feminist epistemology as a "means to resist epistemological racism."[183] I identify as a Chicana scholar of Latino/a/x cultural studies and language. Indeed, if not for Anzaldúa's words in her essay "How to Tame a Wild Tongue," from her groundbreaking *Borderlands/La Frontera*, I would not have found the guidance and affirmation to do this work. In particular, the following formative words continuously serve as a guidepost: "So, if you want to really hurt me, talk badly about my language. Ethnic identity is twin-skin to linguistic identity—I am my language. Until I can take pride in my language, I cannot take pride in myself."[184] Therefore, *Zones of Encuentro* elevates the voices of Latina language scholars such as Valdés, Frances Aparicio, Gonzales-Berry, and Zentella. It also gives me the permission to elevate my voice and those of my antepasados y abuelitos; the beautifully bilingual voices of my familia Sánchez, Aragón, Montoya, Maes, and Gorman están presentes aquí.

Last, I would like to note that because of my position as a hometown ethnographer engaging in homework in my communities, this tenuous position challenges me to be continuously aware of my culturally mediated position as a researcher, rather than operating under illusions of objectivity or solidarity. This simultaneous insider/outsider positionality also exhorts me to heed Aparicio and Chávez-Silverman's[185] warning to be vigilant in not reinscribing power differentials. It is important to recognize certain power asymmetries that might have been at play in my interactions with my participants. Renato Rosaldo reminds researchers that "culture and power are inextricably intertwined" and that "in discussing forms of social knowledge, both of analysts and of human actors, one must consider their social positions. What are the complexities of the speaker's social identity? What life experiences have shaped it? Does the person speak from a position of relative dominance or relative subordination?"[186] These are not easy questions but are necessary when maintaining a necessary vigilance around power differentials.

---

182. García and Sánchez, "Making of the Language," 31.
183. Delgado-Bernal, "Using a Chicana Feminist Epistemology," 556.
184. Anzaldúa, *Borderlands/La Frontera*, 81.
185. Aparicio and Chávez-Silverman, "Introduction," 7.
186. Rosaldo, *Culture and Truth*, 169.

Most of the participants in my study knew me or were aware of the fact that I taught at New Mexico Highlands University. Two of the participants were my former students. I believe that this information may have framed me as having certain "authority" due to my academic position. I also characterize myself as an insider/outsider within this work because I am Nuevomexicana; however, I would not characterize the Spanish that I speak as identifiable as New Mexican Spanish. This is an instance of linguistic dispossession, as previously noted. Having to leave my home to "immerse" myself in Spanish in Mexico reflects a neocolonial reality. Indeed, the G1 Mexican participants often commented during and after our interviews that I spoke Spanish "really well" and that I did not sound like I was from New Mexico. Although I never explicitly stated this, they all seemed to know that I was a native Nuevomexicana. In several of the interviews, the participants would position me in the Nuevomexicano group with various remarks. For example, one G1 participant told me, "Si preguntas a tus abuelos se han de acordar de cómo fue que no permitieron a la gente de aquí hablar español" [If you ask your grandparents they should remember how it was when they didn't allow people from here to speak Spanish]. I am not aware of all of the ways that my participants may have perceived or positioned me, just as I am not completely aware of all the ways that I may have unintentionally positioned them. However, I can say with certainty that I always felt welcomed and like I was with familia when visiting with them. My hope is that they felt the same. In the next section, I describe my puntos de encuentro, or points of entry, with each Mexicano-Nuevomexicano family.

Retratos de Familia: Mexicano-Nuevomexicano Family Portraits

I first met Andrea Guzmán[187] of the Guzmán family in Taos during the summer of 2009 while she was participating in an eight-day Spanish immersion program for New Mexico bilingual education teachers. I was teaching in the program, and I arrived to one of our class sessions early. As I was preparing my materials, I could hear Andrea's conversation with a classmate. With much emotion she was explaining the ways in which her Mexicana sister-in-law insisted on correcting her Spanish. My radar went up as I heard her mention these corrections and her own accounts of defending northern New Mexican Spanish. Andrea seemed to have the attention of the entire class with her

---

187. As mentioned earlier in this introduction, all participants chose a name to be their pseudonym, and these are the names I use throughout the book.

descriptions of her attempts to defend her way of speaking to her Mexicano/a in-laws, and we proceeded to begin class with the retelling of these experiences. The conversation that began in the classroom that summer extended for several years as Andrea and I remained in contact. Almost three years later, I was able to interview thirty-eight-year-old Andrea in her hometown of Taos, where she resides with her family and where she met her husband. Andrea's husband, Manuel, hailed from Uriangato, Guanajuato, and arrived in Taos at the age of sixteen. I interviewed Andrea; her first-generation Mexicano husband, Manuel; her son, Alejandro; and her daughter, Alexa. I conducted Andrea's interview in Andrea's kindergarten classroom in the neighboring community of Arroyo Seco and the other family member interviews and pláticas in the Guzmán living room in Taos.

I also met Alicia Molina of the Molina family in Bernalillo as a student in my class for bilingual teachers in Las Vegas. Alicia was a student-teacher attending New Mexico Highlands University; however, she was native to Bernalillo. One of my colleagues knew Alicia from a previous class and alerted me to the fact that her father was a first-generation Mexicano immigrant, while her mother was a native Nuevomexicana from Placitas, New Mexico. Upon completion of the class, Alicia agreed to introduce me to her family, and I conducted the interviews and pláticas with Mexicana-Nuevomexicana Alicia, her Mexicano-Nuevomexicano brother, Antonio; Nuevomexicana mother, Elizabeth; and Mexicano father, Pancho. Pancho arrived in Albuquerque as a teenager from his hometown of Cuauhtémoc, Chihuahua.

Upon the conclusion of my group plática with the Molina family, Elizabeth and Pancho mentioned that their comadre might also be willing to participate. Alicia texted her and within days I was having a phone conversation with Verónica Fierro of the Fierro family from Algodones. Verónica and I met at her home in the South Valley of Albuquerque, and we held our conversations around her kitchen table. She called her parents, and they also agreed to participate. Through interviews and pláticas, I came to know Verónica's Nuevomexicana mother, Juanita, and her first-generation Mexicano father, Luis. Luis was from San Francisco de Conchos, Chihuahua, and moved to Albuquerque when he was twenty-two years old. Within one year of moving to Albuquerque, Luis met Juanita, eloped with her, and then they moved to Algodones, where they have lived for the past forty years.

Pía Loredo of the Loredo family in Las Vegas works as an educational assistant at the dual-language elementary school in that town. Pía is a first-generation Mexicana immigrant from Mazatlán, and we connected through a mutual friend. Pía was excited to meet with me at her home in West Las Vegas. She told me of the unlikely pairing between herself and her Nuevomexicano husband, Francisco. Pía's story recalls a longer history between Las Vegas and Mexico. Because Pía's parish priest in Mazatlán attended a Mexican seminary that was in operation outside of Las Vegas until about fifty years ago, he was very familiar with Las Vegas. This priest was also especially close with the Loredo family. Many years later the priest organized a trip of young adults from his parish in Mazatlán to visit Las Vegas. Pía took part in this trip, and, while visiting with the Loredo family, she caught Francisco's eye. After months of long-distance phone calls, mediated through the priest, and several visits to Mazatlán by Francisco, Pía agreed to marry him and relocate to Las Vegas. Francisco and Pía have one daughter, Angélica. All of our interviews and pláticas took place at the family home in the living room or outside around the picnic table. I was also able to conduct a follow-up plática with Pía in September 2022 at her home in West Las Vegas.

Pía and our mutual friend connected me with another educator at the dual-language elementary school in Las Vegas. I met Carolina Santos of the Santos family in Leyba, in her classroom at the elementary school. After explaining my interest in the interactions between Mexicanos/as/xs and Nuevomexicanos/as/xs, she eagerly agreed to tell me about her family and to introduce me to her parents and sister. Carolina is a Mexicana-Nuevomexicana from Leyba.

Leyba is located approximately twenty-five miles southeast of Las Vegas. Carolina invited me to her home in El Pueblo (near Leyba), and we spoke for hours in her living room. Carolina then facilitated interviews with her Nuevomexicano father, Juan, and her first-generation Mexicana mother, Marta, which also took place in Carolina's living room. Marta emigrated from Chihuahua to Albuquerque with her own father and stepmother when she was only twelve years old. Carolina met Juan in Albuquerque when she was sixteen, and, after marrying, they moved back to Juan's hometown of Gonzales Ranch / Leyba. This is where they raised their family. I was also able to interview Carolina's youngest sister, Edna. However, this interview took place at my parents' house in Albuquerque. Edna lives and works full-time in Albuquerque as a dual-language teacher and part-time at Home Depot. Because of her busy schedule, she preferred to conduct the interview in Albuquerque, and the location of my parents' house was close to the Home Depot where she worked. The family plática took place in Carolina's living room.

The community of Ribera is only a few miles from Leyba and El Pueblo. Because of this, most of the residents of these communities all attend the same Catholic church of San Miguel. Through this common parish, Carolina was able to connect me with another Mexicano-Nuevomexicano family nearby in Ribera: the Navarro family. I attended Mass together with Carolina and her family one Sunday morning, and after Mass she pointed out two of the daughters in this family. I approached the teenage daughter and spoke to her about my project. Her name was Rosalinda Navarro. She then introduced me to her sister, Milagros, and her mother, Gabriela. Gabriela was a first-generation Mexicana immigrant from Colima. I then scheduled a visit to the family house in Ribera for the following week. At that time, I interviewed Nicolas, Gabriela's Nuevomexicano husband, and Milagros. I returned the following week to interview Gabriela and Rosalinda. I then returned two weeks later for a plática with the entire family together.

Also because of my involvement in the community of Las Vegas, I was able to connect with an additional Mexicano-Nuevomexicano family in Santa Fe: the Jurado family. I was teaching a Spanish conversation course to parents of the children attending the dual-language elementary, and one of the parents mentioned that she had a friend who had a Mexicano father and a Nuevomexicana mother. She called Rose Jurado and told her about the project. I then contacted Rose, and she enthusiastically agreed to participate. I met Rose at her workplace in Santa Fe, and we conducted her interview in her classroom at the elementary school where she taught. We conducted her parents' interviews at their home just outside of Santa Fe in La Cienega, New Mexico. Her father, Armando, was a first-generation immigrant from Santa Bárbara, Chihuahua. Her mother was a Nuevomexicana from Santa Fe, Diana. We conducted the family interview at the parents' home as well. Several weeks later, I conducted a second follow-up plática with Rose and her Nuevomexicano husband, Mike, at their house in La Cienega. In fall 2022 (ten years after the initial interviews), I visited with Rose for an additional plática at her house. Although we had kept in touch over the years through social media, on a September evening we were able to have an extended conversation about her family and current events in Santa Fe over fresh tortillas, chicharrones, and guacamole in her kitchen.

I met Rolando Quintana of the Quintana family in Santa Fe through a family connection. Rolando was very interested in participating in the project and spoke to his Nuevomexicana mother, Ana, and his first-generation Mexicano father, José Luis, about it. They both agreed to participate. Rolando was living and working in Albuquerque, so we conducted the interview in a conference room in my father's office in downtown Albuquerque due to its central location. I conducted his parents' interviews at their home in Santa Fe, and we also conducted the follow-up family plática at the home in Santa Fe. Rolando has one younger sister, who was present in the house in Santa Fe during the interviews and pláticas.

TABLE 2. Family names and demographics

FAMILY NAME	PLACE	NUEVOMEXICANO/A (NMX) PARENT AND AGE	MEXICANO/A (MX) PARENT AND AGE	MEXICANO-NUEVOMEXICANO (MNMX) CHILDREN AND AGES
Guzmán	Taos	Andrea, 38	Manuel, 39	Alejandro, 18
				Alexa, 15
Molina	Bernalillo	Elizabeth, 44	Pancho, 45	Alicia, 23
				Antonio, 17
Fierro	Algodones	Juanita, 56	Luis, 63	Verónica, 39
Loredo	Las Vegas	Francisco, 54	Pía, 45	Angélica, 16
Santos	Gonzales Ranch/Leyba	Juan, 68	Marta, 64	Carolina, 43
				Edna, 29
Navarro	Ribera	Nicolás, 50	Gabriela, 46	Milagros, 18
				Rosalinda, 17
Jurado	Santa Fe	Diana, 60	Armando, 59	Rose, 36
Quintana	Santa Fe	Ana, 51	José Luis, 51	Rolando, 24
Medina	Española	Penélope, 48	José, 60	Adrian, 18
				Olivia, 17
Maestas	Las Vegas	Not available	Not Available	Sylvia, 33

Penélope Medina and I had our first conversation over coffee at the McDonald's in Española. Penélope's brother and I had been close friends for many years; however, I had never met Penélope until that particular morning. Penélope's brother had facilitated the meeting, and, before I even began my explanation of my project, Penélope exclaimed, "You know, the Mexicans are really different from us." Penélope automatically positioned me in the "us" or Nuevomexicano/a/x category and then proceeded to explain to me her family situation. Penélope was married to a first-generation Mexicano, José, from Chihuahua. They had four children together; however, only two were available to participate in the interviews and pláticas. Penélope is originally from Tierra Amarilla, New Mexico, but she had lived in Española most of her adult life. She also met José in Española. Penélope and José, along with their teenaged children Adrian and Olivia participated in the interviews. Our individual plática took place in a conference room at Penélope's place of employment, McCurdy High School. Our family plática took place in Penélope's living room. It is important to note that Penélope and José were in the process of beginning divorce proceedings when I began the interviews. By the time we scheduled the group plática, Penélope and José were divorced. This is the only Mexicano-Nuevomexicano family unit in which a separation or divorce occurred. In August of 2022, Penélope and I reconnected at a celebration of life for her father, and we scheduled some time for the following month to catch up. Seated at her kitchen table in Española, platicamos, and Penélope shared with me that her ex-husband, José, had passed away several years earlier.

Lastly, I met with Sylvia Maestas at her workplace at Luna Community College to conduct our interview. Sylvia was one of my first friends in Las Vegas, when I moved there in summer 2005. At the time, Sylvia worked in the provost's office as a student worker, and I was not aware that she had a Mexicana-Nuevomexicana background. More than a year into our friendship, Sylvia shared with me that her dad was Mexicano. Sylvia was born and raised until high school in Tucumcari, New Mexico, where her parents met. She spent much of her time as a child and adult with her Nuevomexicana grandmother in Tucumcari. Her mother's side of the family has roots in Mora, New Mexico, and Sylvia moved to Las Vegas with her mother and sister after her parents divorced. Sylvia has lived in Las Vegas since the mid-1990s, and she was the only individual from her family that I interviewed.

Table 2 summarizes the names, ages, and Mexicano/a/x (MX), Nuevomexicano/a/x (NMX), and Mexicano/a/x-Nuevomexicano/a/x (MNMX) designations in each family in 2012. I asked the participants to choose their own pseudonyms for their first and last names.

Chapter Summaries

In this closing section of the introduction, I want to highlight some key ideas about the interdisciplinary ways in which I approach analysis of the data and subsequently organize the chapters. This introduction has outlined the key frameworks of contact zones, encuentro, Latinidad, authentication, Chicana feminist epistemology, critical applied linguistics, and sociocultural linguistics as the approaches that guide *Zones of Encuentro*. They are interwoven into my approach and analysis throughout the chapters. In bringing these frameworks together, *Zones of Encuentro* creates a meeting place for (Latino/a/x) cultural studies, critical applied linguistics, sociolinguistics, (linguistic) anthropology, and Chicana feminist studies. Each chapter productively brings together tools and theories from these areas to analyze the narratives and pláticas that comprise the data. For example, chapter 1 examines the notion of "recontact" by putting Cisneros and Leone's work into conversation with Villa and

Rivera-Mills's sociolinguistic proposal, while continuously dialoguing with the process of Latinidad that is at play. This discussion is then advanced toward the notion of "transculturation" and invokes theories from key cultural studies, performance studies, and literary studies to create another dimension of analysis. Each chapter follows this same type of interdisciplinary "unruly" rhythm. Each chapter of *Zones of Encuentro* also begins with the words of a participant or words from Mexicana-Nuevomexicana Mari Luci Jaramillo's memoir.[188] These quotes frame the topic of the chapter with voices from the Mexicano-Nuevomexicano context, thereby centering the Mexicano-Nuevomexicano language experiences from the first page of each chapter.

In chapter 1, "Recontact Zones: Generational Complications, Language Recovery, and Transculturations," I approach the Mexicano-Nuevomexicano couples as concrete cases of linguistic and cultural recontact. Taking as a point of departure Cisneros and Leone's proposal of "recontact," I explore the power dynamics present within the process of recontact, and I examine the multidirectional nature of influence and the ways in which Mexicanos/as/xs and Nuevomexicanos/as/xs mutually transculturate each other. I conclude the chapter with a discussion regarding the ways in which these moments of linguistic and cultural transculturation lead toward reterritorialization.

In chapter 2, "From Language Shift to Language Shaping," I primarily focus on how familial language use patterns reported by the Mexicano/a/x-Nuevomexicano/a/x individuals in the study contribute to a more complex understanding of Spanish language maintenance and shift both within the families and in northern New Mexico overall. I propose that through subtle acts of language maintenance, recovery, and agency the Mexicano/a/x-Nuevomexicanos/as/xs become "language shapers" rather than language shifters.

Chapter 3, "The Weight of Words: Spanish Language Ideologies, Lexical Choices, and Authenticity in Mexicano-Nuevomexicano Families," examines the language ideologies that operate within each Mexicano-Nuevomexicano family unit regarding lexical choice. I primarily draw from the narratives of the Mexicano/a/x-Nuevomexicanos/as/xs in the study in order to understand the authenticating practices of correction that activate language ideologies regarding the Mexican and New Mexican Spanish lexicon. These practices and ideologies ultimately lead to an overall affirmation of the Spanish language within these families, even as a particular variety of Spanish (New Mexican Spanish) is subordinated.

In chapter 4, "Disjunctures and Difference: Theorizing the Mixed Identities of Mexicano-Nuevomexicanos," I explore familial disjunctures around

---

188. M. L. Jaramillo, *Madam Ambassador*.

discussions regarding cultural identities. I highlight the role of language in these identity-making processes. I also unpack the multiple meanings of the identity terms invoked by the Mexicano/a/x-Nuevomexicanos/as/xs in the study and, specifically, the resignification that occurs around the term "Hispanic."

Chapter 5, "'The Spanglish Lives We Live': Reframing New Mexican Spanish through Spanglish and Contemplating Ethnolinguistic Futures," examines ideologies centered around the relationship between Spanglish and New Mexican Spanish. I explore the role of English and the translanguaging practices in the Mexicano-Nuevomexicano families in the study. Additionally, I discuss Mexicano/a/x-Nuevomexicano/a/x ethnolinguistic futures and the possibilities for the persistence of New Mexican Spanish through what I term "linguistic querencias."

I conclude *Zones of Encuentro* by contemplating contemporary discussions in northern New Mexico around "heritage" and "home." I connect these discussions to the notion of "recovery," and I suggest that the Mexicano-Nuevomexicano zones of encuentro are part of a fundamental dimension to northern New Mexico heritage. *Zones of Encuentro* also encourages a reframing of "home" around the Mexicano-Nuevomexicano family that challenges static and limited notions of home.

CHAPTER 1

Recontact Zones

Generational Complications, Language Recovery, and Transculturations

> I would talk in English, and I would try to communicate in Spanish, but my Spanish was not there. So it was like really, really hard.
> —Andrea Guzmán, Nuevomexicana

On a chilly March afternoon in Andrea Guzmán's kindergarten classroom in Taos, she describes her first encounter with her future husband, Manuel. She states, "When I met my husband, um, I think there was some sort of a little bit of a prejudicism [sic] where I didn't realize he was Mexican until he spoke to me. And once he spoke to me then I was kind of, ah, like disappointed." Her reaction highlights the central role of language in recognizing Manuel's Mexicanness. And it is this very Mexicanness that seems to deter Andrea from considering Manuel as a potential romantic interest. She explains, "I was like, oh, my gosh, this guy is very handsome, but he's Mexican, so no, I was like, definitely not, I will not go out with this guy. And I don't even know why, because I didn't know Mexican people, but there was like something where I just didn't feel like I liked Mexican people."

Andrea reveals her negative predisposition toward Mexicanos/as/xs as something somewhat unexplainable to herself, as she clearly acknowledges that her attitude was not based on any previous contact with Mexicanos/as/xs. Despite this lack of prior contact, Andrea does indeed engage in communication with Manuel. Andrea recounts this process in the epigraph above. She elaborates, "But I did understand Spanish so I was able to comm—I mean I was able to understand what he said." Andrea's reference to her Spanish "not being there" exposes a complicated linguistic profile that emphasizes a certain level of comprehension, but downplays an ability to produce Spanish, as revealed in her self-interruption and correction of "comm—," as in "communicate," to "understand." Despite the minimization of her linguistic proficiency in Spanish, Andrea and Manuel do successfully communicate. In fact, their initial unfamiliar interactions transform into more than twenty years of long-term contact and communication. Andrea explains, "We just like became friends and we started talking. And after that it was like we fell in love and we became best friends. And we've been married nineteen years." Andrea and Manuel do not simply put aside negative cultural perceptions and communication challenges for one interaction. On the contrary, the couple's relationship is a testament to long-term cultural and linguistic negotiations that result in a sustained situation of *recontact*.

In this chapter I examine the different positionalities of the romantic partners through an interrogation of their generational groups and the dimensions it adds to the exploration of recontact. I flesh out what the Nuevomexicanos/as/xs' linguistic profiles looked like before recontact and the complexity of the Nuevomexicanos/as/xs' generational status. I also attempt to capture the tensions that reveal power differentials within the initial encounters of the couples, particularly the ways in which the Nuevomexicano/a partners' linguistic histories are minimized and erased. Then I examine several indicators of the impact of recontact on the Nuevomexicanos/as/xs' language use. Next, I provide an in-depth analysis of the transculturative dimensions of recontact and its circulating influence on both the Mexicano/a and Nuevomexicano/a partners. Lastly, I contemplate the ways in which recontact can lead to reterritorialization.

Cisneros and Leone define recontact as "a continuing relationship between early settlers, their descendants, and recent arrivals. Recontact demonstrates the possible influence one group may have on the other with respect to perception of community language experiences and the cultural traditions used by members of the community."[1] Cisneros and Leone's study focuses on "early settlers, their descendants, and recent arrivals" with a common connection to the same country of origin (Mexico). I interpret the concept more broadly and apply it to Latino/a/x groups in the US who both share and do not share the same countries of origin.[2] In a sense, this entire book is about the cultural processes of recontact or (re)encuentro. Recontact fits nicely within the framework of *Zones of Encuentro* due to its emphasis on long-term relationships and mutual influence. In this chapter, it is precisely through the lens of recontact that I unpack the ways in which Mexicanos/as/xs and

---

1. Cisneros and Leone, "Mexican American Language Communities," 185.

2. Lynch, "Spanish-Speaking Miami," also applies a broad interpretation of recontact in the study of different Latino/a/x groups in Miami.

Nuevomexicanos/as/xs culturally and linguistically influence each other. It is important to note that few detailed cases of recontact are documented in previous sociolinguistic studies of US Latinos/as/xs. Consequently, the nine Mexicano-Nuevomexicano couples in this project provide rare and concrete case studies of this phenomenon.

RECONTACT INSIDE AND OUTSIDE OF NUEVO MÉXICO

Recontact is primarily referenced in studies of Spanish language shift in the US as "the social phenomenon that is most vital and favorable to future maintenance of Spanish among U.S.-born speakers."[3] Past studies of Spanish language shift in the US[4] state that it is the continued influx of new Latino/a/x immigrant populations that will continue to keep Spanish alive and will essentially "revitalize" Spanish in the US (particularly in the Southwest) and provide a cultural reinfusion. Yet, this idea of revitalization implies that there is some kind of significant contact between the more established generations of Latinos/as/xs and the new arrivals. However, none of these studies prove if the process of recontact actually occurs. Waltermire's research and Del Angel Guevara's dissertation[5] both find evidence of Mexican lexical items in Nuevomexicano/a/x language use, suggesting the influence of one group on the other. However, their studies do not document sustained or continuing relationships between the groups. With the notable exceptions of Cisneros and Leone and Lynch,[6] there are relatively few documented cases of such sustained linguistic interactions.[7] There is, however, an abundance of documentation of negative linguistic and cultural attitudes between first-generation Mexicans and more established generational groups as in the research of Ochoa, Hurtado and Vega, Hidalgo, Galindo, Rivera-Mills, and Mendoza-Denton.[8] These studies actually provide evidence that new immigration does

---

3. Lynch, "Toward a Theory," 39.
4. See Bills, "New Mexican Spanish"; Rivera-Mills, "Intraethnic Attitudes among Hispanics"; and Hurtado and Vega, "Shift Happens."
5. Waltermire, "Mexican Immigration"; and Del Angel Guevara, "Returning to Northern New Mexico."
6. Cisneros and Leone, "Mexican-American Language Communities"; and Lynch, "Spanish-Speaking Miami."
7. Notably, Ochoa's 2004 research provides an in-depth examination of these interactions from a sociological perspective, while Griswold del Castillo, *Familia*, and Gutiérrez, *Walls and Mirrors*, explore these encounters from a historical perspective.
8. Ochoa, *Becoming Neighbors*; Hurtado and Vega, "Shift Happens"; Hidalgo, "Spanish Language Shift Reversal"; Galindo, "Language Attitudes"; Rivera-Mills, "Intraethnic Attitudes among Hispanics"; and Mendoza-Denton, *Homegirls*.

not lead to sustained relationships or frequent interaction and that mutual processes of disassociation occur precisely because of language difference. The Chicanos/as/xs in Galindo's study avoid speaking Spanish because they do not want to be perceived as recently arrived "wet-backs"[9] and the first-generation Mexican immigrants in Hidalgo's study do not recognize the bilingualism of US-born Latinos/as/xs and "are often surprised, annoyed, and even shocked to hear the abundant borrowing, interference, and inter- and intra-sentential code-switching."[10]

Yet, the Mexicano-Nuevomexicano couples find a way to negotiate these negative perceptions, stereotypes, and lack of knowledge, and their stories allow for the exploration of the everyday lived dynamics of recontact. These everyday lived experiences recall the "complex moments of convergence" embodied in Latinidad.[11] Indeed, recontact and Latinidad consistently and productively inform each other throughout my exploration of the Mexicano-Nuevomexicano zones of encuentro, and I highlight the utility of putting these concepts together in this chapter. Additionally, the couples' accounts provide a type of "laboratory" in which to explore the linguistic implications of recontact. For example, it is clear that a romantic relationship with Manuel challenges Andrea to convert her receptive knowledge of Spanish into productive knowledge and, consequently, may alter trends of intergenerational Spanish language loss through her engagement with an expanded social network of monolingual Mexicano/a/x Spanish speakers. This is a fascinating possibility in and of itself. However, recontact is not simply a one-way process that solely affects the more established generational group by (re)stimulating a heritage language. As Pratt reminds us of the disparities present within contact spaces, the couples' relationships allow us to consider the ways in which recontact impacts both partners and the spaces of unevenness and mutual transculturations that are mapped onto the shifting cultural terrain of this process.

As I mentioned above, there seems to be an assumption that contact between first-generation Spanish-dominant immigrants and subsequent generational groups is common in many parts of the US. The New Mexico studies are no exception. Two related studies by Bills and Bills and Vigil[12] examine New Mexican Spanish and Spanish dialect variation in New Mexico. In both studies the authors conclude that New Mexican Spanish is experiencing a standardization or "Mexicanization" process that is associated with "the greater exposure of the younger generations to the larger Spanish-speaking

---

9. Galindo, "Language Attitudes," 86.
10. Hidalgo, "Spanish Language Shift Reversal," 62.
11. García and Rúa, "Processing Latinidad," 318.
12. Bills, "New Mexican Spanish"; and Bills and Vigil, "Ashes to Ashes."

world."[13] More than twenty years later Waltermire's research and Del Angel Guevara's study[14] confirm these conclusions. From a lexical perspective, it would seem that New Mexican Spanish is in a great deal of contact with Mexican Spanish in northern New Mexico despite its distance from the border. Bills explains that proximity to the border "increases the possibilities for contact with those who are monolingual in Spanish."[15] The fact that seven out of the nine Mexicano/a partners immigrated to New Mexico for work purposes seems to support Bills's claim that proximity to the border can be favorable for recontact.[16] However, because most of the couples met and live at least two hundred miles north of the border, defining "proximity" would be key in linking the Mexicano-Nuevomexicano interactions to Bills's study. Additionally, proximity to the border is not necessarily a determining factor when one immigrates for work. Moreover, Waltermire's and Del Angel Guevara's findings challenge the assumption regarding proximity to the border with their lexical data. However, the data does not necessarily show evidence of sustained relationships between Mexicanos/as/xs. Much research within the Southwest continues to assume that established Latino/a/x communities and newer immigrant arrivals have regular contact.

LINGUISTIC PROFILING: REFRAMING GENERATION

To explore "a continuing relationship between early settlers, their descendants, and recent arrivals,"[17] it is useful to (re)evaluate the notion of generation, as this is the most common method used to distinguish between the groups involved in recontact. The Mexicano-Nuevomexicano context adds a distinct dimension to the model of recontact in that Nuevomexicanos/as/xs and Mexicanos/as/xs do not necessarily see themselves as different generational members of the same group. They engage in continuous and simultaneous processes of disidentifying[18] and identifying. Part of the disidentification lies in the fact that Nuevomexicanos/as/xs do not have any recent immigration to reference in their generational histories. This presents the question, How does

---

13. Bills and Vigil, "Ashes to Ashes," 57.
14. Waltermire, "Mexican Immigration"; and Del Angel Guevara, "Returning to Northern New Mexico."
15. Bills, "New Mexican Spanish," 25.
16. However, this analysis also naturalizes the geographic dimension of the border while erasing its social and cultural dimensions. Tatum, "On the Border," elaborates on these multiple dimensions of "border."
17. Cisneros and Leone, "Mexican-American Language Communities," 185.
18. See Muñoz, *Disidentifications*.

the Mexicano-Nuevomexicano context reframe the notion of generation in a study of recontact?

A three-generation model for language-shift to English has been widely documented among minority language communities in the US. Fishman concludes that, by the fourth generation, English monolingualism is the reality for most immigrant groups.[19] Fishman and Veltman's research underscored these conclusions throughout the 1980s.[20] Silva-Corvalán's sociolinguistic conventions for denoting these generations relies on this "immigrant model." Recall that, according to Silva-Corvalán, G1 denotes an individual born abroad who came to the US after the age of twelve; a G2 designation describes an individual who was born in the US to two G1 parents, or who arrived in the US before the age of six; a G3 individual was born to at least one G2 parent.[21]

Because this model depends on an immigrant generation, it does not match the sociolinguistic history in northern New Mexico. For this reason, Villa and Rivera-Mills problematize the concept of Spanish as an "immigrant language" in the Southwest due to the "continuous Spanish-speaking presence that has existed along the Río Grande corridor that dates back to the arrival of settlers from Zacatecas, Mexico in 1598,"[22] and propose the "contact generation" as a reframing of the classic three-generation model. The contact generation provides a point from which Nuevomexicano families can trace their generational status within the context of English contact, rather than within a context of immigration. Villa and Rivera-Mills explain,

> We introduce the notion of a "contact generation." This consists of a generation monolingual in Spanish that comes into contact with English speakers after the critical period . . . either through its own migration or the arrival of English speakers into its territories. Examples of this generation are . . . Spanish speakers who were born in the U.S. and grew up in closely knit Spanish-speaking communities, who also learned English as adults, either through ESL classes or through joining the English-speaking workforce. Such individuals were typically found, for example, in rural communities throughout the state of New Mexico.[23]

Mexicano-Nuevomexicano couples allow for the opportunity to apply Villa and Rivera-Mills's model in order to closely read the linguistic profiles of the

---

19. Fishman, "Language Maintenance and Language Shift."
20. Fishman, "Rise and Fall"; and Veltman, "Language Shift."
21. Silva-Corvalán, *Language Contact and Change*.
22. Villa and Rivera-Mills, "Integrated Multi-Generational Model," 28.
23. Villa and Rivera-Mills, "Integrated Multi-Generational Model," 32.

Nuevomexicano/a partner and to flesh out the complexity and diversity within their generational status.

After identifying the contact generation, Villa and Rivera-Mills develop a maintenance/loss model based on the language and marriage patterns of the successive generations following the contact generation. Villa and Rivera-Mills trace seven generations within their model with four subsets within each generation.[24] Notably, they divide each generation into a shift/loss category and a maintenance category. In essence, they categorize members of each designation based on whether or not they are "Spanish/English bilinguals" who tend toward maintenance or "Spanish/English receptive bilinguals" who tend toward shift/loss.

Through my participants' narratives, specifically their answers to questions regarding who spoke Spanish in their family, I was able to deduce the contact generation. The interviews with the Nuevomexicano/a participants provided enough information to place many of the Nuevomexicano/a partners precisely within the subsets established in the model. However, many did not know enough background information about grandparents, great-grandparents, and, in some cases, great-great-grandparents for exact placement in the subcategories. For my purposes, I simply want to show the distance from the contact generation and the tendency toward maintenance or shift before the Nuevomexicano/a partner meets the first-generation Mexicano/a partner. It is not necessarily useful for me to fit my participants into all of the subcategories in the Villa and Rivera-Mills model, mainly because my sample is not large enough to lend itself to this type of application. However, my sample of Nuevomexicano/a participants does allow for a fleshing out of Villa and Rivera-Mills' underapplied notion of contact generation. A close reading of my participants' narratives of family language histories and language tendencies before meeting their partner permits the application of the contact generation framework to my project. In what follows I will highlight the generational profiles of each of the Nuevomexicano/a partners in relationship to the notion of contact generation. These profiles allow for a clearer understanding of the impact of recontact on the linguistic tendencies of the Nuevomexicano/a partners. I address the question, What did the Nuevomexicano/a partners' linguistic profiles look like before (re)contact?

Of the nine Nuevomexicano/a partners, the majority belong to the third-generation category. This generation is separated from the contact generation by two generations. Four of the partners are clearly categorizable as third-generation maintenance, while two Nuevomexicano/a partners belong to

---

24. Villa and Rivera-Mills, "Integrated Multi-Generational Model," 37.

the third-generation shift/loss category. It is difficult to categorize one of the Nuevomexicana partners. She is undoubtedly part of a maintenance designation, but, because she does not speak of her grandparents, it is not easy to deduce whether she is second-generation maintenance or third-generation maintenance. She explains that her parents spoke mostly Spanish, but also frequently mixed Spanish and English. However, without the grandparents' information it is not possible to make a clear determination. Regarding the remaining two Nuevomexicano/a partners, one belongs to the second-generation maintenance category (only one generation from the contact generation), and one belongs to the fourth-generation maintenance category (a full three generations after the contact generation). These designations reveal that most of the Nuevomexicano/a partners come to their initial interactions with their Mexicano/a partners with at least one, usually two, generations separating themselves from the contact generation and with a deep-rooted relationship with both Spanish and English.

Zones of Encuentro's application of the contact generation framework illuminates generational stories, experiences, and long-term relationships with Spanish. Additionally, the framework highlights the intricate ways in which each Nuevomexicano/a's experiences overlap with each other and allows for the exploration of the varying degrees of Spanish language persistence within their lives. This persistence reveals pieces of the sociohistorical linguistic legacy of northern New Mexico. For example, Juan (second-generation maintenance) underscores the vitality of his Spanish despite linguistic oppression in the public school system. He explains, "Sí, donde fui yo era puro español y en la escuela nos hacían hablar en inglés pero nos forzaban a hablar porque no queríamos, todos los de aquí naiden quería" [Yes, I was all Spanish and in school they made us speak in English, but they forced us to speak because we didn't want to, nobody from here wanted to]. Juan's words hint at a resistance to learning English present among his peers. Similarly, Francisco of Las Vegas (third-generation maintenance) underscores the effects of these punitive and oppressive linguistic policies. Francisco recounts, "The teacher used to tell us, 'Quit talking in Spanish. . . . Don't talk Spanish 'cause you're gonna get in trouble,' or whatever, no? And a lot of people my age don't know any Spanish 'cause of that I guess . . . I only knew Spanish. Spanish de aquí, ¿no? and I remember that clearly. I would get in trouble for talking Spanish."

Despite this treatment in the schools, Francisco emphasizes that he has always spoken Spanish to his parents and most of his siblings. The linguistic oppression or, in the spirit of Gloria Anzaldúa, the linguistic terrorism[25]

---

25. Anzaldúa, *Borderlands/La Frontera*.

did not deter him from maintaining his Spanish. Perhaps due to the rurality of San Miguel County, the numerical majority of Nuevomexicanos/as/xs in this region, or because they lived in a "closely knit Spanish-speaking community" (as defined by Villa and Rivera-Mills), Juan and Francisco were able to exercise a certain degree of their own agency in the maintenance of Spanish within their language experience. These outcomes certainly go against the assumption of an inevitable shift to English when schooling begins.[26] However, these narratives do not necessarily indicate an emergent stable bilingualism in these communities. Yet, they do reference an "intergenerational persistence of Spanish in this country not commonly found in other non-English, non-indigenous language groups."[27] In the case of Nicolás, he not only spoke primarily Spanish until he began school, but his mother also only spoke Spanish until beginning school. He explains, "Well, when, um, we grew up like I was telling you earlier, I grew up sorta like my mom did. We didn't learn English until we actually started going to school . . . so toda la primera lengua de nosotros siempre fue español y naturalmente el español de aquí, del norte de Nuevo México" [so the first language for all of us was always Spanish and naturally the Spanish from here, from northern New Mexico]. Nicolás's experience, also in San Miguel County, references a symmetry between generations that is not consistent with a shift, but instead with an intergenerational persistence of Spanish.[28]

One factor that seems to affect this persistence among the Nuevomexicano/a partners is the communicative need for Spanish with older family members from the contact generation. Nicolás often references the need to communicate in Spanish with his maternal grandmother, who lived well into Nicolás's adult life. This relationship also solidifies his tendency toward maintenance. Likewise, Juanita of Algodones highlights the key role of a Spanish-dominant grandparent in her life. She describes, "I spoke really good Spanish . . . New Mexican Spanish, because like I said my grandpa lived with us and my grandpa only spoke Spanish, and he was my sitter from the time when I was like nine until I was—until he passed away which I was about twelve or thirteen. So my Spanish was better than my siblings . . . so we communicated only in Spanish." However, Juanita does draw attention to the fact that a relationship with an older Spanish-speaking family member from the contact generation was not necessarily typical of those from her generational group. In fact, it wasn't even typical among all siblings within the same family. This experience recalls

---

26. See Valdés, *Con Respeto*; and Schecter and Bayley, *Language as Cultural Practice*.
27. Villa and Rivera-Mills, "Integrated Multi-Generational Model," 40.
28. Schecter and Bayley, *Language as Cultural Practice*, also examine this notion of "intergenerational persistence."

Francisco's reference to his schoolmates who also belonged to his same generational designation but were impacted negatively by the punitive treatment in school for speaking Spanish. Consequently, these schoolmates shifted to English. This reality draws attention to the diversity of linguistic experience even within one category of the contact generation framework.

In light of this diversity, I would like to revisit Andrea's words about her Spanish: "My Spanish was not there." Where exactly is "there"? What exactly does it take for one's Spanish to be "there"? Because the accounts of Juanita, Nicolás, and Francisco emphasize a continuity of Spanish throughout their life experiences, even before meeting their Mexicano/a partners, does this mean that their Spanish was "there" and had always been "there"? It certainly seems that the close connection to an anciano relative from the contact generation contributed to maintenance of the language. What, then, accounted for the shift/loss tendency within this same generation? When Elizabeth of Bernalillo describes her Spanish at the beginning of her relationship with Pancho, she utters a familiar phrase: "My Spanish just was not there." Elizabeth and Andrea belong to the same third-generation designation as Francisco, Nicolás, and Juanita, yet their narratives emphasize a sense of lacking in their Spanish proficiency. They emphasize the receptive capacities with which they were raised rather than productive abilities. Notably, neither Elizabeth nor Andrea mentions any Spanish-dominant anciano family member with whom they may have had a close relationship. Therefore, there was no presence of older family members from the contact generation that would necessitate the need to speak Spanish. Perhaps, Andrea and Elizabeth embody the communal effects of the linguistic repression referenced by Francisco and Juan. The attitudes that they describe toward their Spanish are indeed representative of generations who share a legacy of oppression. Anzaldúa describes this legacy: "*Pena*. Shame. Low estimation of self. In childhood we are told that our language is wrong."[29] Andrea describes a similar experience:

> And for myself, um, growing up I understood Spanish, but I never spoke it until I met my husband . . . and I think there was—I don't know why I never spoke it, but I think I was embarrassed or maybe I didn't want to speak it, so I never spoke Spanish and it was never encouraged. And I know, I remember my mom talking in Spanish, and like when she didn't want us to know something, she would talk in Spanish. Even though I could understand it, um, but because I wouldn't speak it, she just assumed I didn't know it. . . . But I did understand pretty much like everything in Spanish.

---

29. Anzaldúa, *Borderlands/La Frontera*, 80.

Andrea's account clearly describes the meeting of her husband as a pivotal moment in the reversal of her linguistic tendencies. Andrea's account of her language history before meeting her husband references a designation of what Oh and colleagues, as well as Silvina Montrul, term "overhearers."[30] Andrea emphasizes her high level of comprehension due to frequent overhearing of the Spanish spoken around her, despite the embarrassment and the lack of encouragement for speaking. In fact, more than a lack of encouragement, in Andrea's family Spanish was used as a parental secret weapon. Yet this secret code had a flaw in that the receptive skills of Andrea were indeed present, although unacknowledged. Andrea's linguistic history as a child connects to the importance of what De Houwer terms "impact belief."[31] This is the belief that how and how frequently a child is talked to has an effect on that child's language development. This notion suggests that the nature of the input received by Andrea affected her language development and, ultimately, her lack of production, along with a self-disparaging attitude toward her perceived deficiencies. In effect, both Andrea and her family erase the communicative value of Andrea's receptive skills.

Elizabeth echoes a similar experience growing up with her parents in Placitas, over a hundred miles south of Taos. She explains, "They spoke a lot between themselves, but with us, towards the kids, there was a lot of English. But we understood everything that they were saying, but we never spoke it. . . . We never picked it up ourselves to speak it fluently." Again, Elizabeth's words evoke a simultaneous validation and erasure of her skills in Spanish. She makes clear that English was directed to the kids; however, she also emphasizes that this did not prevent the development of high levels of comprehension in Spanish. Yet, with her third "but" she underscores once more that she and her siblings did not speak the language, thus privileging productive skills over receptive ones in a move that conceals her complex bilingual history and abilities. Further complicating this picture, Elizabeth later reveals that she and her siblings would speak a limited amount of Spanish to grandparents and that her older sister "was able to make herself a little more clear" in Spanish. This information serves to augment the layers of complexity in Elizabeth's linguistic profile and calls attention, again, to the diversity within one generational category through the comparison between Elizabeth and her sister. It also emphasizes Elizabeth's continued minimization of her spoken Spanish skills.

Ana experiences a similar process of erasure. However, she does have a Spanish-dominant anciano in her family to whom she spoke in Spanish. Ana

---

30. Oh et al., "Childhood Language Memory"; and Montrul, "Second Language Acquisition."
31. De Houwer, *Bilingual First Language Acquisition*, 362.

reports consistently speaking in Spanish while growing up, therefore belonging to a third-generation maintenance category. Yet, both her receptive and productive abilities are dismissed. Much like Nicolás and Juanita, she invokes the key role of the older anciano relative: "I think I was fortunate that I always spoke Spanish with my grandmother." Yet, she describes that when her aunts and uncles didn't want the kids to know what they were saying, "they'd do the Spanish, even though I did know what they were saying." Ironically, Ana not only understood but also spoke Spanish at that time. Nevertheless, these abilities are not recognized. Perhaps, because other siblings or cousins of a similar age exhibit a shift/loss tendency, she is categorized with others in her age group. These minimizations recall Lipski's discussion of the "transitional generation of vestigial speakers who spoke the language in question during their childhood, but who have subsequently lost much of their native ability and their standing as true *transitional bilinguals*."[32] The invisibility or lack of recognition of certain linguistic abilities underscores the fluid social construction of a "bilingual standing." The fact that Andrea's, Elizabeth's, and Ana's receptive abilities are minimized or completely unrecognized within their families illustrates this social construct. They even downplay their own abilities as they grapple with their own history, generational status, and linguistic insecurities.

INITIAL ENCOUNTERS: PERCEIVING PROFICIENCY ON UNEVEN GROUND

Regardless of the visibility or invisibility of the Nuevomexicanos/as' receptive Spanish abilities within their families, the future Mexicano/a partners actually depended on the Nuevomexicanos/as' receptive abilities. Shifting to the moment of recontact, José Luis (Ana's husband) explains,

> Siempre le hicimos la lucha, o sea ella le hizo la lucha de hablar español, porque yo no hablaba nada de inglés. Y fue como ella aprendió más, como fue aprendiendo más y más, pero ella tenía más posibilidad que yo, porque ella sí entendía lo que yo le decía, no podía hablar mucho, pero sí entendía lo que yo decía.

> [We always made an effort, I mean she made the effort to speak Spanish, because I did not speak English. And that is how she learned more, how she

---

32. Lipski, *Varieties of Spanish*, 56.

began to learn more and more, but she had more of a possibility for learning than me, because she did understand what I said, she couldn't speak much, but she understood what I said.]

Through the "tenía más posibilidad que yo" phrase, José Luis acknowledges Ana's high levels of comprehension and the history that gave birth to this comprehension. José Luis acknowledges that Ana already had an advantage: her generational status within the contact generation framework. Although he recognizes and depends on her comprehension, Ana's productive abilities remain somewhat unrecognizable to her future husband. José Luis explains that "no podía hablar mucho." Like her family, José Luis minimizes Ana's productive skills. We know that Ana's communication with her grandmother took place solely in Spanish, yet these speaking abilities remain invisible to José Luis.

Similarly, Elizabeth's husband, Pancho, describes his wife's linguistic profile. He states, "Ahora con mi esposa, cuando recién la conocí a ella, pues ella no hablaba español; yo hablaba muy poquito inglés; entonces ahí nos fuimos poco a poco, ¿no?" [Now with my wife, when I first met her, well she didn't speak Spanish; and I spoke very little English; so there we went, little by little, no?] Pancho is clear that Elizabeth did not speak any Spanish. However, when asked about her experiences growing up, Elizabeth denotes some limited Spanish-speaking to grandparents. She states, "We had to. We communicated what little we could in Spanish, but it wasn't a lot." Although Elizabeth clearly believes that her Spanish "was not there," her family's long-term relationship with Spanish allowed for the development of a set of linguistic resources in Spanish. This skill set may have been uneven, but it was present, nonetheless.

Gabriela recognizes these linguistic resources in her future husband, Nicolás, when answering her family's questions about whether Nicolás could speak Spanish. She remembers the conversation:

Nomás dijeron, "¿Y habla español? Porque si es gringo, ya estuvo de que no nos vamos a poder comunicar con él," y les dije, no, sí, habla español, mocho les dije pero lo habla les dije. Pues sus abuelitos hablan español y su mamá también, pero lo hablan mocho, como aquí en Nuevo México. Ya cuando lo conozcan lo van a ver.

[They just said, "Does he speak Spanish? Because if he is gringo, we won't be able to communicate with him," and I told them, no, yes, he does speak Spanish, mocho, I told them, but he does speak as they speak in New Mexico. When you meet him you will see.]

Although she acknowledges both Nicolás's speaking skills and the intergenerational history of Spanish in his family, she qualifies his Spanish with the term "mocho." Here we see the positioning of Nicolás and his family's Spanish as somewhat haphazard, unsophisticated, and not completely competent.

Additionally, the comments of Gabriela, and the other Mexicano/a partners, draw us back to the discussion of one's Spanish being "there." Nicolás describes his Spanish as "el español de aquí" [Spanish from here]. In a similar vein, recall when Francisco recounts his linguistic tendencies growing up. He states, "I only knew Spanish, Spanish de aquí." It is significant that Nicolás, Francisco, and Juanita speak of their high proficiency in Spanish, but also find it necessary to qualify the Spanish they knew well as "el español de aquí." Juanita describes the Spanish she spoke growing up as "really good New Mexican Spanish." Yet, when Luis (Juanita's husband) remembers his wife's Spanish in their first encounter, he characterizes her language as "really bad." It seems that, even when the Nuevomexicano/a partners perceive their Spanish to be "there," the Mexican partners' opinions diverge from this perception. "There" seems to be a moving target. Yet, returning to Gabriela's account of her initial interactions with Nicolás, she remembers that the day she met Nicolás "estuvimos platicando como unas cinco horas yo creo" [we were talking for like five hours I think]. It is significant that despite a perception of Nicolás's New Mexican Spanish as being "mocho," the tension between "here" and "there" does not impede communication.

The deictic use of the adverbs "here" and "there" by the Nuevomexicano/a participants elucidates some key connections between place, proficiency, and Latinidad. "There" seems to point outside of New Mexico and New Mexican Spanish. The Nuevomexicano/a partners would not feel the need to distinguish their Spanish as Spanish "de aquí" if there were not some other reference point or some other Spanish for which it might be mistaken. Francisco underscores this point when he explains that, upon meeting his wife, he became aware that "the Spanish from over there is different 'cause we got the lazy Spanish." The Nuevomexicano/a participants use the distinction of "aquí" as a strategy to not overstate their proficiency in light of the exposure to Mexican Spanish that they have received through recontact. This strategy illustrates how recontact facilitates a process of inter-Latino/a/x linguistic knowledge construction, in line with the key tenet of Latinidad of the production of inter-Latino/a/x knowledge.[33] Yet, the results of this knowledge production in the context of the uses of "here" and "there" highlight an activation of the "competing authenticities" of Latinidad through Spanish. Additionally, it seems that a process of what Zentella has termed "chiquitafication" is

---

33. See Aparicio, "Jennifer as Selena," 94.

occurring between these two Latino/a/x groups. Zentella explains that chiquitafication "diminishes the complexity of the languages and cultures of the more than 22 million Latinos[34] who reside in the U.S., and the repercussions of that process for their linguistic security."[35] Zentella references this process as a dynamic occurring between dominant US Anglo culture and Latinos/as/xs. However, these dynamic spaces of inter-Latino/a/x contact within the Mexicano-Nuevomexicano unions add a new layer to the practice of chiquitafication. That is, Mexican immigrants, like Anglo-Americans, diminish the linguistic value of US Spanish. The Nuevomexicanos/as' use of "aquí" or "here" responds to the chiquitafication of their linguistic history and proficiency as well as to their own linguistic dispossession.[36]

I do not present theses differing perceptions of linguistic skills between the romantic couples to pit one account against another. My goal is not to arrive at some absolute "truth." However, I think it is important to draw attention to the complex generational status of the Nuevomexicano/a partners and to elucidate the moments of erasure, recognition, and, many times, judgment of the linguistic abilities and histories embedded within the generational profiles. Unpacking the diverse and complicated generational status of the Nuevomexicano/a partners provides a lens through which to view the intergenerational persistence of Spanish, and this persistence serves as an important element within the continuous relationship of recontact within these zones of encuentro. By applying the Villa and Rivera-Mills model to the participants' linguistic profiles, it is my hope that we are better equipped to move forward in the analysis of the recontact process due to a deeper understanding of the ground on which the process begins. The tensions between perceptions of linguistic ability among the Mexicano/a and Nuevomexicano/a partners highlight the unevenness of this ground. Yet, the tensions actually serve as a fundamental feature of recontact (and Latinidad) illuminating struggle, power differentials, and simultaneous moments of erasure and recognition.

"NOT [LOSING SPANISH] AS MUCH 'CAUSE I MARRIED A MEXICAN": GAUGING RECONTACT

In Elizabeth's retelling of the initial interactions between herself and Pancho, she highlights the gradual pace of recontact. She recounts,

---

34. This was the figure in the year 1995 when Zentella first presented the notion of "chiquitafication." According to the Pew Research Center's 2021 figures, this number is now over 62.5 million.
35. Zentella, "'Chiquitafication' of U.S. Latinos," 3.
36. See Aparicio, "Of Spanish Dispossessed."

> When we met, I really didn't know Spanish so how we got together I don't know. . . . We met, actually, through church. I always went to the church, the Presbyterian Church in Placitas, and him and his family were helping to rebuild the church there. He was living with a family there in Placitas, and they'd take him to church, and we'd see him working on the church until one day he caught my eye because he always said, "I would look at you and you never looked at me." I'm sorry, but you just didn't catch my eye. Till one day he did. It was funny because it was for an enchilada dinner, and I was like, "Go tell him I want to talk to him." I was telling it to my sister because my sister spoke more Spanish than I did, so she kind of made herself a little more clear. She goes, "Okay." There she goes and she's all, "My sister wants to talk to you." He was like, "Okay." So then he comes over and with what little English he knew, "Let's go for a walk." Okay, let's go for a walk. So then we went for a walk and were just very simple, basic, just barely conversating.[37] But that's how we got together.

Her emphasis on words such as "basic," "simple," and "barely" underscore this slow and steady process. I would like to juxtapose this account of her linguistic tendencies during her initial meeting with Pancho with the description of her present communication with Pancho's family. Elizabeth explains,

> I couldn't communicate very much because my Spanish just was not there, and so I would just speak to them very minimal. . . . "Hola. ¿Cómo estás?" And that's like about it. . . . Right now, my Spanish isn't all that great either. Still, it's tremendous compared to where I started, but it's still not fluent. It's gotten a lot easier for me to talk with his family, his sister, his dad, his mom, all of them. It's gotten a lot easier for me to talk with them. Now we can have, at least, a full conversation instead of just, "Hola. ¿Cómo estás?"

Elizabeth's narrative clearly emphasizes the linguistic implications of recontact in her daily life. Elizabeth's walk with Pancho evolves into a long-term relationship in which she expands her network of individuals to whom she speaks Spanish. Her increased use of Spanish allows her to improve her communication with her in-laws, despite the fact that her Spanish may not match her own notion of "great" or "fluent." How do we describe what occurred in the space from the night of the enchilada dinner to Elizabeth's present-day interactions with Pancho and his family? José Luis's previously mentioned use of the

---

37. The use of the term "conversating" reveals a transculturative effect of Spanish influence on Elizabeth's English. "Conversating" seems to function as a loanword from the Spanish "conversando."

phrase "siempre le hicimos la lucha," and Pancho's description, "nos fuimos poco a poco," shed light on the daily and gradual work that characterize this space. When Pía discusses this process with her husband Francisco, she similarly notes, "Gracias a Dios pues, lo logramos poco a poco" [Thank God we made it little by little]. It is in these phrases that reference patience, struggle, and achievement that we see the inner workings of the long-term process of recontact. Though it is impossible to document all the linguistic struggles, difficulties, and achievements between the Mexicano-Nuevomexicano couples, in what follows I document several indicators of current language tendencies among the Nuevomexicano/a participants. I report on the change in the Nuevomexicanos/as' Spanish-speaking social network since beginning their relationships with their Mexicano/a partners. I also discuss the self-reports of the percentage of Spanish used in a typical week by the Nuevomexicano/a partners. I believe that these indicators of language use provide some specific ways to gauge the impact of recontact on the lives of the Nuevomexicanos/as.

Because the mixture of Spanish and English is a daily reality of communication among many in northern New Mexico, it was difficult to gauge with whom the Nuevomexicano/a partners may have interacted exclusively in Spanish before coming into contact with their Mexicano/a partners. For this reason, I used the phrase "mostly in Spanish," because this is the way that the participants described their interactions with these individuals. With this in mind, my conversations with the couples reveal important trends. Throughout their relationship with their husbands, Elizabeth and Andrea have created an entirely new network of individuals with whom they interact solely in Spanish. No such network existed before contact with their romantic partners. Ana, Nicolás, and Juanita each had one or two individuals in their Spanish-speaking network before initiating the relationship with their Mexicano/a partners. However, some of these individuals were the older relative from the contact generation that passed away before, or soon after, meeting their spouse. As a result of the recontact process, Ana, Nicolás, and Juanita drastically expand their Spanish-speaking networks to include their husband, their husband's family, and individuals in their respective workplaces. Nicolás's wife, Gabriela, notices her husband's increased use due to having a large network of individuals with whom to speak Spanish. She explains, "Pero como te digo, él ha mejorado mucho para su manera de hablarlo . . . pero yo digo que es por eso, de cómo lo está practicando, y luego como convive con más gente también que habla español" [But I tell you, he has greatly improved his way of speaking Spanish, I tell you that it is because of how he practices and then he spends more time with people who speak Spanish]. Penélope, Diana, and Francisco already had a network with whom they interacted mostly in

Spanish before meeting their partners. However, the romantic relationship expanded this network to include their spouse and their spouse's family. Notably, Francisco stated that currently his two best friends are Mexicano and that this is due to his wife's influence. He interacts solely in Spanish with these best friends. The only individual who seemed to experience no change in his Spanish-speaking network was Juan. Juan reports maintaining roughly the same size Spanish-speaking network throughout his entire life. If anything has changed, it has been a slight increase in his English use due to having to speak to his grandchildren in English. He explains, "Mi esposa sabía más inglés que yo.[38] Todo siempre en español . . . pero más inglés que antes con los nietos." [My wife knew more English than me. Everything was always in Spanish . . . but now more English than before because of the grandchildren.] Juan is also the oldest participant in this study. He is the only member of the second-generation maintenance category and has lived in rural areas of northern New Mexico for much of his life. These factors inevitably play a part in the stability of his Spanish use and Spanish-language network throughout his life.

The Nuevomexicano/a participants' reported use of Spanish in a typical week varies from 10 percent to 65 percent. Andrea reports the lowest percentage (10 percent) of Spanish use. However, if we consider that Andrea had no one with whom she spoke Spanish before meeting her husband, this is quite a change. The fact that all the Nuevomexicano/a participants do, in fact, report a regular weekly use of Spanish is notable. Francisco underscores this fact when he laments the loss of Spanish around him: "I figure once a person needs to go to school to learn your own language, something is wrong, don't you think? That's wrong." When I asked him if he thought he was losing Spanish, he replied: "Not as much because I married a Mexican but I would've been losing it." Francisco's use of "would've" emphasizes the role his wife has played in his language maintenance. In his estimation, those of his peer group, including his sister, have shifted to English. He continues, "Oh my sister she's kinda lost it, I don't know why. Se casó con un Gonzales that don't speak no Spanish. . . . If I call my sister now . . . she will just talk to me in English only." Again, considering each Nuevomexicano/a participant's complex generational status and the language shift trends that precede them, the presence of the Mexicano/a partner in the Nuevomexicano/a's life contributes to the regular use of Spanish on a weekly basis.

---

38. Juan and Marta's partnership was unique in that both claimed that Marta knew more English than Juan when they met. It appears that this is due to Marta arriving to Albuquerque as a preteen and attending junior high and high school in monolingual English classrooms, whereas, despite efforts to eradicate Spanish from northern New Mexico schools, Spanish still dominated Juan's interactions through high school.

It is important to mention that eight out of the nine Nuevomexicano/a partners have made regular trips with his or her Mexicano/a partner to Mexico throughout their relationship. Each of these nine couples would visit their Mexicano/a partner's hometown at least once a year, with some couples making up to six trips a year. The trips would last anywhere from a weekend to two weeks. When in Mexico, the percentage of reported Spanish use was consistently 100 percent. This did not come without its challenges, as José Luis explains: "Ella al principio tenía un poco de problema cuando íbamos para allá, como nunca había practicado 100 porciento el español, allá tenía que . . . esforzarse un poquito" [At first she had a few problems when we would go there, since she had never practiced 100 percent Spanish, there she had to . . . make a little bit of an effort]. These brief periods of 100 percent Spanish indicate the key role of the Nuevomexicano/a partner's in-laws in forming his/her network of Spanish speakers. Notably, the frequency of trips to Mexico has changed within the last five years for all the couples due to increased violence in Mexico or due to the fact that their in-laws have moved to New Mexico.

REACQUISITION AND COMMUNAL RECONTACT

Though perhaps momentary and localized in the grand scheme of language maintenance and loss, the Nuevomexicano/a partners' recontact experiences represent a potential halt in language shift. The recontact experience assigns the Nuevomexicanos/as to a "reacquisition generation." According to Villa and Rivera-Mills, "This concept recognizes that individuals who had limited, dwindling or no abilities in Spanish may re-acquire it, to then pass it on to their children (or not)."[39] The recontact process is the key ingredient in creating this reacquisition generation. In the cases of Elizabeth and Andrea, we most definitely see instances of limited abilities that then change shape with both women experiencing a subsequent reinfusion of Spanish into their lives. The remaining partners may never have seen a complete dwindling or fading of Spanish in their lives, yet the recontact process has allowed for a reacquisition of a regular sustained use of the language and, more importantly, a sustained communicative need to continue the maintenance of Spanish.

The presence of the Mexicano/a partner in the respective communities in which the couples reside also creates recontact and, subsequently, reacquisition opportunities beyond the interactions of the Mexicano-Nuevomexicano couple. The relationship has linguistic implications for both the extended

---

39. Villa and Rivera-Mills, "Integrated Multi-Generational Model," 32.

family and the surrounding community. For example, Elizabeth references the fact that her parents and Pancho "could conversate[40] any time. They just 'wedee wedee wedee.' So him and my mom would get together and just go to town talking away." Andrea also recounts that her mom likes to talk to her husband in Spanish. Similarly, José Luis shares the experience that his in-laws have always enjoyed speaking to him in Spanish:

> Todos me hablaban español, todos, mi suegra y los hermanos de ella.... Los cuñados también hablaban español, porque sí saben poquito, pero sí me hablaban español siempre. Pues como entonces pues yo no sabía absolutamente nada, o sea nada, nada ... siempre le hicieron la lucha de hablar conmigo.
>
> [Everyone spoke to me in Spanish, everyone, my mother-in-law and her brothers.... My brothers- and sisters-in-law also spoke Spanish, because they do know a little bit, but they always did speak to me in Spanish. Well, back then since I knew absolutely nothing, I mean nothing, nothing ... they always made the effort to speak with me.]

In this instance, the reference to "haciendo la lucha" points to Ana's family's desire to increase their Spanish language use and, perhaps, to turn around tendencies of shift within their own linguistic profiles. It is also significant that consistently in the couples' interviews both the Mexicanos/as and Nuevomexicanos/as reference the special relationship that the Mexicano/a partner has/had with an older parent or grandparent of the Nuevomexicano/a partner. Nicolás explains his grandmother's reaction to his wife: "Oh my grandmother, she loved her! Oh yes! She had somebody that she could carry a full conversation in Spanish with." The Mexicano/a partner not only reactivates or increases the use of Spanish in the Nuevomexicano/a partner's daily language patterns but also provides opportunities for older members of the contact generation to continue their use of Spanish.

The presence of the Mexicano/a partner in these Nuevomexicano/a/x communities provides the opportunity for other Nuevomexicanos/as/xs to expand their social network of Spanish speakers as well. When Gabriela and Nicolás's daughters began school, Gabriela recalls that the teachers encouraged her to be part of the classroom. She explains, "Ya enseguida me decía la maestra: 'Quédate un rato, unas dos o tres horas aquí para que nos enseñes

---

40. The use of the term "conversate" again reveals the transculturative effect of Spanish on Elizabeth's English.

español.' . . . Ella hablaba en español, aja no muy bien, ¿verdad?, pero sí . . . me podía comunicar mejor con ella." [Right away the teacher told me: "Stay a while, two or three hours here so that you can teach us Spanish." . . . She spoke Spanish, but not very well, right?, but yes . . . I could communicate better with her.] The Nuevomexicana teachers in the local school viewed Gabriela as a resource to reactivate and build upon their own knowledge base of Spanish. Indeed, Valdés[41] highlights the necessity of capitalizing on community and educational resources in maintaining a minority language past the second generation. Similarly, Pía describes how community members in Las Vegas take advantage of the opportunity to converse with her in Spanish:

> La mayoría de la gente se esfuerza por rescatar su español . . . y te digo Las Vegas no es el lugar adecuado para aprender inglés porque la mayoría de la gente habla español y espanglish. ¿Cómo voy a aprender si no me contestan en inglés?
>
> [The majority of the people make an effort to maintain their Spanish . . . and I tell you Las Vegas is not the ideal place to learn English because the majority of the people speak Spanish and Spanglish. How am I going to learn if they don't answer me in English?]

Pía's comments demonstrate the intergenerational persistence of Spanish in the Las Vegas community. She continues, "Yo tengo que reconocer de la gente de aquí de Las Vegas si saben que tu inglés no es tan fluido, ellos hacen un esfuerzo de tratar de hablar un español que ellos pueden y logramos tener una conversación" [I have to recognize that the people from Las Vegas, if they know that your English is not very fluent, they make an effort to speak the best Spanish they can and we are able to have a conversation]. These communicative encounters also illustrate how the Mexicano/a partners put into motion a process of recontact that creates a ripple effect with an impact far beyond their own romantic relationship. One of these "ripples" even extends toward other Mexicanos/as/xs in the community. Juanita tells of an instance when she was registering her granddaughter for school. She explains, "And the day we went to go register her, a lady came in with her son or nephew, I don't know who he was. And she addressed the lady at the front of the counter and said, '¿Alguien habla español?' And the lady looked at her, 'Uhmmm.' She was like, 'Un momento, let me find somebody.' And I stood up and said, 'I can translate for you.' And she goes, 'That'd be awesome.'" The communal

---

41. Valdés, "Ethnolinguistic Identity."

effect of recontact has the potential to be quite "awesome." The presence of the Mexicano/a partner in communities with an intergenerational persistence of Spanish allows for concrete opportunities for sustained recontact outside of the romantic relationship that may in turn contribute to a more widespread reacquisition generation in these locales.

UNCOVERING THE TRANSCULTURATIVE DIMENSION OF RECONTACT

Up to this point I have framed the notion of recontact in terms of initial encounters, tensions, and the linguistic influence within the Mexicano-Nuevomexicano relationship. My analysis has primarily focused on the linguistic implications from the perspective of the Nuevomexicano/a partner. Given that recontact has previously been framed in terms of language maintenance and revitalization, it has been relevant to focus on the ways in which these romantic relationships impact the linguistic trajectories of the partners who have experienced more Spanish language shift. Yet, if we are to truly consider the cultural dimensions of *influence* within the Cisneros and Leone definition of recontact, we must view influence as multidirectional and unpack recontact in terms of mutual influence.

Instead of giving the impression that recontact is simply a one-way process, I would like to draw attention to a transculturative feature within the Mexicano-Nuevomexicano partnerships that speaks to a more circular interplay of cultural influence. This interplay emphasizes cultural movement rather than fixedness in a way that allows for the viewing of mutual influence (albeit uneven). I argue that recontact is always impacting both Mexicanos/as/xs and Nuevomexicanos/as/xs. Diana Taylor's conceptualization of transculturation provides a useful framing for this idea. She explains that transculturation "allows the 'minor' culture (in the sense of positionally marginalized) an impact on the dominant one, although the interactions are not, strictly speaking, 'dialogic' or 'dialectical.' Transculturation suggests a shifting or circulating pattern of cultural transference."[42] Taylor's theory allows for the possibility that recontact's influence exists simultaneously within and between both groups. However, the interactions of Mexicanos/as/xs and Nuevomexicanos/as/xs in northern New Mexico problematize Taylor's designation of "minor" and "major" cultures. In the spirit of Zentella's notion of chiquitafication and Aparicio's examination of linguistic power differentials,

---

42. Taylor, "Transculturating Transculturation," 108.

both groups are positionally marginalized by the dominant Anglo culture.[43] Yet, what happens when we are exploring the dynamics between two "minor" cultures? The framework of Latinidad provides the tools to examine these inter-Latino/a/x convergences, divergences, and competing authenticities and ultimately renders any notion of fixed "major" and "minor" positions as irrelevant. The major and minor positions continually shift as power discrepancies and inter-Latino/a/ x chiquitafications and tropicalizations occur between the two "minor" culture groups. Ramírez addresses this type of shifting under the rubric of "assimilation." She explains, "I define assimilation as a relational process whereby the boundary between unequal groups and between inside and outside blurs, disappears, or, paradoxically, is reinforced. Some boundaries are hard and bright, while others are porous and ambiguous."[44] Both Ramírez and Taylor importantly elucidate the relational nature of "minor" and "major" cultures and emphasize fluidity over fixity. Likewise, Aparicio's "horizontal hierarchies" underscores "the relational, situational, and historically contingent nature of these social dynamics" while also focusing on "the transculturative potential among Latina/o ethnicities as well as on the structured conflicts."[45] This element of Latinidad fits nicely with Taylor's emphasis on the constant cultural movements, shifts, and reciprocities[46] at work in transculturation. The Mexicano-Nuevomexicano couples allow for the exploration of this movement-oriented influence that dismantles fixed categories.

How exactly does this transculturative element of the recontact process play out between the couples? Let's consider the case of reacquisition. I mentioned earlier that the Nuevomexicano/a partners belong to what Villa and Rivera-Mills term a "reacquisition generation."[47] Nevertheless, the Nuevomexicano/a partners consistently articulate a sensitivity toward the specific variety of Spanish that they are (re)acquiring, reminding us that reacquisition (and recontact) do not occur outside of the disparate conditions of a contact zone. These processes are not neutral. Penélope explains, "I speak more Mexican than I do Spanish northern,[48] and, like I tell you, that bothers me." Diana also speaks of an overtaking of Mexican Spanish throughout the course of her relationship with her husband. She explains, "I've learned to talk the Mexican Spanish, you know, so—because I don't use the New Mexico

---

43. Zentella, "'Chiquitafication' of U.S. Latinos"; and Aparicio, "Whose Spanish, Whose Language?"
44. Ramírez, *Assimilation*, 15.
45. Aparicio, *Negotiating Latinidad*, 25.
46. Taylor, "Transculturating Transculturation," 103.
47. Villa and Rivera-Mills, "Integrated Multi-Generational Model," 32.
48. Penélope is referring to northern New Mexican Spanish in this instance.

Spanish anymore." In fact, eight of the nine Nuevomexicano/a partners express some type of predominance of Mexican Spanish in their present daily lives. This is consistent with Waltermire's findings in his 2015 study, as well as with Del Angel Guevara's research.[49] Penélope laments this predominance. When asked which word she knows for "dress" in Spanish, Penélope responds that she knows both "túnico" (the NM variant) and "vestido." She explains emphatically, "I don't say 'túnico' very much anymore . . . and so all of the terms are being lost, because I didn't teach my kids those terms so that their grandparents on their dad's side and their dad would understand, and that makes me angry. It really makes me angry with myself because I see it getting more lost." In this case of influence we see perceived power differentials, notions of dominance, and a sense of loss. In the explanation of their lexical choices, Andrea and Juanita also express a sense that New Mexican Spanish is being relegated to the past. Andrea explains that she used the word 'nodriza'[50] "pienso que cuando yo estaba joven y 'enfermera' ahora que estoy adulta" [I think when I was younger and "enfermera" now that I am an adult]. And again, with the word for "dress" she clarifies, "antes 'túnico' y ahora 'vestido'" [before "túnico" and now "vestido"]. Lastly, with the word for "peas" she states, "antes 'alberjón' y hora 'chícharos' . . . ahora uso 'chícharos' mejor" [before "alberjón" and now "chícharos" . . . now I prefer to use "chícharos"]. Andrea's explanation for her most frequent lexical usages certainly locates New Mexican Spanish in her past. Similarly, Juanita clarifies that "'túnico' is just gone. I say 'vestido' now." Likewise, upon seeing a photo of an "apricot" she states, "that was 'albarcoques.'" Similar to Del Angel Guevara's findings, these Nuevomexicana partners express a familiarity with New Mexican variants, despite their increased us of Mexican variants. Also, similar to Andrea, Juanita's words construct an oppositional relationship in which New Mexican Spanish is aligned with the past and Mexican Spanish is aligned with the present.

These accounts prompt the questions, Does Mexican Spanish actually replace New Mexican Spanish? and Is this a manifestation of the "Mexicanization" of New Mexican Spanish?[51] Perhaps, this is a case of long-term language accommodation.[52] Does the influence of the Mexicano/a partners on Nuevomexicano/a partners from northern New Mexico ultimately result in the acquisition of Mexican Spanish at the expense of New Mexican Spanish? I

---

49. Waltermire, "Mexican Immigration"; and Del Angel Guevara, "Returning to Northern New Mexico."

50. "Nodriza" refers to "nurse" in New Mexican Spanish. However, in most other Spanish dialects it translates to "wet nurse."

51. Bills, "New Mexican Spanish"; Waltermire, "Mexican Immigration"; and Del Angel Guevara, "Returning to Northern New Mexico."

52. Giles and Smith, "Accommodation Theory"; and Trudgill, *Dialects in Contact*.

suggest that the overwhelming influence that the Nuevomexicano/a partners are perceiving is more complicated than simply a binary framework of Mexican Spanish versus New Mexican Spanish, in which the Mexicano/a partners' language and experience remains unaffected by the Nuevomexicano/a partner. As a side note, it is important to emphasize that although my participants may refer to "Mexican Spanish" as if only one homogenous dialect of Mexican Spanish existed, regional variation in Mexico is considerable and multiple Spanish dialects exist. Lipski notes that, in order to understand the Mexican Spanish spoken in the United States, "it is necessary to take a closer look at dialect differentiation within Mexico, particularly the speech of economically distressed regions, which have contributed to the majority of Mexican immigrants to the United States in the last half century or so."[53] Therefore, certain regions may contribute to the specific dialects of Mexican Spanish spoken by Mexicano/a/x immigrants in the United States; however, this does not imply that dialect differentiation does not exist in Mexico. This is important to keep in mind as my participants' use of the phrase "Mexican Spanish" may not imply this dialect diversity.

Returning to the notion of influence, consider the dynamic between dominance and loss occurring with Marta. She explains her struggles with using Mexican Spanish in her relationship with her Nuevomexicano husband, Juan. She remembers,

Sí habían cosas que eran duras al principio . . . habían cosas que eran así que no nos entendíamos . . . y en veces cuando me enojaba con él y le hablaba en mexicano, en mi mexicano y luego me decía, "Si no me vas a hablar bien no me hables." . . . Casi no me dejó hablar mi mexicano, tenía que aprender el de él. . . . Cuando le hablaba a él en mi español, se enojaba . . . porque no me entendía. Y luego me decía él, "Si no me vas a hablar bien, no me hables," porque yo estaba impuesta a todas las cosas en mexicano mío.

[There were things that were hard at first . . . there were things that we did not understand . . . and sometimes when I got angry with him and I spoke to him in Spanish, in my Spanish and then he would say, "If you're not going to speak well to me, then don't speak to me (at all)." . . . He rarely let me speak my Spanish, I had to learn his. . . . When I spoke to him in my Spanish, he would get mad . . . because he didn't understand me. And then he would tell me, "If you're not going to speak well to me, then don't speak to me (at all)," because I was used to everything being in my Spanish.]

---

53. Lipski, *Varieties of Spanish*, 84.

It is significant that during Marta's description she repeats Juan's words to her twice: "If you're not going to speak well to me, then don't speak to me (at all)." These are strong and scolding words. Juan asserts the dominance of Nuevomexicano Spanish over Marta's Mexican Spanish as he positions Marta's "mexicano" as incorrect and unacceptable. In addition to the linguistic hierarchy being established here, there also seems to be a larger gender dynamic at work that propels Juan's attempt to regulate Marta's Spanish.[54] Marta's use of the phrase "cosas duras" and her use of possessive adjectives in denoting "mi mexicano" and "mi español" underscore a deep and personal connection to her variety of Spanish and a sense of loss as it is subordinated in her relationship with Juan. Additionally, Marta laments that she is not more New Mexican: "Yo quisiera ser más de aquí, pero yo sé que no soy. . . . Soy de allá. Y hablo más de aquí, hablo más inglés, y cuando voy a hablar con una persona de allá, cambeo. Pero yo sé que soy de allá." [I wish I was from here, but I know that I'm not. . . . I'm from there. And I do speak more like here, I speak more English, but when I speak with someone from there, I change. But I know I'm from there.] Marta describes an inescapable Mexicanidad that does not allow her to "pass" for Nuevomexicana, despite her husband's reprimands. The case of Juan and Marta illustrates that the roles of "major" and "minor" culture in these inter-Latino/a/x dynamics are not fixed, as we see the strong influence of New Mexican Spanish in Marta's life. Additionally, Marta's "struggle of borders"[55] illustrates a distressing and almost painful dimension to recontact.

With this shifting notion of influence and dominance in mind, I return to the lexical choices of Andrea and Juanita. Although the Nuevomexicano/a partners clarify that they tend to use more, if not exclusively, Mexican Spanish in their daily lives, it is noteworthy that when presented with the pictures of items in the lexical elicitation activity, most of the Nuevomexicano/a participants still offer New Mexican variants first. Six out of nine of the Nuevomexicano/a participants offered the New Mexican variant first for over half of the items. Again, this does not mean that, simply because they uttered these words first, they are the words they use most frequently.[56] However, it is worth noting that although the speakers perceive an erasure of New Mexican Spanish, it is actually recalled when talking about the Mexican variant. Andrea and Juanita do not mention the Mexican variant without recalling the New Mexican lexical choice. This process of recall troubles the construction

---

54. Although not the focus of this chapter, it is important to note that issues of gender and male dominance are a constant theme throughout Marta and Juan's interview. These issues of gender were more prevalent in their interview than in any other.

55. Anzaldúa, *Borderlands/La Frontera*, 102.

56. See Potowski, "Intrafamilial Dialect Contact," 590.

of an oppositional relationship between Mexican Spanish and New Mexican Spanish. Taylor emphasizes that "transculturation . . . does not lock cultures into binaries; it eschews simple oppositions."[57] Indeed, the Nuevomexicano partner may be locating the New Mexican Spanish in the past and the Mexican variant in the present, yet the distance between past and present is minimized as both are recalled almost simultaneously. The interplay of past and present in these discussions of lexical items also references a type of language recovery. Karen Roybal explains her use of the term "(re)conceptualization" in terms of recovery: "I employ the parentheses around the prefix (re) to indicate that we must return to the past to gain a new understanding of the history of dispossession and to redefine our interpretation of the archive."[58] When I ask Juanita about the variety of Spanish in which she feels most proficient, she responds, "Yeah, I do better with the Mexican." I then ask her if she has trouble communicating with other people from New Mexico in Spanish. She explains, "It comes back. It's like riding a bike. . . . It's always there." Juanita's words illustrate a process of (re)conceptualizing language recovery, as well as the continuous presence and vitality of New Mexican Spanish within her linguistic repertoire. Even amidst the lamenting of its loss, New Mexican Spanish stays present. The use of a Mexican variant evokes the New Mexican variant, effectively inserting one into the other. New Mexican Spanish and Mexican Spanish are always already linked.

In this same vein, there is an interesting and analogous process occurring with the Mexicano/a partners. Upon remembering her initial communication with Francisco, Pía recounts the difficulties she experienced, particularly with Francisco's vocabulary. She states, "Y fue difícil al principio, porque él hablaba un español nuevomexicano, y te digo, con palabras que yo no entendía qué era lo que me quería decir; entonces fue difícil" [And it was difficult at first, because he spoke a New Mexican Spanish, and I tell you, with words that I didn't understand what he was trying to tell me; so it was difficult]. To Pía, Francisco's Spanish is foreign. Yet, as Pía and Francisco's relationship progresses, Pía tells of an important discovery. She explains, "Yo jamás había escuchado estas palabras, pero mi mamá cuando empezó a venir a visitarme me decía, 'Sí mija, mi abuelito usaba esa palabra. Yo las escuchaba en mi casa.' Mi mamá no se sorprendía." [I had never heard these words, but my mom when she started to come and visit me would tell me, "Yes mija, my grandfather would use that word. I would hear those words at home." My mom was not surprised.] The words of Pía's mother create a temporal connection and

---

57. Taylor, "Transculturaing Transculturation," 101.
58. Roybal, *Archives of Dispossession*, 14–15.

a sense of linguistic solidarity between Mexican and New Mexican Spanish lexicon. The fact that Pía's Nuevomexicano husband and in-laws speak like her own great-grandparents is actually a marker of familiarity and denotes a much older cultural flow between northern New Mexico and Mexico. When Francisco first begins to pursue Pía, she tells him: "¿Por qué no buscas a una muchacha pues de Las Vegas, de tu cultura, tu idioma?" [Why don't you look for a girl from Las Vegas, from your culture, your language?] Ironically, Francisco's culture and language are more a part of Pía than she imagined. What Pía initially perceived as foreign and unfamiliar indexes a deep relationship of influence that recalls a larger linguistic history and linguistic dispossession that confuses any sense of one-way influence. This recalling of a history of linguistic dispossession makes visible the "the silenced knowledge about each other that has been our educational legacy"[59] and the fragmented histories[60] Latino/a/x groups learn (and don't learn) about each other.

Pía's discovery of a historical linguistic connection to her Nuevomexicano partner, along with the recall of Nuevomexicano lexical choices when utilizing Mexican words, draws attention to moments of linguistic Latinidad occurring within this transculturative process. These moments call to mind the "analogous sociopolitical conditions and colonial and neocolonial legacies"[61] in the zones of encuentro, the similar histories, and displacements between Nuevomexicanos/as/xs and Mexicanos/as/xs. For example, as Andrea categorizes "túnico" with "antes" and as Juanita states that the word "túnico" is "just gone," we remember the linguistic dispossession experienced in northern New Mexico. Francisco's and Juan's experiences again manifest themselves and evoke Nuevomexicanos/as/xs' deterritorialization from a linguistic home. Penélope's sense of loss is real, and it references the intergenerational loss within her linguistic history. If cultural deterritorialization "marks a transformation in the relationship between culture and territory,"[62] then this is an instance of linguistic deterritorialization that marks a transformation in the relationship between *language* and territory. The history of Spanish language repression in New Mexico references a deterritorialization from a linguistic home even while remaining in the same land or territory. Yet, the very presence of Mexican words and Mexicano/a partners in the Nuevomexicanos/as/xs' lives represents a related process of deterritorialization experienced by Mexicanos/as/xs

---

59. Aparicio, "Jennifer as Selena, 94.
60. These fragmented histories recall the words from the Somos Primos campaign PSA: "Nuevomexicanos grew up not knowing the deep roots they shared with their *primos* on the other side. Mexican textbooks do not mention the over 60,000 Mexicans that remained in the conquered territory. What happened to those primos?"
61. Álvarez et al., "Encountering Latin American," 539.
62. Hopper, *Understanding Cultural Globalization*, 52.

from their geographic homelands through their migration to northern New Mexico. This deterritorialization also recalls simultaneous dispossessions from actual tierras: Mexico's loss of half of its territory in 1848, and Nuevomexicanos/as/xs' continual loss of historical lands through contested land grants and recent fires. These analogous postcolonial conditions[63] position both Mexicanos/as/xs and Nuevomexicanos/as/xs as "minor" cultures.

Yet, the knowledge production that occurs within the couples' relationships disrupts this positioning. Consider Pancho's sensitivity to the history of linguistic oppression in northern New Mexico. He explains, "Pues la gente nacida de aquí, que aquellos años tú sabes que no los dejaban ni hablar español en las escuelas, entonces mucho menos estudiarlo" [Well, the people born here, who for those years you know that they didn't allow them to speak Spanish in the schools, much less to study it]. Or think about Andrea's impulse to "get like really defensive over Mexican people's rights." The Mexicano/a and Nuevomexicano/a partners gain an understanding of their partner's sociolinguistic and cultural histories, thus empowering them to challenge the legacy of these segmented histories. This construction of inter-Latino/a/x awareness and knowledge disrupts the "minor" culture category as these groups' sociolinguistic histories are put into conversation with each other. Just as these histories coexist and continuously contextualize each other, the lexical choices and linguistic varieties behave in a similar way. This process evokes Mignolo's theories around "the colonial difference." Mignolo explains the colonial difference as "the space where the restitution of subaltern knowledge is taking place."[64] These examples of inter-Latino/a/x linguistic and cultural knowledge production index a "restitution of subaltern knowledge" taking place within these dynamic zones of encuentro.

Moreover, these multilayered histories of displacement, dispossession, and deterritorialization create a circular interplay of influences that center around language. Hopper explains an aspect of this interplay:

> As migrants interact with locals there will be the possibility of mutual intercultural borrowings and the development of new cultural formations. Hence, cultural deterritorialization does not only affect those who are migrating, but it will also have an impact upon the culture or cultures of host countries. In sum, an important consequence of such movement is that cultures and cultural forms can inhabit or exist within other cultures, albeit often being indigenized in the process.[65]

---

63. Aparicio, "Jennifer as Selena," 94.
64. Mignolo, *Local Histories/Global Designs,* ix.
65. Hopper, *Understanding Cultural Globalization,* 53.

Mexicano/a/x and Nuevomexicano/a/x histories can inhabit each other almost seamlessly through a sharing of postcolonial and globalized conditions of deterritorialization. New Mexico and Mexico's overlapping histories also add an additional layer of complexity to Hopper's explanation because Mexicanos/as/xs migrate to a land that is not necessarily foreign. We see this through Pía's linguistic discovery regarding her great-grandparents' Spanish. Pía's experience also points to an extension of Hopper's theory: not only do cultural forms exist within each other but also linguistic forms. In this context, language serves as a tool to construct cultural memory. The recalling of words acts as what Deborah Paredez has termed a "memory circuit." Paredez describes these circuits as "complex pathways through which currents of past histories often run alongside or intersect with currents that pulse with claims to the present and hopes for the future."[66] Mexican lexical choices and New Mexican lexical choices intertwine in a circuit that recalls New Mexican words to the present, engages language recovery, and evokes intertwining Mexican and New Mexican histories. Through a discussion of lexical choices, Pía discovers a part of her Mexican linguistic history that is New Mexican as well. Pancho and Elizabeth learn about their partners' histories and absorb them as part of their relationship, effectively creating a champion for each other's history, culture, and language. In these cultural and linguistic interconnections, we see how the impact of recontact's influence leads to a certain embedding or inhabiting of the Mexicano/a/x in the Nuevomexicano/a/x and of the Nuevomexicano/a/x in the Mexicano/a/x. Pennycook presents this idea in terms of transculturation. He explains transculturation as "the constant processes of borrowing, bending and blending of cultures to the communicative practices of people interacting across different linguistic and communicative codes, borrowing, bending and blending languages into new modes of expression."[67] This "borrowing, bending and blending" of cultures leads to a new mode of expression embodied within the transculturated daily realities of the Mexicano-Nuevomexicano relationship. Through the long-term recontact interactions, the process of blurring, borrowing, bending, and blending leads to the embeddedness of linguistic varieties and histories within the experiences of the Mexicano-Nuevomexicano couples. Luis (Juanita's husband) clarifies this concept. He states, "You come over from Mexico and then you, that's a lot of culture over here, and then you kind of mix together and changes happen, which is okay for me, I don't mind. I like it." These changes represent a multifaceted transculturation process that culminates in this embedded mode of expression.

---

66. Paredez, *Selenidad*, 9.
67. Pennycook, *Global Englishes and Transcultural Flows*, 47.

CONCLUDING THOUGHTS: RETERRITORIALIZATION THROUGH RECONTACT

Perhaps one of the most interesting ways in which the transculturative dimension of recontact plays itself out is through cases of mistaken identity. Notably, language plays a central role in these stories of mistaken identity. Diana tells of being mistaken for Mexicana. She explains,

> Yeah, but it's funny, because I'm from here and a lot of people think I'm from Mexico . . . by the way I speak Spanish . . . and ask me, "What part of Mexico are you from?" I'm [like], "No, I'm not from Mexico. I'm just from New Mexico. I was born in Santa Fe," I tell them. But there is a lot of people that they do think I was born in Mexico. . . . I think maybe it's just the way I speak, you know, because of the Spanish, you know.

It is fascinating that through Diana's account we see an interesting transformation in the ways in which Nuevomexicanos/as/xs are perceived to speak Spanish. In the initial encounters between the Mexicanos/as and Nuevomexicanos/as, the New Mexican Spanish was often chiquitafied[68] or diminished as "not there" or "really bad." Yet, throughout the course of the relationship, the borrowing, bending, blending, and blurring process of transculturation confuses the Nuevomexicano/a for the Mexicano/a precisely through the way that the Nuevomexicano/a speaks. Interestingly, Mexicana-Nuevomexicana Rose and her Nuevomexicano husband Mike both perceive that Rose's Mexicano father's (Diana's husband's) linguistic profile has shifted toward increased "Nuevomexicanidad." Mike explains, "Uh, it's kinda—it's funny, too, because her dad is Mexican, but I see a lot of his, like—I don't know. It kinda seems like—sometimes, it seems like he's more, like, New Mexican now, after—after so many years." Rose adds that her father uses more New Mexican words and enjoys Nuevomexicano/a/x activities such as attending the Santa Fe fiestas and listening to Spanish music by Nuevomexicano/a/x artists. She emphasizes that these activities are not associated with Mexicanos/as/xs in Santa Fe. The Mexicano-Nuevomexicano Jurado couple illustrates transculturative reversals and a blurring of borders between Mexicanidad y Nuevomexicanidad.

Juanita also references an experience of mistaken identity based on her way of speaking. She states, "But my Spanish is to the point where people that are from Mexico, 'cause I work for H&R Block, people that are from Mexico come into my office and they ask me, 'What part of Mexico are you from?' And I'm like, 'I'm not Mexican. I was born and raised here.' And they go, 'But

---

68. Zentella, "'Chiquitafication' of U.S. Latinos."

you don't speak the Spanish like the people from here.'" After this description, Juanita's husband, Luis, interjects, "Because you are married to a Mexican!" It is precisely because of the long-term relationship and influence between the couple that this transculturative dimension of recontact becomes evident. Juanita clarifies quite emphatically that she was "born and raised here," thereby keeping her Nuevomexicana identity present. However, recontact does lead to a confusion of perceptions regarding who is Mexicano/a/x and who is Nuevomexicano/a/x precisely because of language variety. Juanita continues:

> Even the girls at work . . . I don't know how the conversation came about that they asked me. And I'm like, "I'm not Mexican." And they're like, "Yes, you are Mexican." And I'm like, "I'm not. I'm New Mexican." "But you use language from Mexico. You use a lot of sayings from Mexico." And I'm like, "Yeah, I had been married for so many years that you know you just pick up on it." . . . But even Verónica's kids and my nephew from Phoenix, they came to find out the other day. They didn't know I wasn't Mexican, and I'm like, "How come you didn't know I wasn't Mexican?" And they would go, "We didn't know, grandma." It was crazy.

Juanita's mistaken identity exists on several levels: among clients, coworkers, and family. What also becomes evident through Juanita's retelling is the disbelief surrounding her identity. The apparent mismatch between the way she speaks Spanish and her Nuevomexicana identity reveals that recontact also results in a process of reterritorialization.

Madrid explains reterritorialization as "a moment when the cultural meaning of given spaces is changed (even for a brief period of time) by their novel uses by a group of people different from those who use them normally."[69] These members of Juanita's social network do not consider a Nuevomexicana to be one who "normally" uses Mexican Spanish or who sounds Mexican. Similarly, Luis (Juanita's husband) tells of one of his coworkers questioning his identity with the words, "Are you from Mexico really?" Luis explains that because he spoke English and Spanglish[70] so well, this coworker had no idea that he was Mexican. Luis also adds one last dimension to the notion of reterritorialization when he states, "Well, being here for so many years I feel more New Mexican than Mexican." Not only is Luis mistaken for New Mexican, but he actually feels more New Mexican. Through the transculturative influence of recontact, Luis's sense of self is transformed. He is involved in a process of

---

69. Madrid, *Nor-Tec Rifa!*, 2.

70. In this example Luis is referring to his ability to code-switch. I will engage in a more in-depth discussion regarding "Spanglish" and the contested use of the term in chapter 5.

reterritorialization. If reterritorialization "constitutes a search for a sense of home or place,"[71] then Luis's homeplace becomes New Mexico.

Finally, Elizabeth's account reveals a similar process of reterritorialization that takes place due to her long-term relationship with her Mexicano partner. She explains,

> I've gotten now used to his Spanish so now his Spanish is more comfortable to me and I understand it all. It makes more sense to me, especially if I'm seeing a novela. The novelas, I love the novelas too. But I'm sitting there watching my novela, and my mom's all, "What'd they say? What'd they say?" Some of the words that they use, she doesn't know because she doesn't use them. I was like, "Oh, it means this, this, and this." She's all, "Oh, okay." So, it's just different things like that that are different.

Elizabeth's words do not emphasize a sense of loss or dominance regarding her use of Mexican Spanish, but instead a sense of comfort and home. Not only does Mexican Spanish become her reterritorialized linguistic home, but she is also able to serve as a bridge between Mexican Spanish and her Nuevomexicana mother through her translations. Here we see a culmination of recontact. If before meeting her Mexicano partner Elizabeth's complex linguistic profile represented a legacy of Spanish language shift, the description of her novela watching reveals how the recontact process challenges the historical linguistic deterritorialization that Nuevomexicanos/as/xs have experienced. Through a multidirectional mutual influence, Elizabeth's linguistic profile is now marked by language recovery, illustrating how the multidimensional process of recontact leads to reterritorialization.

---

71. Hopper, *Understanding Cultural Globalization*, 52.

CHAPTER 2

From Language Shift to Language Shaping

Because of Dad's influence, our Spanish language skills were much more developed than those of most of our friends.

—Mari Luci Jaramillo, *Madam Ambassador*

"I hope to God my kids learn Spanish.... I wish THEY (points to her parents) would talk to them more in Spanish!" Rose makes this emphatic declaration as we sit gathered around the dining room table at Armando and Diana Jurado's home just south of Santa Fe. Before Rose can continue, her Nuevomexicana mother responds, "We do, but they just don't know what we're talking about." Rose replies, "Yeah, but that's how they learn!" Then her Mexicano father, Armando, chimes in, "El trabajo de nosotros era que aprendieran español (points to Rose). Y lo aprendieron. Now el trabajo de ellos es que enseñen a sus hijos español." [Our job was to make sure they learned Spanish. And they learned it. Now their job is to teach their children Spanish.] Diana adds, "Yeah. It's not up to us. It's not going to be easy." This lively exchange about the future of Spanish in their family highlights the Jurados' perceptions regarding roles and responsibilities in the area of Spanish language maintenance. Diana's words underscore the difficulties of maintaining a minority language in the US. The fact that the intergenerational transmission of Spanish to Rose's children is not certain, but instead hoped for already points to the language shift occurring between generations in the family. Rose's expectation that her parents be the ones to stimulate and teach Spanish to her children speaks to Rose's belief that her parents are more capable in Spanish. This in turn reveals Rose's own perception that her Spanish skills are inferior to those of her parents and serves as another indicator of intergenerational language shift and individual language attrition or incomplete acquisition.[1]

This pattern is not unique to the Jurado family. Multiple studies regarding Spanish language maintenance among US Latino/a/x populations over the past forty years have concluded that, overall, there is a shift to English by the third generation, and this conclusion is not limited to any one region of the US. Intergenerational language shift is evident in studies conducted in the Southwest, particularly New Mexico,[2] as well as in California, illustrated by Rivera-Mills and Hurtado and Vega.[3] Additionally, studies conducted outside the Southwest in Chicago, Florida, and New York also demonstrate a common three-generation model for language shift from Spanish to English.[4]

In this chapter, I unpack the families' conscious efforts to shape their language use and the ways in which the Mexicano-Nuevomexicano families theorize about their own language shift and maintenance. I suggest that the study of the Spanish language use practices of the Jurado family, and of that of other Mexicano-Nuevomexicano families, contributes to a more nuanced understanding of Spanish language maintenance, shift, and loss in New Mexico. The Mexicano-Nuevomexicano accounts reveal that the families are keenly aware of their language practices and that they do not necessarily perceive language shift to be a one-way process. For example, Rose articulates a conscious decision to increase her Spanish use upon entering high school. Also, Rose and Verónica articulate high Spanish proficiency as a discriminating factor in choosing a romantic partner. Additionally, nearly half of the Mexicano/a/x-Nuevomexicano/a/x adult children have purposefully chosen professions

---

1. Ricardo Otheguy, "Linguistic Competence," 302, disputes the notion of "incomplete acquisition." Whereas Montrul, *Incomplete Acquisition in Bilingualism,* 164, attempts to account for "apparent incomplete L1 knowledge" through either attrition and incomplete acquisition, Otheguy critiques the proposal of incomplete acquisition in favor of an alternative view that frames the linguistic behavior of G2 bilingual US Latinos not as erroneous "as they are frequently described in the literature, but rather points of divergence, dialectal differences if you will, between their Spanish and that of the previous generation due to normal intergenerational language change accelerated by conditions of language contact."

2. Hudson and Bills, "Intergenerational Language Shift"; Bills, Hernández-Chávez, and Hudson, "Geography of Language Shift"; Bills, "New Mexican Spanish"; Bills and Vigil, "Ashes to Ashes"; Bills, Hudson, and Hernández-Chávez, "Spanish Home Language Use"; Bernal-Enriquez, "Factores socio-históricos"; Bills and Vigil, *Spanish Language of New Mexico*; and Jenkins, "Cost of Linguistic Loyalty."

3. Rivera-Mills, "Intraethnic Attitudes among Hispanics"; and Hurtado and Vega, "Shift Happens."

4. Potowski, "Spanish Language Shift in Chicago"; García and Otheguy, "Language Situation of Cuban Americans"; Lynch, "Spanish-Speaking Miami"; and Zentella, *Growing Up Bilingual.*

that require Spanish proficiency. These factors individually may not add up to sustained intergenerational language maintenance, but they are significant in the trajectory of each family and allow for the exploration of complex acts of agency, maintenance, and recovery within larger shift patterns. Thus, the family narratives effectively create a space in which the Mexicano/a/x-Nuevomexicano/a/x subjects can be viewed as "language shapers" rather than "language shifters." These narratives are the focus of this chapter.

Schecter and Bayley emphasize that "research in bilingual and multilingual communities is now beginning to focus on the dynamic nature of language practices, particularly in societal or situational contexts where individuals have choice with regard to the use of the minority or the dominant language."[5] The Mexicano-Nuevomexicano families contribute to the exploration of the dynamic nature of language practices and the linguistic agency associated with this dynamicity. In this chapter, my analysis of the Mexicano-Nuevomexicano family answers the question, "Who speaks what to whom in your family, and how has this changed over time?" The responses provide more detailed insight into the families' own theories regarding their language maintenance and shift. First, I provide a brief background to the study of Spanish language maintenance and shift in New Mexico. I then provide family language socialization and language use portraits to unpack the families' remarkable acts of maintenance, agency, and recovery. I next call for a reframing of Spanish language maintenance and shift in the context of the Mexicano/a/x-Nuevomexicano/a/x subjects. I conclude with some thoughts around symbolic associations with Spanish language maintenance within the Mexicano-Nuevomexicano families.

LANGUAGE MAINTENANCE AND SHIFT IN NEW MEXICO

As discussed in the previous chapter, because Nuevomexicanos/as/xs do not fit neatly into traditional generational distinctions, the added layers of the contact generation model, the recontact process, and the fact that Nuevomexicanos/as/xs many times become part of a "reacquisition generation" problematize G1, G2, and G3 designations for the Nuevomexicano/a/x partners and for the children in these mixed families.[6] Yet, regardless of model or terminology, the Jurado family mentioned above is aware of a reduction in Spanish language use and ability between the grandparents (Diana and Armando)

---

5. Schecter and Bayley, *Language as Cultural Practice*, 15.
6. See Villa and Rivera-Mills, "Integrated Multi-Generational Model," for the "reacquisition generation" and "contact generation" model.

and grandchildren (Rose's children). However, simply chalking the family's story up to one piece of a larger predictable pattern of Spanish language loss obscures the complexity of the family's own awareness and agency. Studies that rely on census data also contribute to the invisibility of family agency.

A good number of previous studies of language shift and maintenance in New Mexico have relied on census data from the Southwest. Bills, Hernández-Chávez, and Hudson's 1995 study[7] examines the 1970, 1980, and 1990 US Census data regarding Spanish language maintenance and shift to English in five states of the Southwest, including New Mexico. The study utilizes the proportion of Spanish language loyalty, or those who claim Spanish language use in the home, among younger and adult generations to calculate Spanish language retention and intergenerational transmission of Spanish. The study concludes that lower education level was the best predictor of Spanish language loyalty and intergenerational transmission of the language. Utilizing the same census data, Hudson, Hernández-Chávez, and Bills' 1995 study[8] also concludes that the number of years of education completed by those of Hispanic origin predicts the shift from Spanish to English. Additionally, the authors conclude that proximity to the border favors retention of Spanish and greater distance favors a shift to English.[9] In a later study, Bills, Hudson, and Hernández Chávez[10] similarly claim that Spanish language use diminishes with increased education level. Additionally, the study concludes that English language proficiency is an indicator of language shift from Spanish to English. Devin Jenkins[11] extends the Bills, Hernández-Chávez, and Hudson model[12] with the data from the US Census from the year 2000. Jenkins finds similar results to the 1995 study in all but one area. He explains, "The most notable change after 20 years took place in the measures of language loyalty and retention. . . . in 2000 both loyalty and retention showed a decreased relationship, or none at all, with socioeconomic measures of income, education and occupation among the Hispanic population."[13] This is an important deviation from the 1995 study because it indicates a potential closing in the societal gap between socioeconomic status and Spanish language retention. The findings from all of these census-based studies contribute significantly to the study of Spanish language maintenance and shift among US Latinos/as/xs, but they do

---

7. Bills, Hernández-Chávez, and Hudson, "Geography of Language Shift."
8. Bills, Hudson, and Hernández-Chávez, "Spanish Home Language Use."
9. Bills, Hudson, and Hernández-Chávez, "Spanish Home Language Use," 25.
10. Bills, Hudson, and Hernández-Chávez, "Spanish Home Language Use."
11. Jenkins, "Cost of Linguistic Loyalty."
12. Bills, Hernández-Chávez, and Hudson, "Geography of Language Shift."
13. Jenkins, "Cost of Linguistic Loyalty," 23.

not necessarily flesh out the individual and familial stories that accompany the shift patterns. Also, because census-based studies have not distinguished between Nuevomexicano/a/x participants and those of a Mexicano/a/x immigrant background, or the participants have simply all been identified as Nuevomexicano/a/x, this chapter allows for a more fine-grained analysis of language use patterns among children whose parents belong to different generational and Latino/a/x origin groups.

Several studies focusing on familial language patterns in New Mexico do provide more detailed analysis of family stories. An early and extensive study examining Spanish language shift in the small northern New Mexico town of Arroyo Seco by Leroy Ortíz[14] examines to what extent the community is maintaining Spanish. The study utilizes a sample of forty-eight Nuevomexicano/a/x children and their respective parents and families. The study concludes that, generally, older members of the families interviewed tended to use more Spanish and Spanish was used almost exclusively when addressing parents in the household. Interestingly, Ortíz also indicates that males claimed to speak more Spanish than females. An additional New Mexican study that explores family patterns of Spanish language use is that of Hudson and Bills[15] in the historic neighborhood of Martíneztown in Albuquerque. Through a series of interviews with fifty-five Hispanic families, the study concludes that the signs of language shift from Spanish to English were evident within one generation due to the discrepancy between the number of participants who claimed Spanish as their mother tongue and the number of participants who were fluent in the language. A shift to English among each generation of speakers in the families interviewed demonstrated an increased shift to English in the home. The study concludes that Spanish in Martíneztown is still very much alive. However, because of the signs of language shift, both within one generation and from one generation to the next, the long-term maintenance of Spanish is doubtful.

Roberts's 2001 ethnography[16] also documents language use within the family setting through a focus on cultural identity among school-age children (K–12) in a northern New Mexico school. She administered a home language survey that reveals family language patterns, and she observes a generational change when comparing what language(s) parents and children use at home. Her study reports that, "although 32% of the parents speak only English to their children, 71% of the children speak only English to their

---

14. Ortíz, "Sociolinguistic Study."
15. Hudson and Bills, "Intergenerational Language Shift."
16. Roberts, *Remaining and Becoming*.

parents."[17] Roberts highlights how the language habits of her participants are dependent on multiple factors including place of residence, religious affiliation, the language preference of the extended family, the home language, the participant's spouse's first language, sibling order, gender, occupation, amount of formal Spanish instruction, and the age of the people involved in the conversation.[18] Many of these same variables influence the language use practices in the Mexicano-Nuevomexicano families.

Lastly, Schecter and Bayley's extensive 2002 monograph with four case studies on families of Mexican descent in California and Texas provides a coherent and nicely structured analysis of families across the two regions. Specifically, the authors' objective to "articulate a more fully developed model for the study of language socialization"[19] aligns with the aims of the present chapter. The authors argue that "language socialization, instantiated in language choice and patterns of use in sociocultural and sociohistorical contexts characterized by ambiguity and flux, is both a dynamic and fluid process."[20] Schecter and Bayley question the conceptualization of language socialization as a unidirectional process. They underscore that "support for a strategy of maintenance may well ensue not from a one-time decision on the part of caregivers regarding family language practice but rather from a series of choices that constitute affirmations and reaffirmations of a commitment to the minority language."[21] These notions of dynamicity, fluidity, and multidirectionality are useful when considering language use patterns within the Mexicano-Nuevomexicano context.

"SOMEWHERE IN THE MIDDLE": LANGUAGE SOCIALIZATION PRACTICES AND LANGUAGE USE PORTRAITS

"My dad always spoke Spanish and my mom always spoke English, and I was somewhere in the middle." Rolando Quintana's description of being "somewhere in the middle" highlights the complexity of language choice within his family. In fact, the notion of "somewhere in the middle" could describe the linguistic location of all of the Mexicano-Nuevomexicano families with regard to their language use patterns. If we consider these practices to reside along a

---

17. Roberts, *Remaining and Becoming*, 56.
18. Roberts, *Remaining and Becoming*, 56.
19. Schecter and Bayley, *Language as Cultural Practice*, xv.
20. Schecter and Bayley, *Language as Cultural Practice*, xv–xvi.
21. Schecter and Bayley, *Language as Cultural Practice*, 110.

continuum, as in Valdés's proposal of a "bilingual continuum"[22] with English monolingualism on one side and Spanish monolingualism on the other, these families find themselves along shifting positions of this continuum throughout different moments of their lives. García and Sánchez extend this continuum further beyond regimented notions of "English" and "Spanish" and discuss a continuum of bilingual practices. They state,

> Latinx families' language goes beyond what schools call 'English' or 'Spanish.' Even when parents speak Spanish at home, children often reply in English; and when parents insist that only Spanish be spoken at home, television, radio and social media, besides friends and neighbors, bring English into the mix. In Latinx families that are said to be 'English speaking,' there are relatives who speak Spanish. There is a continuum of bilingual practices in all Latinx families, regardless of experiences and ideologies, that needs to be recognized.[23]

For instance, Rolando reports that his parents always used a mix of English and Spanish with each other throughout his life. His father tended to use more Spanish and his mother used more English. Rolando remembers speaking all Spanish to both of his parents before entering school. However, after beginning school at age four,[24] Rolando reports a pattern of speaking English with both his Nuevomexicana mother and his Mexicano father. His mother spoke English with Rolando and his father spoke to him in Spanish. Yet, Rolando notes that recently the language use with his father is different from what it was when he was in high school. His father agrees. José Quintana explains,

> Últimamente se me hace que hablamos más español. Cuando estaban chicos es otro. No quieren hablar así jovencitos. Ya nada más empiezan a agarrar edad y yo creo que se sienten más confortables. Es lo que creo yo en cuanto a Rolando. Le gusta hablar conmigo ya más en español. De hecho, en veces texteamos.
>
> [Lately, it seems to me that we speak more Spanish. When they were younger it was another story. They didn't want to speak when they were little. I think they feel more comfortable as they get older. That's what I think the case is

---

22. Valdés, "Heritage Language Students."
23. García and Sánchez, "Making of the Language," 29–30.
24. This is consistent with Valdés, *Con Respeto*, and Schecter and Bayley, *Language as Cultural Practice*.

with Rolando. Now he likes to speak with me more in Spanish. In fact, sometimes we text in Spanish.]

Valdés reminds us that "over the course of a lifetime, a single individual's bilingual profile can vary immensely."[25] Indeed, Schecter and Bayley's entire project emphasizes that language choice and familial patterns are not static and that individual language behavior is dynamic. Gabriela Navarro reiterates this dynamicity when she assures me that she does want her daughters to speak both Spanish and English: "Sí quiero que hablen los dos idiomas y yo digo que ahora les están interesando un poco más porque pueden platicar más con sus primos que están allá" [I do want them to speak both languages and I think that now they are more interested because they can speak more with their cousins who are over there]. In response, her daughter Milagros emphasizes, "I want to spend a lot more time in Mexico now that I'm older." The Mexicano/a/x-Nuevomexicano/a/x answers to the question, "Who speaks what to whom in the family, and how has this changed over time?" allow for a more detailed portrait of language use and describe the perceptions of how familial linguistic patterns may change direction. Essentially, these Mexicano/a/x-Nuevomexicano/a/x responses flesh out the notion of being "somewhere in the middle." In line with Schecter and Bayley's objectives, these responses contribute to a deeper understanding of "the complexity of individual language behaviors observed over years and across a spectrum of family contexts."[26] The responses to this question and the narratives that it triggers make visible the multidirectional language use patterns within each family.

Although there is no one-size-fits-all paradigm for the language behavior in each Mexicano-Nuevomexicano family unit, below I attempt to group the families together according to certain commonalities in the directionality of the language flows between the family members. For example, both the Guzmán and Molina families report a predominant use of English by both parents and by both children in each family throughout most of their lives. This is represented in figure 2.

Alexa Guzmán explains that she has always spoken English with her parents and that they have always spoken English with her. Alejandro Guzmán reports a slight difference in that he and his Nuevomexicana mother speak English to each other and that throughout most of his life he has responded to his father in English; however, his father uses some Spanish with him. Both Alexa and Alejandro report English as the primary language between their

---

25. Valdés, "Heritage Language Students," 42.
26. Schecter and Bayley, *Language as Cultural Practice*, 173.

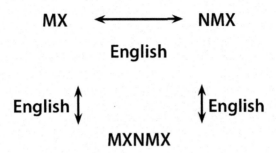

FIGURE 2. Family language use patterns of directionality in Guzmán and Molina families.

parents. They specify that if their father spoke Spanish to their mother, she would respond in English. Likewise, Alicia Molina reports speaking English to her Nuevomexicana mother and her mother speaking English to her. She describes her Mexicano father speaking both English and Spanish, but mostly English to her. She reports responding in English to her father. She describes speaking only English to her brother, Antonio, as well. She explains that her parents speak Spanish and English to each other, with her father speaking more Spanish and her mother using more English. Antonio only remembers his father speaking English with the immediate family during most of his life. Antonio also reports speaking English with his parents and sister.

The Quintana, Medina, Maestas, and Jurado families also report English to be the dominant language in their interactions; however, these four families denote more Spanish use by the Mexicano parent than the Guzmán and Molina families. See a visual representation of these patterns in figure 3.

Like Rolando Quintana, Rose Jurado reports her father speaking both English and Spanish with her. She explains that she has always spoken English with him. Rose also notes that she has always spoken English with her Nuevomexicana mother and that her mother has always spoken English with her. Adrian Medina reports that his Nuevomexicana mother has always spoken a mix of Spanish and English with him. However, Adrian has always responded to his mother in English. Adrian explains that his Mexicano father has always spoken to him in mostly Spanish and that he responds in mostly English. Olivia describes that her mother has always spoken English to her and that her father has always spoken mostly Spanish. She speaks English to both parents. Both Olivia and Adrian report that they have always spoken English to each other. They both also note that their parents speak mostly Spanish to each other.

FIGURE 3. Family language use patterns of directionality in Quintana, Medina, Maestas, and Jurado families.

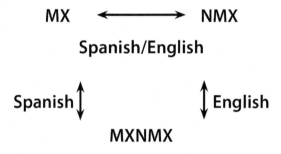

FIGURE 4. Family language use patterns of directionality in Loredo and Navarro families.

The Mexicano/a/x-Nuevomexicano/a/x subjects in the Loredo and Navarro families report almost exclusive Spanish use between the Mexicana parent and the Mexicano-Nuevomexicanos. These households, overall, report more Spanish use. This is illustrated in figure 4.

Interestingly, both families have Mexican mothers. Angélica Loredo reports that she has always spoken Spanish to her Mexicana mother and that her mother has always spoken Spanish to her. Her father has always spoken English to her, and she speaks English to him. Her parents speak both English and Spanish to each other, but they tend toward predominantly Spanish conversations. Like the Loredo family, the Navarro sisters report a similar linguistic pattern in their household. Milagros and Rosalinda state that Spanish was the only language in the home until they started preschool. They both report that their Mexicana mother has always spoken to them in Spanish and that they have always spoken to her in Spanish. Both Rosalinda and Milagros

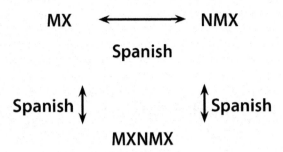

FIGURE 5. Family language use patterns of directionality in Fierro and Santos families.

report using English and Spanish with their father; however, they reveal that they typically use more English with him. Both sisters report that their father has consistently used English and Spanish with them equally throughout their lives. The sisters explain that English and Spanish have always been used between their parents; however, Spanish has predominated. Rosalinda reports using English and Spanish with Milagros. However, Milagros reports using almost all English with Rosalinda.

Mexicana-Nuevomexicana Verónica Fierro describes mostly Spanish use in her family as well. Like Rolando, upon beginning school she describes a shift to speaking English outside of the house with her friends and sister; however, she reports the linguistic patterns between her parents and herself to be relatively consistent. Verónica explains that growing up it was Spanish all the time in the house between her parents and with her parents. Carolina Santos describes a similar scenario in her family growing up. She explains, "Everything was Spanish. There was no English. Everything was Spanish, Spanish, Spanish." Carolina grew up speaking Spanish to her parents and her parents spoke Spanish to her. Figure 5 represents Verónica's and Carolina's experiences growing up.

However, Carolina's younger sister, Edna, describes a different experience. She says that she never wanted to speak or learn Spanish. She explains that she heard more Spanish from her Nuevomexicano father than from her Mexicana mother. She reports that her parents spoke Spanish between each other; however, she always spoke English to both of her parents. Edna reflects on this pattern: "And I don't know how I really communicated with my parents a lot because they would speak a lot of Spanish, my dad in particular. I just, I never really wanted to learn it or anything when I was younger." Edna's different experience in language use patterns from that of her older sister highlights the diversity of experience even with the same family.

The ten-year age difference between Carolina and Edna may account for the differences in familial linguistic experience.[27] Younger siblings oftentimes are less proficient in the minority language than older siblings, and Roberts[28] emphasizes the influence of sibling order in Spanish language maintenance. This is consistent with MaryAnn Parada's finding[29] that with a higher birth order among siblings, the older sibling's Spanish tends to be more proficient and used more frequently. The Navarro sisters also highlight a difference between their Spanish language abilities and those of their eight-year-old sister. Milagros explains her worry about this situation: "I'm concerned about it, too, 'cause sometimes I feel that she speaks more English than what she does Spanish than when I was at her age 'cause I knew a lot more and understood a lot more." Similarly, although both Alexa and Alejandro Guzmán speak of English dominating their household while growing up, Alejandro tells of writing articles in Spanish for the local newspaper, and he speaks of a recent increase in his use of Spanish, particularly with his father. Yet, Alexa still emphasizes that she communicates in English with her immediate family, and, in her words, "My Spanish is bad. Because I like sort of stopped speaking it. Like I don't speak it like as much as I should. And like I don't like really feel comfortable speaking it." These cases of younger siblings highlight the different positionalities along the maintenance/shift continuum, even within the same family.

LANGUAGE SHAPING: ACTS OF MAINTENANCE, AGENCY, AND RECOVERY

The language use portraits of each Mexicano-Nuevomexicano family challenge notions of clear-cut language boundaries within families. There are no realities of homogeneous language use in these households. Phrases like "mostly English" and "mostly Spanish" reveal the coexistence of Spanish and English within each family member's linguistic repertoire. Different from both Potowski's findings and those of Ortíz,[30] the Mexicano-Nuevomexicano family exhibits a diversity in linguistic and generational profile among the parents that most definitely influences the overall familial language use patterns. Even if the family reports a dominance of English among most family members,

---

27. See Silva-Corvalán, "Narrating in English and Spanish."
28. Roberts, *Remaining and Becoming.*
29. Parada, "Sibling Variation."
30. Potowski, "Spanish Language Shift in Chicago"; and Ortíz, "Sociolinguistic Study."

the Spanish "overhearing"[31] or receptivity is still present. Fishman[32] highlights the notion of domains and role relations. He underscores that one approach to multilingual language use in the family domain is to recognize that "interacting members of a family (as well as the participants in most other domains of language behavior) are hearers as well as speakers (i.e., that there may be a distinction between multilingual comprehension and multilingual production), but it also recognizes that their language behavior may be more than merely a matter of individual preference or facility, but also a matter of role-relations."[33] Fishman's words illustrate the diversity of interaction within the families and how one individual is usually not defined by one language alone with all interlocutors. These profiles also demonstrate the variability between families and within families. Schecter and Bayley comment on this variability:

> Our agenda . . . has involved elucidating processes of language maintenance and shift both within and across time. In pursuing this inquiry, we have discovered that various enabling or constraining factors do not necessarily have the same effects for different actors, or for the same actors at different times in their evolutions. Although some of these processes have proven responsive to sociolinguistic hypotheses, we have also learned that in some situations when people have choice, there is a limit to how accurately one can predict how they will choose.[34]

Schecter and Bayley's words emphasize that unpredictability of language choice. They note that the study of variability, as in Labov's work,[35] implies systematicity and the controls provided by such structure. A rigid framework of systematicity may not capture the variability within the families studied in Schecter and Bayley or within the different Mexicano-Nuevomexicano family units.

Hornberger[36] examines a similar situation when studying community language choice between Quechua and Spanish in a Peruvian community. Although Quechua use is largely favored in the family/home/community domain, and Spanish is usually the language of choice outside of this domain, circumstances such as setting–role mismatch or interactions occurring in what Hornberger terms a "comunidad" domain[37] dis-

---

31. DeHouwer, *Bilingual First Language Acquisition*.
32. Fishman, "Who Speaks What Language?"
33. Fishman, "Who Speaks What Language?," 75.
34. Schecter and Bayley, *Language as Cultural Practice*, 177.
35. Labov, "Notion of System."
36. Hornberger, *Bilingual Education and Language Maintenance*.
37. Hornberger, *Bilingual Education and Language Maintenance*, 107.

rupt strict associations between one language and one domain. Additionally, in her examination of code-switching and lexical borrowing, she states that individual factors "influence language choice above and beyond generalized domain" and that "when factors of individual bilingualism are added to the domain . . . there is room for an almost infinite variety of language use."[38] Hornberger reminds us that community language use is complex and that "there are no simple generalizations to be made about language use in the community."[39] Hornberger's discussion complements Schecter and Bayley's work in that it allows for the loose association of certain domains with certain languages, for example, "mostly English" in the house, but also highlights the complexity and variability present at the individual level. This variability underscores the notion of Mexicano/a/x-Nuevomexicano/a/x "language-shaping." The Mexicano/a/x-Nuevomexicano/a/x descriptions of the language use patterns make visible the subtle acts of maintenance, recovery, and agency over time. Although six of the Mexicano/a/x-Nuevomexicano/a/x subjects from four of the ten families (Medina, Jurado, Loredo, and Navarro) report no change in language use patterns over time, the majority report movement along the continuum of Spanish/English language use throughout their family life. These movements along the continuum constitute Schecter and Bayley's "affirmations and reaffirmations," of commitment to the minority language. In some cases slight and in other cases more dramatic, the change indexes moments of "language shaping" and sheds light on the families' theories about their language behavior.

Notably, this language shaping can also manifest itself as linguistic refusal, rather than affirmations and reaffirmations. Sylvia Maestas's language experience embodies the tensions of an estranged relationship with her Mexicano father and the emotions embedded in this experience. Sylvia consciously moves away from Spanish language use. She explains,

> I don't really know Spanish as well as I should. I think it's just from trying to, like, disassociate myself with that 'cause, you know, the experiences and stuff. But when I was little, I spoke pretty fluent Spanish. . . . But once he and my mom kind of divorced, he kind of divorced us all, I guess. . . . That's where I kinda started getting mad, and then I started kind of rebelling and trying to not talk Spanish anymore.

The upset caused by Sylvia's parents' divorce affects her linguistic trajectory. Her choice to stop speaking Spanish illustrates her agency in rejecting Spanish

---

38. Hornberger, *Bilingual Education and Language Maintenance*, 115.
39. Hornberger, *Bilingual Education and Language Maintenance*, 115.

language use due to its painful associations. Thus, subtle acts of linguistic agency are not necessarily synonymous with language maintenance.

An additional case of a change toward increased English use within the Mexicano-Nuevomexicano families is that of the Fierro family. Verónica Fierro reports her present language use to be almost all English with her Nuevomexicana mother and half and half with her Mexicano father. That is, she speaks almost all English with her mother and her mother speaks all English with her. Verónica's father speaks half English and half Spanish with her and she responds using half English and half Spanish. She attributes her father's work, his desire to better his English, and the desire to communicate with the grandchildren (the children of her sister) for the increased English use within the family unit. This shift to English might seem somewhat expected given previous studies. However, it is significant that Verónica (one of only four married Mexicano/a/x-Nuevomexicano/a/x subjects) has chosen a first-generation Mexicano husband. She reports speaking mostly Spanish with her husband. In a fascinating move, as Verónica's Spanish with her parents has decreased, she has shaped a new home environment with her husband in which Spanish dominates.

In addition to the Quintana family denoting a recent increase in Spanish use,[40] the Guzmán and Molina Mexicano/a/x-Nuevomexicano/a/x subjects also describe a recent increase in Spanish use within their families. As I mentioned above, Alejandro Guzmán reports an increase in Spanish use with his Mexicano father. He explains that, if Spanish was spoken in the house when he was growing up, it was by his father. When he was younger, he always responded in English. However, as he has grown older, he responds in Spanish. Similarly, while growing up, Alicia Molina describes that she only spoke English with her younger brother, Antonio. Now, however, she explains that her brother prefers for her to speak more Spanish. Antonio echoes this when he states that he usually speaks English to his sister but wants her to "mix it up" and speak more Spanish to him now. He also reports that now that they are older, their father speaks more Spanish to both him and Alicia and that he perceives that his parents are speaking more Spanish between the two of them as well. Antonio's father, Pancho, describes the language use patterns in the family over the years. He explains,

> Nos fuimos por la ruta más fácil. . . . Te empiezas a meter en una guerra de cada rato: "Háblame en español, no hables inglés, y no esto, y no lo

---

40. Zentella, *Growing Up Bilingual,* also finds an increased use of Spanish among her participants later in their lives. However, Zentella connects this to her participants becoming mothers.

otro," entonces ya son muchos "no, no, no." Desgraciadamente escogieron no hablarlo mucho. Alicia ahora se interesó. Antonio ahora está muy interesado, y ahora les ayudo. En todo lo que me piden ayuda, les ayudo. Pero sí, cuando estaban chiquitos, no se interesaron.

[We took the easy way. . . . You start getting into a fight all of the time: "Speak to me in Spanish, don't speak English, and don't do this, and don't do that," so it's a lot of "no, no, no." Unfortunately, they chose not to speak much Spanish. Now Alicia is now more interested. Now Antonio is very interested, and now I help them. I'll help them with anything they ask. But, yes, when they were little, they were not interested.]

Pancho highlights the English dominance in the household when his children were younger, and he clarifies that it was a conscious choice. To avoid conflict in the home and not stifle communication within the family, he and his wife chose not to demand Spanish. His words reveal his own agency in issues of language choice.

Pancho's words also illustrate Schecter and Bayley's comments regarding directionality in language socialization. Schecter and Bayley explain,

> Clearly, interpretations of patterns of variation and choice within a framework where language socialization is a one-way process in which mothers, teachers, and other caregivers inculcate the values, knowledge, and linguistic repertoire of their culture into children are increasingly problematic in reference to contemporary Western settings where adolescents, and even preadolescents, exercise a fair amount of autonomy within family units.[41]

Pancho speaks of not wanting to get into a fight or "meter en una guerra" because of his children's resistance to speaking Spanish. The notion of the Mexicano/a/x-Nuevomexicano/a/x subjects playing an active role in their own language socialization is important to consider. The concept of directionality is expanded in this case through the idea that children can also socialize parents. However, the directionality of language shift is also challenged within the Molina family because both Alicia and Antonio speak of increasing their Spanish use recently. Alicia had just taken a trip to visit her grandmother in Mexico when I interviewed her. This was the first time she had ever stayed for an extended period without her father. She remarks that after this trip she feels more confident and wants to speak more Spanish in her family. Additionally,

---

41. Schecter and Bayley, *Language as Cultural Practice,* 173.

she was also student-teaching in a dual-language immersion elementary school classroom the semester before our interview. Antonio speaks of his favorite norteño bands and how he enjoys going to Mexico with his father and spending as much time with him as possible in "his world." The Molina family, Rolando Quintana, and Alejandro Guzmán illustrate that the Mexicano/a/x-Nuevomexicano/a/x subjects can recover, reinfuse and restimulate their Spanish use even as young adults.

The case of the Santos family also challenges notions of directionality within language socialization patterns and language shift. Recall that Edna Santos reported speaking almost all English growing up and that she strongly disliked speaking Spanish. However, now she currently reports speaking 63 percent Spanish in a typical week. What accounts for such a drastic change over her lifespan? Just as Potowski[42] has underscored that the language used with peers predicts language maintenance, Edna's primary socialization with Mexicano/a/x monolingual Spanish-speaking coworkers and friends has propelled her Spanish dominance in recent years. Previous employment at Wal-Mart and current employment at a dual-language immersion middle school and Home Depot assure daily Spanish use with friends, coworkers, customers, and students throughout her workday. Edna describes her educational assistant's perceptions of her abilities. She explains, "When I started there, she said she was really nervous for me. She goes, 'You tried your hardest, but, eh—you were bad.' And she says now, she said I've improved like 100 percent." Edna's older sister, Carolina, also works as a teacher in a dual-language immersion school, and she reflects on this change in Edna: "Yeah, so it's really weird that Edna ended up a Spanish teacher because she hated it. Now her BFFs are all Mexicanos. . . . Her aide and her hang out three times a week, go do lady stuff, and do all kinds of stuff. Now she's thinking of going to Colombia. Her two friends from work, a husband-and-wife team, came back from Colombia from doing a two-year stint out there." Not only has Edna's Spanish use increased, but she is actively considering opportunities to continue to enrich her Spanish.

Yet, as both Carolina's and Edna's Spanish language use has become a consistent and dominant force in their everyday lives, the Santos parents' Spanish use has followed a different trajectory. Edna explains,

> Yeah, my dad would always speak Spanish. And it's really weird to see my parents just now speaking more English than Spanish. . . . When I call I'll try to talk in Spanish and sometimes they answer in English . . . it's reversed. I'm

---

42. Potowski, "Spanish Language Shift in Chicago."

like, "Ah." I get so frustrated. So yeah, it's really weird. . . . A year ago, I think, we went to the Mexican consulado for my mom to try and get her birth certificate from Mexico and, um, there was a lawyer from Mexico there, from Chihuahua. And they were talking and they were asking my mom questions. And, I mean, they were talking really fast and they asked my mom a question and she was like—she didn't know how to answer. Like, her and my dad just, like, looked at each other and they didn't know how to, like, talk back to him. And I just looked at him and so I answered for her and I told him what we were looking for and I go, when we left, I go, "Mom what happened?" I mean like—and she goes, "I didn't know how to respond." She goes, "I didn't know what to say. I didn't know how to say it," she goes. . . . I called my sister and I said, "You will not believe what happened to Mom today." And then my sister had seen it the other day at a restaurant. They went to a Mexican restaurant and the waiter—the waitress talked to my dad in Spanish and my dad talked English. And it never used to be like that, never.

Edna and Carolina report amazement at their own parents' language shift to English. The fact that Edna was able to intervene in the communication between her parents at the Mexican consulate speaks to her own confidence and the shifting role that Spanish has played in her life. Much like Rivera-Mills's study in Fortuna, California,[43] the moments described by Edna highlight the shift to English that can occur within one generation. It seems that as Marta and Juan have expanded their domains of English use and, thus, reduced their domains of Spanish use, the opposite has occurred in the cases of the Santos daughters. Zentella reminds us in her introduction to Schecter and Bayley's work that

> as bilinguals, we do not live double lives, with the exact same range of speakers, locales, and discourse demands in both of our languages. For most of us, one language is dominant. As the rich case studies in this book reveal, the dominant language may change as our lives change, and the authors argue persuasively that the deep emotions that accompany these changes are not given the attention they deserve.[44]

Edna and Carolina have deep emotions about family language use and about the changes in this use. Carolina asserts, "I love to speak Spanish because I still feel that it's respectful for me to speak Spanish to my parents." The changes in

---

43. Rivera-Mills, "Intraethnic Attitudes among Hispanics."
44. Zentella, "Foreword," xi.

her parents' linguistic patterns and in her younger sister's use of Spanish both challenge fixed notions of directionality and underscore the many layers of language maintenance and shift.

Edna's case not only highlights a fascinating instance in which the younger sibling now utilizes more Spanish than both her parents and older sister, but it also illustrates the importance of domain expansion in influencing Spanish language maintenance. The expansion of Spanish language use in the work domain is key to the Spanish language increase and maintenance in the cases of Edna, Carolina, Alicia, and Alejandro. Alejandro specifically sought out a job in the Latinx cultural and student services organization at his university to be able to utilize his Spanish in the workplace with his peers. Alicia, Carolina, and Edna all hold positions at dual-language immersion elementary and middle schools. Dorian[45] defines the association of one language with a particular domain with "language allocation." In the case of these four Mexicano/a/x-Nuevomexicano/a/x subjects, an instance of language reallocation seems to be occurring. In choosing jobs that require Spanish, they illustrate an important act of agency in shaping their language use.

However, even Rose, who does not report an increase of Spanish in her immediate family and does not hold a job that requires the use of Spanish, has taken measures to increase her Spanish in her adult life. Like Verónica, she also made choosing a husband who was proficient in Spanish a priority. She explains, "Well, when I was in—in college, one of the—one of the biggest things for me is I wanted to meet somebody that spoke Spanish. Plain and simple." In the plática with her Nuevomexicano husband, Rose tells him, "What drew me to you was the Spanish. Oh, yeah, I remember telling him all the time, 'Talk to me in Spanish, sing to me in Spanish.'" This conscious choice in a romantic partner serves as an act of agency in language maintenance due to Rose's desire that her own children know Spanish. All the Mexicano/a/x-Nuevomexicanos/as/xs take intergenerational transmission of Spanish seriously. One hundred percent of the subjects expressed that they want their children to speak Spanish and that, with the help of their parents, they will teach them Spanish.

There is one additional trend that I would like to highlight regarding the Mexicano/a/x-Nuevomexicanos/as/xs' opinions about language use patterns within their families: a discourse of blame. For example, Rose is not pleased with the fact that Spanish use has not increased with her parents. She explains,

> Yeah. That's what I tell my dad. It's your guys' fault that my Spanish isn't all that great. [Laughs] . . . They laugh at me because they know it's—you know,

---

45. Dorian, *Language Death*.

it's not really true. It's just a joke we have. But, honestly, it really is—that's how I feel anyways, that if it would have been spoken to me or made me—or if they would have made me speak it to them.

But they—they blame it on me. They say it's me that I never spoke it. I'm like I didn't speak it because you told me to talk to you in English. Or you would only speak to me in English. . . . I mean her—my grandma and grandpa, that's all they spoke to each other was Spanish. They spoke to them in Spanish. My mom grew up speaking Spanish. That was her first language. Um, but she didn't teach it to us as a first language.

Rose may not be able to change the language use patterns between herself and her parents, but this does not mean she does not form her own theories about these patterns. This discourse of blame embodies the ways in which the Mexicano-Nuevomexicano families make sense of the zone of encuentro that is their household. Consider Schecter and Bayley's words:

> In situations of language and dialect contact, or what Pratt (1987) has described as the "contact zone," a fair amount of "online" decision making takes place that is not circumscribed by schematic behavior related to who speaks what language to whom. To be sure, this decision making is ideologically motivated, but ideology, we must insist, is not impervious to individuals' immediate best interests.[46]

The Mexicano-Nuevomexicano families exist in a society in which Spanish continues to be the minority language and in which ideology and "best interests" matter. Diana's Nuevomexicano/a/x family represents the Nuevomexicano/a/x historical legacy of the imposition of English and the gradual dispossession from Spanish. Rose's father learned firsthand the necessity of English proficiency to succeed as an immigrant in the US. Throughout his interview he references suffering discrimination from Anglos and Chicanos alike. These larger sociohistorical issues play themselves out within the households through language use patterns that lead to maintenance and/or shift. Rose's parents, as well as many Latino/a/x and first-generation immigrant parents more generally, are faced with the perceived dilemma of either actively maintaining a minority language or social advancement. The influence of the ideology of normative monolingualism eclipses good intentions to maintain a minority language. Furthermore, I suggest that the Mexicano-Nuevomexicano families make sense of these larger sociopolitical issues through the discourses of blame and responsibility. Returning to Milagros

---

46. Schecter and Bayley, *Language as Cultural Practice,* 177.

Navarro's comments about her younger sister's Spanish proficiency, we see another dimension to the blame. She explains, "I think my parents have kind of emphasized it on her a little bit more, but, um, I guess they are also leaving it to us. It just feels kind of unfair because, uh, I'm just her sister. I'm not supposed to raise her, I'm supposed to just help her in whatever she needs help with, and so it's my parents' job to teach her Spanish." Reminiscent of the Jurado family exchange at the beginning of this chapter, Milagros assigns the responsibility for intergenerational transmission of the language to her parents, rather than to siblings.

REFRAMING MAINTENANCE AND SHIFT AROUND THE MEXICANO/A/X-NUEVOMEXICANO/A/X SUBJECTS

In eight out of the ten families, English has consistently dominated the communications of the Mexicano/a/x-Nuevomexicano/a/x adult children. Even when the Mexicano/a (or Nuevomexicano/a) parents speak in Spanish, twelve out of the fifteen Mexicano/a/x-Nuevomexicanos/as/xs speak mostly English with their parents. These results differ from both Ortíz's study, in which Spanish was used almost exclusively with parents in the household, and Potowski's findings, in which Spanish was used 75 percent of the time with parents.[47] The most notable exceptions to this trend are the Navarro, Loredo, and Santos households (all with Mexicana mothers).[48] Yet, even when the Mexicano/a/x-Nuevomexicanos/as/xs speak pejoratively of their Spanish skills or claim to only spend a fraction of their week in Spanish, they all report being able to conduct themselves completely in Spanish with members of their Mexicano/a/x extended family. This generally includes grandparents, aunts, and uncles.

Alexa and Alejandro report spending every Sunday with their grandmother, aunts, and uncles on their Mexicano father's side of the family. During these Sunday dinners, they speak all Spanish with this extended family. Rolando tells of this same type of Sunday tradition with his Mexicano father's side of the family. Adrian and Olivia both report spending regular weekly time with their aunts, uncles, and Mexicano/a grandparents. The remaining Mexicano/a/x-Nuevomexicanos/as/xs report that their Mexicano/a/x family members still live in Mexico. However, when speaking on the phone, or when visits occur, Spanish is the exclusive language between these

---

47. Ortíz, "Sociolinguistic Study"; and Potowski, "Spanish Language Shift in Chicago."
48. This fact might suggest that the dominant language in the home follows the dominant language of the mother just as Potowski, "I Was Raised Talking," finds a correlation between Spanish lexical choices and phonological production with the background of the mother.

grandparents, aunts, uncles, and the Mexicano/a/x-Nuevomexicanos/as/xs. Notably, the Mexicano/a/x-Nuevomexicanos/as/xs do not report speaking Spanish with their Mexicano/a/x cousins unless the cousins live in Mexico. The Mexicano/a/x-Nuevomexicano/a/x narratives reveal that their Spanish use tends to be widely person-specific and based on communicative need. Generally, their older Mexicano/a/x relatives living in New Mexico and all Mexicano/a/x relatives living in Mexico are Spanish dominant. This presents a communicative need to speak in Spanish. Despite the fact that Mexicano/a/x-Nuevomexicano/a/x Spanish use appears to be mostly limited to certain individuals, rather than to larger domains,[49] and that the majority of the Mexicano/a/x-Nuevomexicano/a/x subjects speak less Spanish than their parents, it is crucial to note that all report some weekly use of spoken Spanish. Additionally, 25 percent of the Mexicano/a/x-Nuevomexicanos/as/xs speak the same amount of Spanish or more as one or both of their parents. This is important given the rapid shift patterns reported over thirty years ago in Martíneztown by Hudson and Bills and even in Arroyo Seco by Ortíz.[50]

Indeed, Bills and Vigil are quite aware of the dwindling number of participants under the age of forty who could participate in their project. They explain, "One of the biggest obstacles to achieving the desired balance of consultants across ages was lining up persons under the age of forty who had sufficient skills (and confidence) in Spanish to participate."[51] Bills and Vigil highlight the decreasing numbers of younger Nuevomexicanos/as/xs who were able to converse in Spanish in the 1990s. In addition to lamenting the loss of Traditional Spanish in New Mexico in their work, Bills and Vigil also predict the overall loss of Spanish. They declare, "Continued reduction of proficiency in the ethnic language is sure to culminate in the death of the Traditional Spanish dialect and in the death of the Spanish language in general for many persons of Hispanic heritage in the NMCOSS region."[52] More than twenty years later, it might be expected that these predictions would already be a reality, in particular for Nuevomexicanos/as/xs in the age group of the Mexicano/a/x-Nuevomexicanos/as/xs (ages 15–35). However, the Mexicano/a/x-Nuevomexicano/a/x subjects represent a departure from this trend.

Also, the Nuevomexicano/a partners, and the Mexicano/a/x-Nuevomexicanos/as/xs themselves, are well aware of their children's higher Spanish proficiency when compared to that of their Nuevomexicano/a/x peers. Verónica speaks of differences between herself and her Nuevomexicana friends. She

---

49. This is generally a sign of language shift.
50. Hudson and Bills, "Intergenerational Language Shift"; and Ortiz, "Sociolinguistic Study."
51. Bills and Vigil, *Spanish Language of New Mexico*, 243.
52. Bills and Vigil, *Spanish Language of New Mexico*, 260.

explains, "I remember very vividly having friends who had grandparents who only spoke Spanish, and they—how they understood each other I still don't know, um, because the—the grandchild spoke English, and the grandparents spoke Spanish. They could understand each other, but they couldn't respond in the appropriate language." On the other hand, Verónica and her sister always understood when their parents and their friends' families spoke in Spanish. This would cause a wrinkle in other Nuevomexicano/a/x parents' practice of speaking in Spanish so that the children would not understand. Juanita explains,

> We could never do that with our girls because we spoke both Spanish and English in the house. Also, Verónica and Brianna always knew what was going on. . . . The kids were like, "Can we go to this party?" and the parents would be like, "¿La dejamos ir? ¿No la dejamos ir? ¿Con quién van?" [Should we let her go? Do we not let her go? Who are they going with?] So Verónica and Brianna would be standing there, and the kids were like, "I don't know what my parents are going to say!"

Juanita explains that her daughters would translate, "Well, they are saying that they don't know who we really are because we just came," and that their friends would respond with surprise, "'Oh my God. You know what they are saying?' So we could never get away with that with the girls." Francisco Loredo comments on his daughter Angélica's bilingual abilities when compared to those of her Nuevomexicano boyfriend. He states, "It's una bendición que ya sabe los dos idiomas. Most kids nowadays no saben. Como éste que anda con Angélica . . . este Anthony, you know? Oh, this guy don't know nothing. . . . He knows a couple of words. He is learning more that he is hanging here at the house. But . . . it's gonna take him a lifetime." In the previous chapter, I highlighted Francisco's belief that marrying a Mexicana had contributed to his Spanish language maintenance. In the case of Angélica, we see a potential for another recontact process between Mexicana-Nuevomexicana Angélica and her Nuevomexicano boyfriend. Similarly, Rose's Nuevomexicano husband, Mike, has benefitted from the Spanish use among his in-laws. Mike reveals, "My Spanish has gotten better from talking to her dad, you know . . . what's helped me a lot, too, is, like, when we go visit her—her grandma, in Juárez. We go and—and I met her uncles and aunts and all that. It's helped me because I have better conversations with them 'cause I've learned stuff over the years." Mike's experience with increased Spanish language use and linguistic confidence demonstrates the ripple effects of his Mexicana-Nuevomexicana wife's language shaping and acts of agency, maintenance, and recovery.

The Mexicano/a/x-Nuevomexicano/a/x subjects' weekly Spanish language use may not be surprising when compared to language shift studies among Latino/a/x populations with mostly G1, G2, and G3 populations. However, when compared to the Nuevomexicano/a/x peers of the Mexicano/a/x-Nuevomexicanos/as/xs and earlier studies of Nuevomexicano/a/x family language maintenance patterns, the Mexicano/a/x-Nuevomexicanos/as/xs represent a different profile of language maintenance and ability. In a sense, the Nuevomexicano/a/x peers of the Mexicano/a/x-Nuevomexicanos/as/xs represent the trajectory of shift that the Nuevomexicano/a partners may have continued along if they had not married their Mexicano/a partner and reaped the benefits of recontact. Like their Nuevomexicano/a parents, the Mexicano/a/x-Nuevomexicanos/as/xs represent what Villa and Rivera-Mills term "an intergenerational persistence of Spanish"[53] even amidst patterns of English dominance.

CONCLUSIONS, SYMBOLIC ASSOCIATIONS, AND LANGUAGE MAINTENANCE

Schecter and Bayley explain that "language socialization ... is able to elucidate changes in the symbolic associations of the use of different language varieties. It is also able to document changes in family and community ideologies concerning the importance of different languages."[54] It has been my objective in this chapter to reveal the complex language use patterns within the Mexicano-Nuevomexicano families and to challenge unidirectional conceptualizations of language shift by presenting the Mexicano/a/x-Nuevomexicanos/as/xs' perceptions and theories about their familial linguistic behavior. How the Mexicano/a/x-Nuevomexicanos/as/xs symbolically associate the languages, and the dynamicity in these associations, adds an additional layer to this portrait. The Mexicano/a/x-Nuevomexicano/a/x narratives from the Santos family provide an example of how symbolic associations with Spanish and English change over time. Edna now associates socializing, professional advancement, and the ability to aid in familial communications with her use of Spanish. Her parents also view their use of English as a positive route to communication with their grandchildren. These flows constantly in motion between Spanish and English are key to understanding the language use patterns of the Mexicano-Nuevomexicano family units and the linguistic sophistication

---

53. Villa and Rivera-Mills, "Integrated Multi-Generational Model."
54. Schecter and Bayley, *Language as Cultural Practice*, 15.

and competency[55] that is activated to navigate these flows. Pennycook invokes "transcultural flows"[56] as a continuous reorganization of the local that occurs at the intersection of language and cultural identities. The flows of language use in the Mexicano-Nuevomexicano families signal a continuous movement and reorganization of their local family language use patterns according to shifting symbolic associations.

The patterns of communication between the Mexicano/a/x-Nuevomexicanos/as/xs and their Nuevomexicano/a/x extended family members underscore their linguistic sophistication. Except for Adrian, who reports speaking Spanish frequently with his maternal Nuevomexicano grandfather, and Carolina, who spoke exclusively in Spanish to her Nuevomexicano grandparents, 86 percent of the Mexicano/a/x-Nuevomexicanos/as/xs report speaking English with their Nuevomexicano/a/x grandparents, aunts, uncles, and cousins. As Fishman[57] indicates, this does not necessarily mean that Spanish is not present within the soundscape of the interactions between the Mexicano/a/x-Nuevomexicanos/as/xs and their extended Nuevomexicano family. For example, Angélica explains that her Nuevomexicano grandparents speak Spanish with her, but she responds in English. She states that "it's awkward to respond in Spanish." Alexa reports speaking in Spanish "sometimes" to her maternal Nuevomexicana grandmother. She explains, "That's the thing all the viejitos have." She characterizes her maternal grandmother as one of those viejitas who "has" Spanish. Angélica's reference to awkwardness in using Spanish with her Nuevomexicano grandparents and Alexa's categorization of Spanish as "belonging" to the Nuevomexicano viejitos reveal coexisting symbolic associations with language use.

First, in terms of day-to-day communication, English is symbolically associated with Nuevomexicano extended family; that is, Nuevomexicanos/as/xs view English as the most natural language to use with Nuevomexicano/a/x extended family members. Indeed, the Mexicano/a/x-Nuevomexicanos/as/xs do not perceive any communicative need to use Spanish with their extended Nuevomexicano family because they are all bilingual. Yet, the fact that they still "have" Spanish acknowledges an additional association of Spanish with Nuevomexicanos/as/xs. Schecter and Bayley underscore this linguistic ability. They explain, "A speaker's choice of one or another variety represented not only a linguistic decision, but, perhaps, more importantly, a choice of

---

55. Zentella, *Growing Up Bilingual*, and Zentella, "Latin@ Languages and Identities," highlight this competency.

56. Pennycook, *Global Englishes and Transcultural Flows*.

57. Fishman, "Who Speaks What Language?"

identity."[58] The Mexicano/a/x-Nuevomexicanos/as/xs possess a sophisticated competency in distinguishing when it is appropriate to utilize Spanish and when it is not. Simply because they and their Nuevomexicano extended family may both have proficiency in Spanish does not necessarily dictate its use. Angélica's labeling of speaking Spanish to Nuevomexicano/a/x extended family members as "awkward" contributes to an understanding of this act as artificial. Simply because one has bilingual ability and is Latino/a/x does not necessarily dictate the use of Spanish. This assumes a "lamination of culture and language"[59] and ignores that English and Spanish are both Nuevomexicano/a/x and Mexicano/a/x-Nuevomexicano/a/x languages. The Mexicano-Nuevomexicano families can and do utilize both. Additionally, their narratives speak of their agency to restimulate their Spanish use. The Mexicano-Nuevomexicano families may be in the midst of larger language shift trends; however, it is imperative that these language shift trends not eclipse the nuanced and complex acts of language shaping that occur within the family unit.

---

58. Schecter and Bayley, *Language as Cultural Practice*, 14.
59. Urciuoli, "Whose Spanish?"

CHAPTER 3

The Weight of Words

Spanish Language Ideologies, Lexical Choices, and Authenticity in Mexicano/a/x-Nuevomexicano/a/x Families

> My mother spoke the Spanish from New Mexico. . . . On the other hand, my father had a much more cosmopolitan and literate vocabulary. His Spanish was beautiful and I loved its refined sound from the very beginning.
>
> —Mari Luci Jaramillo, *Madam Ambassador*

"You did it again!" interjects one of Nicolás Navarro's daughters. She continues, "Es casi!"[1] The living room was full of activity as Nicolás and I conversed together on a warm Thursday night. Music and laughing provided pleasant interruptions to our interview. Because the living room was situated in the center of the house, his four daughters would occasionally pass through the room and provide commentary on our conversation. This was one such moment. Nicolás remarks to me, "¿Ves? Ella anda corrigiéndome otra vez." [You see? There she goes correcting me again.] Laughter then followed the exchange. In the seconds preceding his daughter's interjection, Nicolás was describing the nature of Mexican immigration to New Mexico. He explained, "Porque en ese tiempo cuaji los hombres se vinían a trabajar y no traían a su familia" [Because at that time the men almost always came to work and didn't bring their family]. His daughter was particularly bothered by his use of the variant "cuaji" for the more standard pronunciation of "casi." She explains to him, "Sorry. . . . When you say 'cuaji' . . . it's like 'Kawaii.' It's a place in Hawaii or something . . . it's something in Hawaii, Dad, just to let you know." Then a second daughter adds, "New Mexico changes the Spanish language a lot I've noticed." This interaction afforded me the unexpected opportunity in my

---

1. Here, the discussion centers around the variant "cuaji" for "casi" for the English word "almost."

fieldwork not only to be told by my participants about their linguistic attitudes but also to actually witness a manifestation of these attitudes through the activation of specific language ideologies within the family unit.

I highlight this conversation to draw attention to the weight of words and the ideologies that accompany them. Far from neutral, words matter in the Mexicano-Nuevomexicano families. In this chapter I focus on the ways in which the Mexicano-Nuevomexicano families talk about words, and I identify the dominant language ideologies circulating within the families. The articulation of a lexical difference is central to the ways in which the Mexicano/a and Nuevomexicano/a partners frame each other's Spanish within their narratives. These narratives reveal that lexical choices have consequences. The conversation in the Navarro living room reveals several significant elements within the family dynamic regarding linguistic practices and attitudes. First, Nicolás uses a stigmatized variant of the word "casi." Second, his daughters are aware of this usage and seem to reject it. Third, with Nicolás's observation, "Ella anda corrigéndome otra vez," we learn that the practice of correction seems to be a commonplace occurrence in the Navarro home. Lastly, the second daughter's comment illuminates the perception that New Mexico, in a general sense, engages in linguistic practices that, in her opinion, change the Spanish language (as if there was one Spanish language). These brief moments in the Navarro living room demonstrate that the New Mexican "changes" to Spanish are not necessarily well received.

In what follows, I examine the intricate links between beliefs about language and beliefs about authenticity, correctness, difference, and power. In the first part of the chapter, I highlight a process of linguistic validation among the Mexicano/a and Nuevomexicano/a partners that then gives way to what I term "slippages" or moments of dissonance that emerge in the family members' descriptions of each other's language. It is in these moments of slippage when the subtle, and sometimes not so subtle, practices of correction and linguistic hierarchies are revealed and reproduced. I suggest the notion of an intergenerational transmission of these "insidious linguistic hierarchies"[2] through acts of correction. I then explore the practice of correction more deeply and the standard language ideology[3] it constructs to reveal uneven relationships between language and power.

My analysis draws primarily from the participants' direct responses to questions that ask them to characterize their Spanish, their family members' Spanish, and any differences or similarities that they note between family

---

2. Zentella, "Dime con quién hablas," 36.
3. Lippi-Green, *English with an Accent*.

members' Spanish varieties (i.e., Mexican vs. New Mexican Spanish). I also incorporate portions of the narratives in which the participants bring up these types of descriptions without elicitation. This chapter focuses predominantly on the responses of the fifteen Mexicano/a/x-Nuevomexicanos/as/xs, but also includes the narratives of the Mexicano/a and Nuevomexicano/a parents in order to contextualize the family dynamics and to better comprehend how ideologies simultaneously overlap, intersect, and diverge within the same family. Overall, I approach these ideological sites as an additional zone of encuentro in which different faces of Latinidad again manifest themselves in the dynamic meeting place of the Mexicano-Nuevomexicano family.

TRACING LANGUAGE IDEOLOGIES

Before advancing with my analysis of language ideologies in the Mexicano-Nuevomexicano context, I would like to discuss several key definitions regarding "ideology" that guide the theoretical framework of this chapter. Joseph Errington describes language ideologies as simply ideas about language structure and use.[4] Silverstein explains language ideology as "a set of beliefs about language articulated by users as a rationalization or justification of perceived language structure and use."[5] Silverstein's use of the term "perceived" is particularly important because this chapter seeks to explore not only the families' perceptions but also how these perceptions coexist with and contradict each other. Kathryn Woolard defines language ideologies as "representations, whether explicit or implicit, that construe the intersection of language and human beings in a social world."[6] I approach the family narratives as representations of this intersection. Also, Paul Kroskrity addresses the importance of validating a speaker's perceptions and beliefs about their language. He explains,

> The dominant and disciplinary institutionalized approaches to language . . . denied the relevance—to linguistics, certainly—of a speaker's own linguistic analysis and valorized the referential functions of language to the exclusion of others. . . . Today, although students of language ideology recognize the limitations of members' explicitly verbalized models (Silverstein 1981, 1985), they do not view these knowledge systems as competing with expert or scientific models. . . . Rather, these local models are valued as constructs that emerge as part of the sociocultural experience of cultural actors.[7]

---

4. Errington, "Ideology."
5. Silverstein, "Language Structure and Linguistic Ideology," 193.
6. Woolard, "Language Ideology," 3.
7. Kroskrity, "Regimenting Languages," 7.

How the Mexicano/a/x-Nuevomexicano/a/x participants may or may not change their linguistic and discourse forms in response to these ideological constructs is not necessarily the focus of this chapter. I have not tracked the Navarro father's usage of "cuaji" versus "casi" to document if the Navarro father actually changes his use of "cuaji" in response to his daughters' correction tactics. However, Nicolás's perceptions of his usage, and his reactions to the correction, are the relevant points to my analysis. They index his own local knowledge system. Like Kroskrity, Rosina Lippi-Green recognizes the importance of social context and speaker perceptions. She states, "However objective linguistic definitions of a given language may be, no matter how detailed the description of phonology, intonation, lexicon, syntax, semantics, and rhetorical features, nonlinguists will define the language on the basis of their personal relationship to the sociocultural context in which the language functions."[8] In the spirit of Kroskrity and Lippi-Green, my analysis of Mexicano-Nuevomexicano family language ideologies does not seek to challenge the veracity of my participants' perceptions, but rather to explore what these belief systems allow Mexicanos/as/xs, Nuevomexicanos/as/xs, and Mexicano/a/x-Nuevomexicano/a/x subjects to do as cultural actors in their own daily lives.

An additional significant framework for the discussion of language ideologies arises from Glenn Martínez's 2006 analysis of Mexican Americans and language. Martínez invokes Kroskrity in highlighting four facets of language ideologies relevant to Mexican American communities. Particular to my study are the lenses of multiplicity, awareness, and interest.[9] Regarding multiplicity, Martínez explains, "The multiplicity of language ideologies within the Mexican American community suggests that there is no one Mexican American language ideology, but rather that a confluence of ideologies emerges from within and from without, penetrating inwards and extending outwards."[10] Martínez's words recall Gloria Anzaldúa's declaration: "There is no one Chicano language just as there is no one Chicano experience."[11] These multiple language experiences and ideologies mutually and dynamically inform each other within and between the Mexicano-Nuevomexicano families.

Although I intend to draw correlations between individual and familial belief systems, I approach my discussion cognizant of this multiplicity, as well as of the contradictions among multiple ideologies. Martínez also underscores that speakers may not be aware of these contradictions due to "varying degrees of awareness of local language ideologies."[12]

---

8. Lippi-Green "That's Not My Language," 232.
9. Martínez, *Mexican Americans and Language*, 9–17.
10. Martínez, *Mexican Americans and Language*, 15.
11. Anzaldúa, *Borderlands/La Frontera*, 80.
12. Martínez, *Mexican Americans and Language*, 13.

Kroskrity reminds us of the utility of such contradictions. He explains that "clashes or disjunctures in which divergent ideological perspectives on language and discourse are juxtaposed" result in "conflict, confusion, and contradiction."[13] Furthermore, he explains that this "contestation and disjuncture thus disclose critical differences in ideological perspectives that can more fully reveal their distinctive properties as well as their scope and force."[14] This notion of contradiction relates to the feature of "interest" in language ideologies. Often, contradictory ideologies are based in opposing interests. Martínez explains that "a language ideology represents a perception of language and discourse that is constructed in the interest of a specific social or cultural group."[15] Yet, often these interests are opposed. He continues, "Language ideologies are oppositional in the sense that one always challenges and attempts to subvert the other."[16] On a related note, Terry Eagleton explains ideology as "something that is used and possessed by the powerless in order to challenge the perpetuation of asymmetric power relations."[17] The relationship between language and power is clear in both Martínez's and Eagleton's explanations. Irvine and Gal[18] identify the three processes of iconicity, fractal recursivity, and erasure as part of a framework that allows for the conceptualization of social difference and distinction as it is related to language and power. Shifting asymmetrical power relations reveal themselves in the present chapter through the activation of these processes and ideological frameworks within the families.

One last element that is important when mapping out relevant definitions of "ideology" as it pertains to language are the notions of language panic and language pride. Again, related to the idea of "interest," Martínez reminds us that "language ideologies are, then, fundamentally about social and political control of linguistically distinct groups."[19] Two cultural processes that highlight this control are embodied in language pride and language panic. Martínez explains language pride: "I understand language pride as the belief that the language of one's home and community is a viable public language and a real option to be used and infused in expressing one's voice."[20] In my analysis, I uncover how the familial language ideologies connect to notions of language

---

13. Kroskrity, "Regimenting Languages," 13.
14. Kroskrity, "Regimenting Languages," 13.
15. Martínez, *Mexican Americans and Language*, 9.
16. Martínez, *Mexican Americans and Language*, 11.
17. Eagleton, *Ideology*, 6–7.
18. Irvine and Gal, "Language Ideology and Linguistic Differentiation."
19. Martínez, *Mexican Americans and Language*, 9.
20. Martínez, *Mexican Americans and Language*, 13.

pride in Mexican Spanish and New Mexican Spanish. Jane Hill[21] coins the term "language panic," and Martínez interrogates this notion as "a period of intense debate and heightened emotions over relatively obscure and technical issues."[22] Martínez expands Hill's definition in order to highlight language panics in everyday routine affairs.[23] Martínez emphasizes the application of language panics to such continuous occurrences as the use of mock Spanish[24] and other manifestations in which "whiteness" and English are elevated by the dominant society. Because my study is about inter-Latino/a/x relationships, rather than Anglo versus Latino/a/x interactions, the examples of mock Spanish and other manifestations of the elevation of "whiteness" by dominant Anglo society are not as relevant. However, that is not to say that "language panics" do not occur within Latino/a/x communities. Behaviors of "dialect dissing" and "Spanglish bashing" do, indeed, occur within Latino/a/x groups.[25] These are important forms of chiquitafication[26] that fall under the umbrella of language panics and are particularly useful behaviors for observing the manifestation of power within language ideologies. Martínez reminds us, "It would be a grave error to suppose that language pride is always and only expressed and reproduced within the Mexican American community and that language panic is always and only expressed within the dominant culture."[27] These behaviors occur routinely between Latino/a/x groups and, in my study, between Latino/a/x family members.

In summary, as I move forward with my analysis of language ideologies, I seek to validate local systems of perception and Latinos/as/xs' own theorizations about language grounded in their daily life experiences. I am aware of the power differentials embedded in these ideologies and their multiplicity. These concepts naturally fit in with the framework of Latinidad. Through the manifestation of Latino/a/x language ideologies, we see moments of convergence and divergence, competing authenticities,[28] and inter-Latino/a/x knowledge produced through the activation of these belief systems. Indeed, Martínez emphasizes that "the degree to which our speech patterns conform to or differ from one another has to do with our lived experiences in social encounters. Language ideologies are thus embodied in these lived experiences."[29]

21. Hill, "Racializing Functions of Language Panics."
22. Martínez, *Mexican Americans and Language*, 11.
23. Martínez, *Mexican Americans and Language*, 12.
24. Hill, "Mock Spanish."
25. Zentella, "Latin@ Languages and Identities."
26. Zentella, "'Chiquitafication' of U.S. Latinos."
27. Martínez, *Mexican Americans and Language*, 14.
28. Aparicio, "Reading the 'Latino.'"
29. Martínez, *Mexican Americans and Language*, 9.

Martínez's approach to language ideologies implicitly evokes the theoretical framework of Latinidad by recalling Rúa's 2001 study of mixed-Latino/a/x identities in Chicago and the ways in which "ordinary people, in this case individuals who are of both Puerto Rican and Mexican ancestry, theorize *latinidad* from their lived experiences."[30] Here I will highlight how Mexicanos/as/xs, Nuevomexicanos/as/xs, and Mexicano/a/x-Nuevomexicano/a/x subjects theorize linguistic Latinidad from lived experiences embedded within ideological constructs.

SLIPPERY CONSTRUCTS: MOMENTS OF IDEOLOGICAL CONTRADICTIONS

One process that allows for the viewing of the contradictory nature of language ideologies within the families is a fascinating interplay between validation and correction. For instance, Manuel Guzmán, a G1 Mexican, married to Andrea from Taos, explains about the differences between his Spanish and that of his in-laws. He states,

> Sí hay mucha diferencia porque su familia de ella usa muchas palabras que no las entiendo. Dicen palabras muy diferentes que nosotros. Porque su mamá de ella habla muy bien el español, pero también hay palabras que significan diferentes cosas, que yo nunca las había oído. Entonces, para mí, sí hay diferencia. . . . Ellos tienen su forma y nosotros tenemos nuestra forma de hablar. Pero ninguno es mejor que otro.
>
> [There is a difference because her family uses many words that I don't understand. They say words that are very different from ours. Because her mom speaks very good Spanish, but there are also words that have different meanings that I had never heard of. So, for me, there is a difference. . . . They have their way of speaking and we have ours. But neither is better than the other.]

Manuel's words emphasize lexical distinction while not imposing any notions of linguistic deficiency. His affirmation of his mother-in-law's "very good" Spanish confirms that difference does not imply superiority. Manuel's wife, Andrea, expresses a similar recognition and appreciation for the differences in their lexicon:

---

30. Rúa, "Colao Subjectivities," 118.

Our vocabulary is totally different. Like we say 'calzones' for pants, and he says 'calzones' for underwear. And I would be like, "No! Calzones are pants," and he'd be like, "No! They're underwear." I would always tell him, "You know what? Your Spanish is different than mine. I'm not saying that my Spanish is better, and I'm not saying that your Spanish is better. . . . Our Spanishes are just different, and we need to adapt."

Within both Andrea's and Manuel's characterizations of each other's lexical choices we see a clear move to give equal footing to both New Mexican Spanish and Mexican Spanish. This move reveals an ideology of linguistic equality as well as a sense of pride in their respective varieties and respect for their partner's variety. Additionally, Manuel and Andrea's relationship has created the setting for certain inter-Latino/a/x linguistic knowledge to be produced, theorized, and negotiated in their daily lives. The couple's interactions have resulted in the "increasing consciousness among U.S. Latinos" to which Sandoval-Sánchez[31] refers.

Yet, moments later in Andrea's interview she laments her husband's tendency to overcorrect her. She explains, "When I say words he'll be like, 'No. That's not a word.' Or if I put the wrong ending on a word, he'll be like, 'Oh babe, you still don't know that?' . . . And then he would keep correcting me. . . . He'd be like, 'No babe, you don't say it like that.' . . . He'd be like, 'That's not even a word.' . . . I'm like, excuse me, that is a word." Andrea's description of Manuel's overcorrection of her lexical choices, particularly in his use of the word "still," undermines the equal footing attributed to both varieties of Spanish and consequently relegates Andrea's Spanish to a position of inferiority. In highlighting this subtle linguistic hierarchy, it is not my intention to question Manuel's sincerity regarding his equal regard for New Mexican Spanish. However, Andrea's account of Manuel's linguistic policing draws attention to an inconsistency that is potentially indicative of a larger belief system that Mexican Spanish is always ultimately more correct than New Mexican Spanish.

A similar dynamic occurs in the Loredo family from Las Vegas. The G1 Mexicana, Pía, explains how she's always emphasized to her daughter that she has three languages: New Mexican Spanish, Mexican Spanish, and English. She also explains how she stresses that her daughter must respect her father's side of the family's Spanish. When describing an incident at her daughter's paternal grandparents' house, Pía states, "Ella los quería corregir, por los términos. . . . They would tell her, 'Hija, pásame el teléfono' . . . y ella les decía '"Teléfono," abuelito, tiene acento.' Le digo pues, 'Angélica, así es el idioma de

---

31. Sandoval-Sánchez, *José, Can You See?*

aquí . . . "zanhoria" por "zanahoria," la "silleta" por "silla."' [She wanted to correct them because of their words. . . . They would tell her, "Hija, pass me the telefón" . . . and she would tell them, "'Teléfono,' grandpa, it has an accent." I would tell her then, "Angélica, this is how the language is from here . . . 'zanhoria' for 'zanahoria,' la 'silleta' for 'silla.'"][32] Pía's discovery of the historical linguistic connections between these words that she initially stigmatized[33] now influences the validity she attributes to her in-laws' Spanish. However, it is important to note that the fact that Pía must discourage her daughter's attempts to correct her grandparents already implies that certain linguistic hierarchies may be at work in this household. Pía's next anecdote illuminates this implication. She elaborates, "Yo oía que decían, 'Voy a mopear' y le digo a mi esposo, 'No me enseñes eso porque voy a aprender mal' y hasta Angélica está aprendiendo así porque su maestra también le habla así. Entonces ella también estaba cayendo en esas cositas." [I would hear them say, "I'm going to mop," and I would tell my husband, "Don't teach me that because I am going to learn incorrectly," and even Angélica is learning that because her teacher also speaks like that. So she is also falling into those types of little things.] These "cositas" again reveal the presence of a certain hierarchy, albeit subtle, between the two varieties of Spanish. Pía's discourse validates New Mexican Spanish only to subordinate it with the correction of her daughter's Spanish. Here we see the coexistence of ideologies of equality and "correctness" that are only revealed through these slippages or moments of dissonance. Milroy and Milroy provide some insight into these moments. They explain that "it seems to be virtually impossible to rely on speakers' reports of their own usage or of their attitudes to usage. . . . People's overt claims about language are inaccurate and often contradict their own actual usage."[34] In the case of Pía, we see this contradiction. She articulates an attitude of linguistic equality and in the same conversation undermines this equality. Pía's account corroborates Milroy and Milroy's assertion that "it is extremely difficult for anyone to calculate the extent to which his general attitudes to language have been coloured by prevailing prescriptions."[35] Although Pía may defend and, even, use New Mexican Spanish, these moments of dissonance reveal the power of previously "learnt attitudes."[36]

---

32. "Zanahoria" and "zanhoria" are words for "carrot." "Silla" and "silleta" are words for "chair."
33. See chapter 1.
34. Milroy and Milroy, *Authority in Language*, 15.
35. Milroy and Milroy, *Authority in Language*, 87.
36. Milroy and Milroy, *Authority in Language*, 87.

In describing her husband's family's Spanish, Gabriela also highlights a tension between linguistic validation and subtle subordination. She emphasizes that New Mexican Spanish "es diferente al que yo hablo . . . pero habían muchas palabras que eran casi igual que las que yo hablaba . . . una diferencia de palabras, pero . . . era la misma cosa. Pero ella la llamaba de un modo, y yo la conocía de otro modo diferente." [is different from what I speak . . . but there were also a lot of words that were almost identical to what I would say . . . a difference in words, but . . . it was the same thing. But she would say it one way, and I knew it as something different.] In this account, Gabriela speaks of difference, but consistently minimizes the difference. She makes it clear that the differences in words do not necessarily impede comprehension. In this instance she is referring specifically to the communication with her husband's grandmother. Yet, when I asked her a few minutes later to elaborate on any perceived differences between the way she speaks and the way her husband's family speaks, she states, "Yo creo—la manera de pronunciar las cosas que no las decían correctamente—Antes decía, 'Te truje.' Le dije, 'No digan "truje," es "traje." "Te traje esto," pero no es "truje."' Les decía, 'No, así no es.'" [I think—the way of pronouncing things that they did not say things correctly—Before he would say, "Te truje." I told him, "Don't say 'truje,' it's 'traje.' 'Te traje esto,' but it's not 'truje.'" I told them, "That's not the way."] Gabriela's downplaying of difference gives way to a critique of this difference as "incorrect."

In an almost identical instance, Luis also indicates equality between linguistic varieties when he states, "I speak three languages, English, Mexican, and New Mexican, so after a while you get used to it, so you don't even pay attention no more." Luis normalizes the variation. He then explains, "You get to the point after so many years that you don't notice it; you know what they mean, like "Te truje"—that's another word, "Te truje" instead of "Te traje," which in Spanish is "Te traje" in Mexico. "Truje," it's just a slang . . . because you know the New Mexican language is different than the real Mexican." In his efforts to naturalize the differences, he actually draws attention to the non-neutral state of these differences. By using the terms "slang" and "real Mexican," Luis reveals a belief that Mexican Spanish is ultimately more authentic. Although "real" and "correct" are not necessarily synonymous, Luis still reveals the construction of a hierarchy in which Mexican Spanish is modified by the term "real" and New Mexican Spanish is equated with "slang."

In highlighting these moments of dissonance, I do not wish to imply that the sentiment of equality is not there. However, it does point to the feature of awareness in language ideologies, in that the speakers may not be aware of these contradictions. Yet, the slippage is important because it speaks to a system of beliefs that reveals a hierarchy between Mexican Spanish and New Mexican Spanish through the process of correction. The ideologies of linguistic equality give way to notions of "real" and "correct" language. These tensions are notable because they speak to active embodiments of the convergences and divergences associated with Latinidad. Manuel's assurances that his mother-in-law does speak "very good" Spanish and Pía's urging to her daughter to respect her grandparents' Spanish actually denote moments of linguistic solidarity between Mexicanos/as/xs and Nuevomexicanos/as/xs. Yet, these moments of solidarity are not without the manifestation of the competing authenticities also active in moments of Latinidad that become visible through references to the practice of correction. This practice highlights an ideology of linguistic correctness and notions of "real" Spanish.[37] This interplay between validation and correction, revealed through the slippages, also underscores a simultaneous manifestation of language pride and panic. The ideology of equality references a sense of pride, while dialect dissing occurs through the practice of correction.

INTERGENERATIONAL TRANSMISSION OF LINGUISTIC HIERARCHIES

In the case of Angélica, I alluded to the possibility that some of the parents' ideologies are also present in the Mexicano/a/x-Nuevomexicano/a/x's perceptions about language. I propose that the moments of dissonance played out by the Mexicano/a and Nuevomexicano/a parents contribute to the transmission of linguistic hierarchies to their Mexicano/a/x-Nuevomexicano/a/x children. Although the couples may demonstrate varying degrees of dialectical acceptance and openness towards negotiation of meaning with regards to lexical choices, the Mexicano/a parents seem less likely to be accepting of features that denote an "un-Mexican" Spanish from their children. This degree of intolerance, in many cases, is transmitted to the Mexicano/a/x-Nuevomexicano/a/x subjects in the form of linguistic policing, as reflected in the practice of correction. Even Mari Luci Jaramillo's account of her language use in her childhood during the 1940s suggests these same ideologies. She describes one memory from her childhood:

> I began school using Mexican Spanish, while the other kids were speaking New Mexican Spanish. We didn't quite understand each other. When we did,

---

37. See Train, "'Real Spanish,'" for a critical inquiry regarding the ideologies surrounding "real" Spanish and language standardization in foreign language education.

I thought my words prettier. I remember playing on the school's swings, yelling at another child, *"empújame"* (push me). All the kids started laughing. One little girl said, "you mean *pushe.*" This is an English word with a Spanish ending and Spanish pronunciation. I said, "Yes," and quickly learned *pushe.* After saying it at home once, Father quickly straightened me out as to which word was correct.[38]

Jaramillo's mention of her Mexican words being "prettier" than New Mexican Spanish demonstrates a subtle linguistic hierarchy despite the numerical majority of New Mexican Spanish speakers in her community and school. Her description of her Mexicano father's Spanish from the epigraph at the beginning of this chapter, "his Spanish was beautiful, and I loved its refined sound,"[39] is evidence of Jaramillo's elevation of Mexican Spanish. Her reference to her father's act of correction sheds some light on the factors that contribute to the construction of this hierarchy.

The moments of dissonance within the families reveal ideologies of prescriptivism, and these seem to override the transmission of notions of linguistic equality. An important point of departure when considering language and notions of "correctness" is the study of Standard English by Milroy and Milroy.[40] Providing a significant critique of prescriptivism, Milroy and Milroy explain, "Prescription depends on an ideology (or set of beliefs) concerning language which requires that in language use, as in other matters, things shall be done in the 'right' way."[41] We clearly see the workings of language prescriptivism at play in constructing linguistic hierarchies. In some instances, these hierarchies seem to be quite stable and clearly demarcated as in the case of Angélica. When I asked Pía's daughter, Angélica, about any differences between the Spanish that her mom speaks and the Spanish that her dad speaks, she explains bluntly, "My mom speaks it right." She continues, "I think that it's the right vocabulary because she's originally from Mexico, and just people from here like of course their grandparents and great-great-grandparents brought it over, and they just left a couple of pieces on the road and they just put whatever words they had and made a new word." Angélica clearly differentiates her mother's Spanish as correct, right, and real. For Angélica, New Mexican Spanish is unorderly and random. In a related example, during the lexical elicitation activity, when asked which word she uses for "light bulb," Angélica responds, "I don't know what the right word in Spanish is, but sometimes they call it here 'globo.'" Angélica creates a dichotomy

---

38. Jaramillo, *Madam Ambassador*, 19.
39. Jaramillo, *Madam Ambassador*, 19.
40. Milroy and Milroy, *Authority in Language.*
41. Milroy and Milroy, *Authority in Language*, 1.

between "right" and "here," thus emphasizing that here in New Mexico they don't speak right. Milagros Navarro expresses a similar ideology of realness and correctness regarding Mexican Spanish. She states, "I try and speak more like they do in Mexico. I hope my Spanish is more Mexican." Milagros's hope that she speaks more Mexican reflects a transmission of the superiority of Mexican Spanish over New Mexican Spanish.

Yet, in other cases, the Mexicano/a/x-Nuevomexicano/a/x subjects' ideologies are not so clearly aligned with strict notions of correctness. In the cases of Rose and Carolina, the belief systems reveal not only a shifting nature but also tensions between linguistic pride and panic. Often this occurs within the same utterance. Consider Rose's explanation of the differences between the ways her parents speak:

> Um, like there's a lot of words that are very different. But my mom's more accustomed to saying 'em the right way or—not the right way, but the Mexican way. I don't know what to say—how to say it. You know, because the Mexicans are saying they're right and, you know, New Mexicans always thought that they're right. So, you know, it's just whoever is right.

Rose begins by activating the notion of difference to describe New Mexican Spanish. With her use of "right" immediately following this statement, it seems as if she is equating "different" with not right or incorrect. After expressing the thought about her mom "saying the right words," Rose seems to become aware of the dialect dissing in which she engaged and expresses bewilderment at how to address this idea of saying things "the right way." She is caught within competing ideologies regarding the notion of "right." Her account ends with a potential activation of the linguistic equality ideology with the last line, "So, you know, it's just whoever is right." However, Rose's slippages and backtracking reveal the complexity and multiplicity of ideologies that are also transmitted to the Mexicano/a/x-Nuevomexicano/a/x subjects simultaneously along with the hierarchies.

Carolina's account reveals a similar dynamic. Like Rose, Carolina activates the notion of difference. However, in this case she does not necessarily utilize it as a euphemism for "incorrect." Carolina downplays the difference in favor of an alternative perception of "fusion." Upon reflection of her language perceptions while growing up, she explains, "I don't think that even then that I thought that there was a difference. I mean, I knew there was a difference in the way she spoke, and the way he spoke, and my grandma and grandpa spoke. But after a while, I think it kind of meshed all into one, if you will. It just kind of all fused into one Spanish." Carolina's words minimize difference.

She indexes her awareness of the difference without associating it with an ideology of correctness. In this example we see the tactics of intersubjectivity of adequation and distinction that Bucholtz mentions in her discussion around authenticity/authentication.[42] Bucholtz outlines the tactic of adequation to allow for the emphasis on shared commonality and distinction as a differentiating process that downplays likeness.[43] In essence, Carolina downplays difference in favor of accentuating a shared commonality to the components that make up her familial linguistic soundscape. For Carolina, the awareness of difference does not undermine the reality that the fusion was the norm for her. Like Luis, she naturalizes the fusion or mixing. Carolina then reflects on how, with exposure to schooling, she develops an awareness regarding "proper" Spanish. She explains,

> I mean I always tell people—like I told you, trilingual because of his Spanish, her Spanish, and then English. But my dad's Spanish . . . it's not always the proper way to speak. . . . I think now that I'm getting older, and I teach Spanish at school, it's had me realize that there are some words that we grew up with that are not the right way to say things. When I'm teaching at school, I always tell the kids, "Yes, we do say 'chopos,' but that's not the proper term. That is in New Mexico for 'slipper' but not the proper term."

Carolina begins with the activation of linguistic equality yet undermines it with an apparent subscription to the ideology of correctness. This moment of dissonance illuminates linguistic validation with subtle subordination. Additionally, Carolina's words clearly reflect what Lippi-Green terms "standard language ideology" or SLI. Lippi-Green explains, "(SLI) is defined as a bias toward an abstracted, idealized, homogenous spoken language."[44] She explains that it is "a powerful idea that most people subscribe to without thought: the belief that there is a homogenous, perfect language, a language stripped of ethnic, racial, economic, religious diversity."[45] The ideology of correctness inherently assumes that there is a "right" language and a "proper" way of saying things. Carolina identifies her father's Spanish, and the terms that she and her students may have grown up with, as invalid, while holding up the dictionary as a symbol of a proper, standard language ideology.

Standard language ideology as well as the previously mentioned ideology of correctness center around the notion of authenticity. References to ideas

---

42. Bucholtz, "Sociolinguistic Nostalgia," 408.
43. Bucholtz, "Sociolinguistic Nostalgia," 408.
44. Lippi-Green, *English with an Accent*, 64.
45. Lippi-Green, *English with an Accent*, 244.

about "real," "proper," "right," and "correct" language point to ideologies of authenticity. Even the beliefs about language equality and linguistic difference are related to authenticity. Linguistic equality subscribes to the notion that there is no one real or authentic language (or perhaps that all are real or authentic). Linguistic difference often uses the term "different" as a synonym for "incorrect." This belief assumes that there is a correct or authentic word or pronunciation. Mary Bucholtz's framework regarding authenticity provides a useful lens through which to view these language beliefs.

LINGUISTIC POWER PLAYS: DECONSTRUCTING CORRECTION AS AN AUTHENTICATING PRACTICE

Recall that Bucholtz suggests the concept of authentication rather than authenticity. She explains,

> Where authenticity presupposes that identity is primordial, authentication views it as the outcome of constantly negotiated social practices. . . . This perspective does not deny the cultural force of authenticity as an ideology but emphasizes that authenticity is always achieved rather than given in social life, although this achievement is often rendered invisible.[46]

Bucholtz's focus on "constantly negotiated social practices" allows us to focus on the central social practice that evokes authenticity within the families' narratives: the practice of correction. This practice falls under what Bucholtz designates as a "tactic of authentication that produces authenticity as its effect."[47] The tactic of authentication coexists with the tactic of denaturalization.[48] The process of authentication involves asserting one's (or another's) identity as credible. Denaturalization emphasizes the artificial nature or incredible nature of one's (or another's) identity. The Navarro family provides an initial glimpse at this authenticating practice. All the preceding narratives have reported instances of correction. The authenticating practice of correction allows the Mexicanos/as/xs, Nuevomexicanos/as/xs, and Mexicano/a/x-Nuevomexicanos/as/xs to express beliefs about correct (authentic) or incorrect (inauthentic) Spanish. Primarily focusing on the narratives of the Mexicano/a/x-Nuevomexicanos/as/xs, I unpack two case studies in correction

---

46. Bucholtz, "Sociolinguistic Nostalgia," 408.
47. Bucholtz, "Sociolinguistic Nostalgia," 408.
48. Bucholtz, "Sociolinguistic Nostalgia," 409.

to highlight these authenticating practices and the denaturalization that results in linguistic power plays.

The first case study centers around the narratives of the Santos daughters. Both Mexicana-Nuevomexicana daughters in the Santos family describe instances of correcting their Nuevomexicano father's Spanish. Carolina explains,

> In a way, I'm kind of teaching my dad too because I'm always correcting him, not meanly, but trying to teach him that there's another way to say something. You know, he'll say "Crismes," and I'm like, "Dad, that's not how you say it." "What do you mean? I've been saying that forever." "I know Dad, but it's 'Navidad.'" It's just the better term. So it's funny. My mom just giggles in the back because I know she still remembers. When she gets with her people, with the cousins from Albuquerque, that's not very often, but when we got together for a funeral, her Spanish changed within seconds. I have always seen it because that's the way she is.

Carolina's correction privileges the term "Navidad" over the term "Crismes" even though "Crismes" is the only term her father has ever used as well as the dominant variant in northern New Mexico.[49] Carolina mentions that her mother "still remembers" the term "Navidad." It is interesting that Carolina identifies this as the "better" term despite the fact that her mother does not describe any moments in which she corrects her Nuevomexicano husband or her children. Carolina and her sister also do not reference any linguistic policing by their Mexicana mother. Yet, Carolina aligns her Spanish more clearly with the non–New Mexican lexical choice. Carolina's reference to her mother's "remembering" highlights this lexical choice as part of her mother's Mexican past. Edna, Carolina's younger sister, engages in similar corrective practices with her father. She explains,

> The way my dad talks he's like—one time, I don't know where we were at, and my dad goes, "¿Dónde está la línea?" And they looked at him, and they were Mexican immigrants, and they looked at him, and I went like this and I go, "Dad, it's not 'línea.'" I said, "For a line you don't say 'línea.'" And he goes, "Yes, you do." And I say, "No, you say 'fila.'" And then he'll say, "No."

Edna's correction of her father places the presence of "Mexican immigrants" at the heart of her concern for her father to speak with the "proper" lexicon. Edna does not want her father to use a marked lexical choice. Edna's narrative

---

49. See Bills and Vigil, *Spanish Language of New Mexico*.

constructs the word "fila" as the unmarked lexical item. Edna's corrections imply that Mexican word choices are the unmarked norm. Beyond instilling notions of Mexican Spanish as the correct, better, and real Spanish, I suggest that Edna and Carolina's corrective practices actually reveal a reworking of a familial relationship between language and power that is then mapped onto a linguistic hierarchy that favors Mexican word choices. In chapter 1, I referenced the interactions between Marta and Juan when they first met. Recall the following exchange:

> MARTA: Y cuando le hablaba a él en mi español, se enojaba.
> LG: ¿Por qué?
> MARTA: Porque no me entendía.
> JUAN: Las palabras eran diferentes, bueno como ahora la comida o la ropa.
> MARTA: Todo me decía, me decía tráeme mis calzones y le traía los calzoncillos. Me decía, "¿Por qué me traes mis calzoncillos? Quiero mis pantalones."
> JUAN: Yeah, porque eran diferentes.
> MARTA: Y luego me decía él, "Si no me vas a hablar bien, no me hables." Porque yo estaba impuesta a todas las cosas en mexicano mío. Y cuando me enojaba con él, porque después de que nos casamos mi comida era diferente a la de él, y hacía yo mi comida y me decía, "Esta comida no es como la que cocina mi mamá." Y le dije yo, "No, pero es la que cocinamos nosotros." Ya me tuve que imponer a cocinar como él.

> [MARTA: And when I spoke to him in my Spanish, he would get mad.
> LG: Why?
> MARTA: Because he didn't understand me.
> JUAN: The words were different, like with food or clothes.
> MARTA: Everything he would say to me, he would tell me to bring me his pants and I would bring him his underwear. And he would ask me, "Why did you bring me my underwear. I want my pants."
> JUAN: Yeah, because the words were different.
> MARTA: And then he would tell me, "If you are not going to speak well, don't speak to me at all. Because I was used to everything being in my Spanish. And when I would get mad at him, because after we were married my food was different from his, and I would make my food and he would say, "This food is not like the food my mom makes." And I would tell him, "No, but it is how we cook." But I had to get used to cooking his food.]

Not only does Marta retell this interaction twice within her interview, but Carolina and Edna also reference it in their individual interviews. This patriarchal linguistic hierarchy seems to have made a significant impact on all three women. I propose that the corrective practices of Carolina and Edna serve to reinstill power and authenticity into their mother's Mexican Spanish and Mexican culture because of the asymmetrical power relationship established by their Nuevomexicano father from the beginning of the Mexicano-Nuevomexicano partnership. When Edna asks her father how he feels when she corrects him, he responds, "No muy bien, pero estoy impuesto al mexicano mío" [Not very good, but I'm used to my Spanish]. Here the authenticating practice reveals key connections between power, language, and gender. The social practice of correction remaps gender power dynamics onto language ideologies. It is significant, and a point for future analysis and research, that the linguistic policing itself seems to be a gendered activity. The clearest examples of this behavior exist between Mexicana-Nuevomexicanas and their Nuevomexicano fathers. The authenticating practice of correction in the Santos family serves to rewrite the power dynamic between their parents and to establish the "standard language" as Mexican Spanish.

The second case I highlight revolves around discourses regarding the use of the variants así/asina. The narratives of the Navarro daughters in particular index the relationship between language, power, and the use of "así" and "asina."[50] The term "así" translates to "like this" or "like that" in English. In another moment of linguistic policing in the Navarro living room, Nicolás is chastised for his word choice. Nicolás explains, "La única que me corrige aquí es mi hija" [The only one who corrects me here is my daughter]. At this very moment his daughter walks in the room. It is her birthday, and the family is preparing a barbeque while I am interviewing Nicolás. The exchange between the two is documented below:

NICOLÁS: Happy birthday, mi jita.
DAUGHTER: Thank you, Dad.
NICOLÁS: ¿Cuál palabra siempre me . . . ?
DAUGHTER: ¡Asina!
NICOLÁS: Asina es como nosotros dicimos aquí. Asina semos nosotros aquí.
DAUGHTER: ¡Asina, no! ¡Así!

---

50. Lipski, *Varieties of Spanish*, 95, categorizes the standard form así vs. the variants asina/ansina/ajina under "urban" vs. "rural." Although my participants associate the "rural" variants exclusively with New Mexico, Lipski emphasizes that they "are not peculiar to Mexico or Mexican-American Spanish, but are found in many rural Spanish dialects throughout the world."

The choice between "así" and "asina" proves to be contentious within the Navarro family. Nicolás's daughter's correction implies that Nicolás's use of "asina" must be frequent. However, during Nicolás's entire eighty-four-minute interview, he only uses the variant "asina" twice. Yet, he uses the variant "así" twelve times.[51] There seems to be a perceived proliferation of the variant "asina" in the family that does not necessarily match real speech. Nicolás's other daughter, Rosalinda, mentions her own confusion with "así" versus "asina." She explains,

> Sometimes I'll say asina y es así. I try to say así, but sometimes I catch myself and my mom will correct me. . . . I think I try to use así, but I still catch myself sometimes saying asina, 'cause like I've heard that a few times and like people say, "Oh, no puedes hacerlo asina," and I'm just like "Huh?" But I always catch myself and I say, "Okay, no, es así," and my mom will correct me too.

Rosalinda's struggle with "así" versus "asina" quite literally functions as an embodiment of the competing authenticities of a linguistic Latinidad converging in her own linguistic repertoire. Additionally, it also invokes the tactics of authentication and denaturalization. Interestingly, the Navarro daughters' correction practices seem to diverge from commonly held ideas around "authenticity." Woolard explains,

> That which is authentic is viewed as the genuine expression of a community or of a person's essential "Self." This ideology of authenticity locates the value of a language in its relationship to a particular community. Within this logic, a speech variety must be perceived as deeply rooted in social and geographic territory in order to have value.[52]

Despite the fact that "ajina"/"asina" are deeply rooted in New Mexico, the Navarro Mexicana-Nuevomexicanas discard this use as inauthentic and incorrect.

Rosalinda acknowledges the difficulty in consciously disciplining herself to use a word (así) that is not like the variant (asina) that she hears in her community. Rosalinda's self-policing and the linguistic policing Nicolás receives from his daughters both reveal an apparent language panic around the así versus asina binary. After all, Nicolás overwhelmingly uses así rather than asina, and Rosalinda is acutely aware of the need to use así and "catches"

---

51. This suggests that "así"/"asina" are in free variation within Nicolás's narrative.
52. Woolard, "Singular and Plural," 22.

herself if she slips up. What, then, accounts for these corrective practices, if the actual use of asina does not seem to be dominant in the Navarro family? What is really at stake if one uses asina versus así? Rosalinda's older sister, Milagros, sheds some light on the beliefs that lie beneath this language panic. When I asked Milagros if any of her family in Mexico ever comments on the way she speaks Spanish, she responded, "There may have been one time, that was a very long time ago, and 'cause over here we say asina [laughs], and then my cousin, '¿Asina? Asina, ¡no!' [laughs] and he made, oh gosh, and he made us look, it was me and my sister actually, and he made us look so stupid. And we were just like, 'Oh no!'" Milagros's memory illuminates the consequences of using a term like asina in Mexico among Mexican family members: embarrassment and shame.

Indeed, Gabriela (Milagros and Rosalinda's mother) tells of warning her husband about being made fun of if he uses terms specific to New Mexico in Mexico. She says, "Y le explicaba yo a Nicolás, le dije: 'Eso no lo digas allá porque se van a reír de ti'" [And I explained to Nicolás, I told him: "Don't say that there because they will laugh at you"]. It seems that the corrective practices of both the Mexicano/a partners and the Mexicano/a/x-Nuevomexicano/a/x subjects are rooted in a larger fear of being corrected by Mexicano/a/x family members in Mexico. The authenticating practice of correction among the Mexicano-Nuevomexicano families reproduces Mexican family members' language ideologies regarding linguistic correctness and provides an example of Irvine and Gal's process of fractal recursivity,[53] in that we see the inscribing of social and linguistic distinctions being reproduced on different levels. Valdés discusses a similar situation with a mother of a student. She explains,

> Deeply influenced by the ideologies we as scholars problematize . . . parents often explain their focus on 'good' Spanish for their children (as a mother recently did to me), saying: "No quiero que me le vayan a hacer burla." For this parent, burla, mockery, is real. So too is her own perspective on its consequences. . . . What she means is that they (relatives, los primos, friends, "real" speakers of "Spanish") will mock her child, and this burla will affect her deeply. . . . She is a fighter and an idealist who teaches social studies informed by an anticolonial orientation. And yet, her views relating to "Spanish" are based on hegemonic, deeply rooted ideologies of language that are a part of her family's pre-migration understanding of the world.[54]

---

53. Irvine and Gal, "Language Ideology."
54. Valdés, "Afterword," 292.

Valdés calls attention to the disconnect between critical approaches to language held by scholars and the real lived experiences in families. Pía's and Angélica's corrective practices function based on a similar fear. Pía expresses concern about her daughter Angélica speaking "incorrectly" in Mexico: "Un error y se la comían en viva" [One error and they'll eat her alive]. Additionally, I asked Pía if she felt her Spanish had changed throughout her years of living in Las Vegas. She explains, "No ha cambiado. No puede cambiar. Es muy difícil porque cuando tú regresas a México, se ríen de ti." [It hasn't changed. It can't change. It's very hard because when you return to Mexico, they laugh at you.] Pía's self-regimenting linguistic practices may, in fact, contribute to her daughter Angélica's acts of correction. In her comments about Spanish spoken in the Las Vegas area, Angélica gives an example of a "made-up" word. She says emphatically, "Like ajina . . . ¡es asina! Not ajina, you know?" Interestingly, Angélica adds another layer to the asina versus así debate. Angélica's zeal to correct leads her to unknowingly correct one stigmatized item (ajina) with another (asina). We see here how the awareness of certain consequences (primarily embarrassment) fuels this fervor to correct. The practices of correction around así reveal the desire of the Mexicano/a/x-Nuevomexicano/a/x subjects to avoid these consequences.

Beyond functioning as a strategy to safeguard against embarrassment, the authenticating practice of correction also serves as a contestatory practice that addresses uneven power dynamics. The Mexicano/a/x-Nuevomexicanos/as/xs use correction to legitimize themselves as valid speakers of authentic Spanish. Whereas their Mexicano/a parents may express anxieties about Mexicano/a/x family members making fun of changes to their Spanish, the question as to whether or not the Mexicano/a parents can speak Spanish is not up for debate. The Mexicano/a/x-Nuevomexicanos/as/xs, on the other hand, may not enjoy the same level of linguistic legitimacy. Like their Nuevomexicano/a parents, the Mexicano/a/x-Nuevomexicanos/as/xs were all born and raised in New Mexico and have grown up hearing stories and witnessing their Nuevomexicano/a parents' linguistic abilities in Spanish be questioned, corrected, and chiquitafied. For example, Rosalinda explains that her father initially needed her mother's help with Spanish. She explains, "With my mom's family, the first time she met him, she had to help him in Spanish a lot cause like even though my grandma spoke it and my great grandma, my dad was like not a very fluent speaker." Rosalinda emphasizes that her father's Nuevomexicano linguistic abilities were not sufficient. Similarly, Verónica retells her Nuevomexicana mother's first interaction with her Mexicano/a grandparents in Mexico:

I'll tell you the story about when my mom and dad—when my mom and dad eloped and they went to Mexico. Um, my mom went to my abuelita and said to her, "Necesito un cajete para lavar las lonas de Luis." And the only cajete that my abuelita knew of was the molcajete and lonas is, of course, a tarp, and she—she turned to Mom, and she said, "Luis no tiene lonas." "Sí, tiene muchas lonas." It took quite a while to figure out—you know, they—they still didn't understand each other, and then it wasn't 'til my dad walked in, and he said, "Quiere la tina para lavar los pantalones de mezclilla." Oh, okay, you know, that kinda thing. Um, you know, she asked for un pitcher para hacer limonada. They didn't know what a pitcher was. So it's kinda that—it's that—I call it New Mexican Spanish. . . . It is Spanish, but it has this certain spin on it that you go to Mexico and they're confused.

With these stories in mind, the corrective practices of the Mexicano/a/x-Nuevomexicano/a/x subjects reflect a desire to avert this confusion by asserting themselves as linguistic experts. Indeed, Rosalinda describes her father's Spanish as "still a work in progress," and Alicia explains that her mom has "come a long way" with her Spanish. Both of these reports of "progress" indicate that becoming proficient in a Mexican Spanish is the desired goal and positions the Mexicano/a/x-Nuevomexicano/a/x subjects as evaluators of this "improvement." Even Rose applauds her Nuevomexicano husband for being mistaken for a Mexicano at work: "I give him props because he's come a long way. And, in fact, he—he was so excited a while back. He works out in the field. He works for the gas company. . . . He works with a lot of Mexicans. And he came home one day, and he was like all excited. He was like, 'Guess what? This Mexican said that he thought I was from Mexico.'" For Rose, and her husband, sounding Mexican enough to pass for Mexicano/a/x is an accomplishment and a measure of good Spanish. Therefore, correction is a symbolic practice that continuously reinforces the notion of authenticity and allows the Mexicano/a/x-Nuevomexicanos/as/x to establish themselves as valid Spanish speakers.

However, in achieving this empowerment, the Mexicano/a/x-Nuevomexicano/a/x subjects do, in fact, inscribe a linguistic hierarchy within their New Mexico communities and among family members. In resetting the power differential between themselves and potential Mexicano/a/x correctors, they reenact it onto Nuevomexicanos/as/xs. This is clear as Angélica corrects her Nuevomexicano grandparents and as Edna, Carolina, and Milagros correct their respective Nuevomexicano fathers. The acts of correction highlight a "process in which ideology, in simplifying the sociolinguistic field, renders some persons or activities invisible."[55] The practice of correction, and the ideology of authenticity it constructs, renders Nuevomexicanos/as/xs and their variety of Spanish invisible. Considering that Zentella's findings in El Barrio in New York emphasize that "children in neighborhoods like el bloque learn to negotiate the linguistic diversity that surrounds them in keeping with the central cultural norm of respeto ("respect"), which requires that the young defer to their elders and accommodate the linguistic abilities of their addressees wherever possible,"[56] the Mexicano/a/x-Nuevomexicano/a/x subjects' impulse to correct seems to trump the notion of deferring to and accommodating their Nuevomexicano/a/x elders. Is this a case of lack of respeto? Are the Mexicano/a/x-Nuevomexicano/a/x subjects complicit in a process of linguistic oppression through their acts of correction? The practice of correction does, indeed, reveal another example of shifting power relationships in the Mexicano-Nuevomexicano context.

However, the Mexicano/a/x-Nuevomexicanos/as/xs' linguistic power play cannot be reduced to a one-way binary relationship between oppressor and oppressed or to a case of disrespect. Despite the hierarchical view of their parents' linguistic varieties, every Mexicano/a/x-Nuevomexicano/a/x subject emphasizes in each of their interviews that they identify equally with Mexico and New Mexico. Often, the subject uses expressions such as "I'm half and half" or "I'm both." They are very careful not to claim one identity over another in order to honor both parents. This fact problematizes any notion of clear-cut disrespect. I do not believe it is necessarily an issue of blaming the Mexicano/a partners and Mexicano/a/x-Nuevomexicano/a/x subjects for linguistically subordinating Nuevomexicanos/as/xs, but of recognizing that the Mexicano-Nuevomexicano impulse to correct represents a response to a larger framework of historical linguistic oppression in the New Mexico context.

A focus on the intersection between correction, authenticity, and standard language ideology illuminates this framework of oppression. Specifically, Lippi-Green discusses the implications of this intersection:

> In the simplest terms, the disciplining of discourse has to do with who is allowed to speak, and thus, who is heard. A standard language ideology, which proposes that an idealized nation-state has one perfect, homogeneous language, becomes the means by which discourse is seized, and provides rationalization for limiting access to discourse.[57]

---

55. Irvine and Gal, "Language Ideology and Linguistic Differentiation," 38.
56. Zentella, *Growing Up Bilingual*, 327.
57. Lippi-Green, *English with an Accent*, 64.

Lippi-Green highlights the process by which New Mexican Spanish is silenced in favor of the "standard" Mexican Spanish. She connects this disciplining to ideas about nation. One of the driving forces in the practice of correction is the fear of being made fun of in Mexico. The Mexicano/a/x-Nuevomexicano/a/x subjects attribute so much validity to Mexican Spanish because, as Angélica reminds us, her mom speaks "the right vocabulary because she's originally from Mexico." The Mexicano/a/x-Nuevomexicano/a/x subjects are able to attach this variety to a "legitimate" Spanish-speaking nation-space, and this nation-space, in turn, validates its own authenticity. This hegemonic ideology of "one nation, one language" emphasizes that New Mexican Spanish does not have a national identity; therefore, it cannot function as the standard Spanish. In a sense, New Mexican Spanish exists as a language without a nation. Likewise, when Gloria Anzaldúa speaks of "Chicano Spanish," she references this absence of a nation to "legitimize" the language:

> For a people who are neither Spanish nor live in a country in which Spanish is the first language; for a people who live in a country in which English is the reigning tongue but who are not Anglo; for a people who cannot entirely identify with the standard (formal, Castilian) Spanish nor standard English, what recourse is left to them but to create their own language? A language which they can connect their identity to, one capable of communicating the realities and values true to themselves.[58]

Spanish in New Mexico has an over four-hundred-year-old presence that has lived through several changes in nation. Absorbing influences from Pueblo Indian languages, Nahuatl, early and contemporary Mexican Spanish, and English, as well as reflecting its own internal innovations,[59] it embodies a language reflective of Nuevomexicanos/as/xs' continuously changing realities. Part of this reality consists of a historical trend of linguistic silencing that began long before the Mexicano/a partners and Mexicano/a/x-Nuevomexicano/a/x subjects initiated their correction practices. From the beginning of the US conquest of New Mexico in 1846, New Mexico has experienced an extensive history of linguistic oppression.[60]

The ideological inter-Latino/a/x linguistic hierarchies constructed within the Mexicano-Nuevomexicano families represent a legacy of this historical

---

58. Anzaldúa, *Borderlands/La Frontera*, 77.
59. See Bills and Vigil, *Spanish Language of New Mexico*.
60. See Nieto-Phillips, "Spanish American Ethnic Identity"; Roberts, *Remaining and Becoming*; MacGregor-Mendoza, "Aquí no se habla español"; Gonzales-Berry, "Which Language?"; and Bills and Vigil, *Spanish Language of New Mexico*.

linguistic oppression. The Somos Primos campaign underscores the obscured histories between Mexicanos/as/xs and Nuevomexicanos/as/xs that contribute to this dynamic. The campaign's video states, "History textbooks in New Mexico schools did not include the history of the region before the U.S. occupation. Nuevomexicanos grew up not knowing the deep roots they shared with their primos on the other side. Mexican textbooks do not mention the over 60,000 Mexicans that remained in the conquered territory."[61] Yet another example of Latinidad, the video recalls the (post)colonial analogies,[62] similar histories, and displacements between Nuevomexicanos/as/xs and Mexicanos/as/xs. This lack of inter-Latino/a/x knowledge creates fertile ground for authenticating practices that construct linguistic hierarchies. Take the case of así versus asina. Mexicanos/as/xs and Nuevomexicanos/as/xs interact around this variant, seemingly unaware that both variants are used in Mexico and New Mexico.[63] Artificially associating only one variant with one region conceals the heterogeneity within these communities. The notion that New Mexican Spanish is so different from Mexican Spanish relies on the premise of separate linguistic histories and language experiences, when, in reality, these histories and experiences overlap. Bills and Vigil capture this notion when they argue that "all of New Mexican Spanish is 'Mexican.'"[64]

When positioned within the framework of a larger sociolinguistic history of repression, I suggest that the Mexicano/a/x-Nuevomexicano/a/x practice of correction operates on a critical level to combat the linguistic invisibility of Spanish in New Mexico. Catherine Walsh describes critical bilingualism as "the ability to not just speak two languages, but to be conscious of the sociocultural, political, and ideological contexts in which the languages (and therefore the speakers) are positioned and function, and of the multiple meanings that are fostered in each."[65] In the context of the Mexicano/a/x-Nuevomexicano/a/x subjects, it seems that we have a critical bidialectalism in which they choose their lexicon based on certain sociocultural and ideological contexts and consequences. Zentella complements Walsh's definition with her own critical perspective on bilingualism that attempts "to understand and facilitate a stigmatized group's attempts to construct a positive self within an economic and political context that relegates its members to static and disparaged ethnic, racial, and class identities, and that identifies them with static and disparaged linguistic codes."[66] The critical frameworks of Walsh and Zentella allow us to

---

61. Somos un Pueblo Unido, "Somos Primos."
62. Aparicio, "Jennifer as Selena," 94.
63. See Lipski, *Varieties of Spanish*.
64. Bills and Vigil, *Spanish Language of New Mexico*, 7.
65. Walsh, *Pedagogy and the Struggle*, 126–27.
66. Zentella, *Growing Up Bilingual*, 13.

see beyond binaries of correct and incorrect, linguistic oppressor/oppressed, and real/unreal. Rather than focus on the ways in which New Mexican Spanish is disparaged in the cases of correction, it is possible to view this authenticating as a response to a larger system of linguistic oppression. It serves as the Mexicano/a/x-Nuevomexicano/a/x way out of a legacy of linguistic terrorism and represents a critical strategy to construct a positive sense of self. Through the practice of correction, and the ideologies it constructs, the Mexicano/a/x-Nuevomexicanos/as/xs actually confront a larger silencing of Spanish in New Mexico and assert their linguistic skills amidst the tides of language shift. The Mexicano/a/x-Nuevomexicanos/as/xs make Spanish visible in New Mexico, albeit by correcting it, but at the very least this potentially creates a dialogue about Mexican and New Mexican lexical choices within the families. In a sense, the practices of correction reinsert Mexico into New Mexico. Although their corrections may index Mexico as the legitimate Spanish-speaking nation, the Mexicano/a/x-Nuevomexicano/a/x subjects simultaneously, and perhaps unknowingly, (re)construct New Mexico as a vibrant Spanish-speaking space through their own language pride and zeal to speak the "right" Spanish.

CONCLUDING THOUGHTS: SPANISH LANGUAGE AFFIRMATIONS

Bonnie Urciuoli reminds us that "people's metalinguistic sense—how they define and analyze the elements of a language—is worked out over the course of their lives. A metalinguistic sense involves both private and public perceptions and experiences of language."[67] The Mexicano-Nuevomexicano family context contributes a distinct dimension to Bonnie Urciuoli's notion of metalinguistic sense. Although this is not a longitudinal study in which I can truly explore how these families "work out" their perceptions about language over the course of their lives, through the contradictions, slippages, and moments of dissonance we are able to see an active process of the Mexicano-Nuevomexicano families working out their definitions of the multiple Spanishes in their daily lives. The families' metalinguistic sense is not fixed but is instead continuously (re)constructed and influenced by authenticating practices such as correction. Interestingly, rather than a public/private dichotomy, as Urciuoli suggests, in which private might be thought of as in-group (or at least in-family) and "public" as "out-group," the Mexicano-Nuevomexicano family complicates this division. Consider Urciuoli's description of the "inner sphere" and "outer sphere" in order to understand the public/private

---

67. Urciuoli, *Exposing Prejudice*, 91.

complication. In the context of code-switching, she describes these analogous concepts: "The inner sphere is the place where, ideologically, Spanish and English can 'mix' or coexist as code-switching.... What is normal to 'us' is a mistake to 'them,' that is, to a 'teacher' as exemplar and monitor of order or correctness."[68] The acts of correction and policing that occur within the same family position the Mexicano-Nuevomexicano family as a microcosm of a public/private or inner/outer sphere. The monitors of correctness exist within the same family. Through the activation of the specific language ideologies of correctness and authenticity, as well as linguistic equality, the Mexicano-Nuevomexicano family again proves to be a dynamic zone of encuentro in which inter-Latino/a/x convergences and divergences occur around the perceptions of certain marked and unmarked lexical choices. We might also consider the familial zone of encuentro as an example of Quijano's "coloniality of power"[69] or a space where a conflict of knowledges and structures of power occurs. These ideological conflicts contribute to Zentella's call for the study of diverse US Latino/a/x linguistic portraits. She states,

> In the end, speakers shape ideologies brought from the homeland in ways that help them make sense of situations and groups they encounter in specific Unites States locales. All the changes wrought in different areas and eras, and by different generations, genders, classes, or races, have yet to be analyzed for any one group of Latin@s. The partial portraits that we do have indicate that some members of the second generation learn to communicate in ways that resist the 'chiquitafication' of their language skills.[70]

The study of language ideologies within the Mexicano-Nuevomexicano families allows me to add a piece to the partial portraits to which Zentella refers. Yet, the notion of homeland changes in the context of Mexico and New Mexico. The Mexicano/a/x-Nuevomexicanos/as/xs resist chiquitafication of their skills through the authenticating practice of correction and the affirmation of Mexico as the measure of linguistic authenticity. Although they may then subsequently chiquitafy New Mexican Spanish, it is clear that, in all of the dominant ideologies circulating throughout the families, Spanish is, indeed, being affirmed. The next chapter provides an in-depth exploration of Mexicano/a/x-Nuevomexicano/a/x identities and of the crucial role that language experiences and language ideologies play in their constructions.

---

68. Urciuoli, *Exposing Prejudice*, 97.
69. Quijano, "Coloniality of Power."
70. Zentella, "Latin@ Languages and Identities," 326.

CHAPTER 4

Disjunctures and Difference

Theorizing the Mixed Identities of Mexicano/a/x-Nuevomexicanos/as/xs

Am I Mexican, am I Chicana, am I Latina, am I Hispanic—what am I?
—Alicia Molina, Mexicana-Nuevomexicana

On a late summer afternoon in the Molina living room, I was interested in developing the discussion about identity that I'd had individually with Alicia several weeks before. On this particular day the entire Molina family was present in the living room, and the term "Chicano" had been used several times during our conversation. I asked Pancho (MX) if he considered his children to be Chicanos. He then replied with an emphatic "No!" Below is the conversation that followed this response:

ALICIA: You told me, I've asked you before, 'cause when I was little I was confused as to what I was, and you told me once that I was Chicana.
PANCHO: Quizás, pero no. Para mí, los chicanos chicanos vienen siendo de que los papás son de aquí siempre. Los niños también, hasta los abuelitos. Al menos es lo que he aprendido de la gente de aquí de Nuevo México. Si te dije eso, no sé por qué. Les digo que son americanos, que son de aquí.... Me preguntan, "¿Estás casada con una americana? ¿Una chicana?" Sí, les digo. Es hispana. Pero es americana. Siempre les he dicho que es americana.

[PANCHO: Maybe, but no. To me, Chicanos Chicanos are those whose parents have always been from here. Their kids too, even the grandparents.

At least that is what I've learned from the people from here from New Mexico. If I told you that, I don't know why. I tell you that you are Americans, that you are from here. Sometimes I'm asked, "Are you married to an American? To a Chicana?" Yes, I tell them. She is Hispanic. But she is American. I've always told them that she is American.]

At this point in the conversation, I noticed Pancho's wife, Elizabeth (NMX), shaking her head in disagreement and frowning. Pancho continued, "Aunque sean hispanos, nuevomexicanos, chicanos, son americanos. Yo los considero americanos." [Even though they are Hispanic, New Mexican, Chicanos, they are American. I consider them American.] I then asked Elizabeth, Alicia, and Antonio, "Is that how you would identify? As American first, before anything else?" Alicia answered, "I would say hispana before americana." Elizabeth then added, "I would say Hispanic." Antonio echoed his mother's response as he stated: "I'd say Hispanic."

In a space of about ten minutes, the Molina family invokes four different identity terms. These terms are simultaneously defined, explained, accepted, and contested. Elizabeth's disapproving expression and shaking of her head signal a rejection of her husband's use of "americana." Similarly, Alicia and Antonio clarify that they would identify as "hispana" or "Hispanic" before using "americana." The convergences and divergences between the Mexicano/a/x-Nuevomexicanos/as/xs' notions of identity and their parents' conceptualizations reveal tensions between nationality, citizenship, ethnicity, and regional identity.

Rather than simply report on the descriptive terms used by the Mexicano/a/x-Nuevomexicanos/as/xs to define themselves culturally, in this chapter I focus on what the contradictions reveal within these meaning-making processes. It is not my intent to arrive at some overarching or all-encompassing fixed identity term to which the Mexicano/a/x-Nuevomexicanos/as/xs subscribe. The words of the Molina family highlight that these terms, and the identity conversations they trigger, seem to be in a constant state of flux, and I approach these discussions through a framework of "identity flows" that illustrates the movement within and between these meanings. In what follows, I explore several additional examples of familial disjunctures around discussions of cultural identities. I then highlight the role of language in these identity-making processes. Lastly, I unpack the multiple meanings of the identity terms invoked by the Mexicano/a/x-Nuevomexicano/a/x subjects and, specifically, the resignification that occurs around the term "Hispanic."

IDENTITIES, MOVEMENT, AND LATINIDAD

I utilize a movement-oriented framework recalling Arjun Appadurai's 1996 work on global flows and Pennycook's "transcultural flows."[1] Appadurai explains that "global cultural processes today are products of the infinitely varied mutual contest of sameness and difference on a stage characterized by radical disjunctures between different sorts of global flows and the uncertain landscapes created in and through these disjunctures."[2] I suggest that the Mexicano-Nuevomexicano families are not isolated from these landscapes, flows, and disjunctures. Like transcultural flows,[3] the identity flows reveal a continuous reorganization of local cultural identities and the construction of new meanings attached to these identities.

Stuart Hall's work illustrates that movement and flow are always present in conceptualizations of cultural identity and are particularly relevant to the Mexicano-Nuevomexicano context. Hall explains,

> Cultural identity . . . is a matter of "becoming" as well as "being." It belongs to the future as much as to the past. It is not something which already exists, transcending place, time, history and culture. Cultural identities come from somewhere, have histories. But, like everything which is historical, they undergo constant transformation. Far from being eternally fixed in some essentialised past, they are subject to the continuous "play" of history, culture and power . . . identities are the names we give to the different ways we are positioned by, and position ourselves within, the narratives of the past.[4]

Hall highlights movement in his theories through the simultaneous processes of "being" and "becoming" as well as the emphasis on the temporal interplay between distinct positionalities. I explore these positionalities, and their histories, with the Mexicano-Nuevomexicano couples in chapter 1. The present chapter expands on this analysis to include the ways in which the Mexicano/a and Nuevomexicano/a parents position their children's identities and how the Mexicano/a/x-Nuevomexicanos/as/xs position their own cultural identities. In theorizing Asian American identity, Lisa Lowe stresses "heterogeneity, hybridity, and multiplicity" as tools to address hegemonic positionalities "between

---

1. Appadurai, *Modernity at Large*; and Pennycook, *Global Englishes and Transcultural Flows*.
2. Appadurai, *Modernity at Large*, 43.
3. Pennycook, *Global Englishes and Transcultural Flows*.
4. Hall, "Cultural Identity and Diaspora," 225.

'dominant' and 'minority' positions."[5] It is important to recognize these power differentials within the Mexicano-Nuevomexicano familial language experiences and the role they play in positioning each other's identities. In particular, Lowe's conceptualization of "multiplicity" provides a tool to describe "the ways in which subjects located within social relations are determined by several different axes of power."[6] Lowe's multiplicity illuminates intra-Latino/a/x and intrafamilial positionality practices.

Appadurai's framework of "-scapes" adds an additional dimension to the process of positioning. When explaining his proposition of different global landscapes, he explains that the suffix "-scape" "indicates that these are not objectively given relations that look the same from every angle of vision but, rather, that they are deeply perspectival constructs, inflected by the historical, linguistic, and political situatedness of different sorts of actors."[7] The Mexicano-Nuevomexicano identity narratives undergo continuous situating and (re)positioning according to the distinct perspectives represented by the Mexicano/a, Nuevomexicano/a, and Mexicano/a-Nuevomexicano/a "angles of vision."

The constitutive notion of flows within this movement-based identity framework also indexes the relational nature of identities. Clary-Lemon discusses this relational movement:

> The idea that one's individual and collective identity may be seen as fluid, and always in relation to the Other, has offered a long-standing basis for understanding the constructs of "identity," which rests specifically in determining what one is by virtue of what one is not. . . . This model . . . allows that identities not be fixed in time or space, even by linguistic construction.[8]

Thus, we have a model that not only emphasizes the fluidity (identity flows) but is also relational, situational, and contingent in nature.[9] Within the larger framework of Latinidad, the relational feature of identity is fundamental to both Aparicio's concept of "horizontal hierarchies" and José Esteban Muñoz's notion of "feeling brown." Horizontal hierarchies provide an additional tool for viewing "internal asymmetries of power" from within the Mexicano-Nuevomexicano families. Aparicio explains, "As a critical concept, horizontal hierarchies acknowledge the potential for solidarity, alliances, and community

---

5. Lowe, *Immigrant Acts*, 66.
6. Lowe, *Immigrant Acts*, 67.
7. Appadurai, *Modernity at Large*, 33.
8. Clary-Lemon, "'We're Not Ethnic, We're Irish!,'" 8.
9. Aparicio, *Negotiating Latinidad*, 76.

while also recognizing the fissures from within."[10] She emphasizes that "horizontal" is not equivalent to "sameness," but "refers to the subordination we face—to various degrees—as racial and historical minorities and as immigrants egregiously constructed as un-American and as perpetual foreigners."[11] Additionally, she clarifies that "hierarchies" refers to "the power differentials behind race, gender, social class, education, legal status, and other factors."[12] Horizontal hierarchies are not fixed. Together, the term allows us "to integrate both shared experiences under US imperialism and our internal asymmetries of power"[13] and for moments of collective identities amidst intrafamilial cultural differences. Similarly, Muñoz theorizes "feeling brown" to think through "feeling together in difference."[14] Like Aparicio, Muñoz underscores the coexistence of difference and power asymmetries in feeling "an apartness together through sharing the status of being a problem."[15] Feeling brown and horizontal hierarchies complement each other in highlighting the relational realities of subordination from both outside and within Latino/a/x groups.

Lastly, I highlight the related notions of "difference" and "hybridity" circulating in this movement model of relational realities. Hall underscores the importance of "difference" when he considers cultural identity in the context of the diaspora experience. He states,

> The diaspora experience . . . is defined, not by essence or purity, but by the recognition of a necessary heterogeneity and diversity; by a conception of "identity" which lives with and through, not despite, difference; by hybridity. Diaspora identities are those which are constantly producing and reproducing themselves anew, through transformation and difference.[16]

The concepts of transformation, difference, and positionalities infuse cultural identity with notions of continuous movement. Additionally, Lowe builds on Hall's notion of "difference" by outlining "heterogeneity" to index "differential relationships within a bounded category."[17] Thus, the heterogeneity within difference also attends to asymmetrical power relations.

---

10. Aparicio, *Negotiating Latinidad*, 42.
11. Aparicio, *Negotiating Latinidad*, 35.
12. Aparicio, *Negotiating Latinidad*, 35.
13. Aparicio, *Negotiating Latinidad*, 35.
14. Muñoz, *Sense of Brown*, 39.
15. Muñoz, *Sense of Brown*, 38.
16. Hall, "Cultural Identity and Diaspora," 35.
17. Lowe, *Immigrant Acts*, 67.

Along with difference, Hall references "hybridity" as a means through which identity lives. In later work, Hall clarifies that hybridity does not simply describe an individual or the mixed racial composition of a population. He defines it as "a cultural logic of translation" and a process through which "cultures are required to revise their own systems of reference, norms, and values by departing from their traditional . . . rules of transformation."[18] In this way, hybridity embodies movement through a transformative process of cultural translation. Similarly, Homi Bhabha's vision of hybridity invokes a space from which the coexistence of many identities simultaneously coalesce and contradict.[19] It is important to note that "hybridization is not the 'free' oscillation between or among chosen identities."[20] Hybridity allows for the coexistence of contradictory and complementary identities, yet power asymmetries do not disappear. Aparicio has cautioned that "it is essential to acknowledge that hybridity is not parity and that new power and social differentials emerge in these mixed national social spaces."[21] Therefore, when I reference "hybridity" in the context of Mexicano-Nuevomexicano identity flows, I do so attentive to its uneven power relations, contradictions, and heterogeneity.

FAMILIAL DIVERGENCES, DISJUNCTURES, AND DIFFERENCE

The conceptual divergences regarding identity that occur in each Mexicano-Nuevomexicano family allow for a window into the continuous processes of "becoming" and "being." In this section I unpack two specific case studies to gain better insight into how identity flows in this process. First, I return to the Molina family's conversation regarding "americana." This disjuncture, seen most clearly in Elizabeth's frown and headshaking, is significant because it speaks to the desire for difference. Here, Elizabeth deploys Bucholtz's tactic of distinction.[22] Elizabeth's headshake insists on difference. Elizabeth, Alicia, and Antonio all indicate that their primary identification is with the term "Hispanic." Pancho perceives this disapproval and continues, "Es su país, sus leyes, no más el color de la piel es diferente. O sea no quiere decir que son americanos gringos." [It's their country, their laws, it's just the color of their skin that is different. I mean, it doesn't mean that they are American gringos.] Elizabeth

---

18. Hall, "Multicultural Question," 113.
19. Bhabha, *Location of Culture*, 5.
20. Lowe, *Immigrant Acts*, 82.
21. Aparicio, "Intimate (Trans)Nationals," 274.
22. Bucholtz, "Sociolinguistic Nostalgia," 408.

agrees and strongly says, "NO!" I then ask Elizabeth what "gringo" means to her. She responds, "That's white!" I then ask the Mexicano/a/x-Nuevomexicanos/as/xs if they have ever been called "gringa" or "gringo." Alicia states that her Mexicana grandmother recently used this term in reference to her when Alicia was visiting in Mexico. Alicia explains that a friend of her grandmother's asked if Alicia was from Chihuahua and her grandmother responded with the words, "No. Es gringa." Alicia recalls, "I took it as kind of an insult, but I didn't tell her nothing." Equally insulted, Carolina Santos tells of feeling outraged at Wal-Mart when a Mexicano man complained to his wife about her with the reference of "esa gringa" because he thought Carolina was holding up the line. Carolina comments that she was surprised that this man perceived her as Anglo. She recounts that she thought to herself, "Dude, do I look Anglo? I don't think I look Anglo!"

I propose that the feelings of insult, offense, and visible disapproval through the reactions described above are a rejection of a perceived process of homogenization. Appadurai states that "the central problem of today's global interactions is the tension between cultural homogenization and cultural heterogenization. . . . for polities of smaller scale, there is always a fear of cultural absorption by polities of larger scale, especially those that are nearby."[23] This tension becomes present in the negative reactions to "americana" and "gringa." The Mexicano/a/x-Nuevomexicanos/as/xs in these cases (as well as Nuevomexicana Elizabeth) equate both terms with "Anglo" or "white." The insistence on "Hispanic" as a primary identity seeks to fight the absorption of their ethnic identity into an overarching national identity infused with unmarked whiteness. Alicia, Antonio, and Carolina seem to be at odds with an identity classification based on nationality due to its erasure of cultural difference. This recalls Pablo Vila's emphasis on the ethnic minority classification systems that take shape only once one is part of the US.[24] In the same way that the term "Latino" only becomes meaningful once in the US,[25] the Mexicano/a/x-Nuevomexicanos/as/xs do not wish for their Hispanic identities to become less meaningful, or specific, by taking on a homogenous "American" or "white" identity. Even when Pancho explains to his family that his mother's use of "gringa" simply "quiere decir que vive en Estados Unidos y nació en Estados Unidos" [means that she lives in the United States and was born in the United States], the sociohistorical association of the term "gringo" with "Anglo" and "white" still holds power in this discussion. The preoccupation with cultural absorption seems especially relevant given that most of the

---

23. Appadurai, *Modernity at Large*, 32.
24. Vila, "Polysemy of the Label."
25. Oboler, *Ethnic Labels, Latino Lives*.

first-generation Mexicanos/as in my study were not even aware of a Hispanic/Chicano/a/x identity in New Mexico prior to their immigration.

Consider José Luis's (Ana's husband's) words about his preconceived notions about New Mexico: "Los chicanos ni existían con nosotros hasta que llegamos. Nosotros siempre nos lo imaginábamos gringos, gringos, todo el tiempo gente güera y gringa hablando inglés." [Chicanos didn't even exist to us until we got here. We always imagined it here with gringos, gringos, all the time light-skinned, blond, and gringo people speaking English.] Manuel Guzmán (MX) of Taos echoes this reality: "In Mexico, we call them güeros, even if they are Chicanos from here." Manuel's use of "güero"[26] adds to the discussion around "gringo" and "americano." For Pancho, and perhaps the other first-generation Mexicano/a partners, the importance of a primary Hispanic identity over a national American identity is not a familiar paradigm. The disjunctures around the meanings of "americano" and "gringo" reference two hundred years of historical Anglo–Hispanic relations in New Mexico in which cultural erasure was at the center.[27] Perhaps the dominance and whiteness of Anglo-American culture in the contemporary Latino/a/x US continues to fuel this disassociation and disapproval among Mexicano/a/x-Nuevomexicanos/as/xs like Alicia and Antonio.

Another fascinating point of disjuncture within the Mexicano-Nuevomexicano families centers around hybridity. Whereas the Molina children and Carolina desire to make visible their distinctly Hispanic identity, rather than a homogenized "American" identity, the Navarro daughters reject their father's affirmation of a hybrid Hispanic identity. Nicolás Navarro explains,

> I call my kids Hispanos. I tell them this is why you are Hispanic: because you come from Spanish ancestors, the whole mixture of our different cultures and, um, we fall under the umbrella of being an Hispano, . . . that's the way I teach them because, um, because I tell them that you're not only, um, Mexican and Indian, you also are of, um, Spanish culture, because there is still a lot of Spanish culture in our area.

Navarro's description of Hispanic/Hispano indexes notions of mixture, pan-ethnicity, and a multiplicity of identities congruent with Lowe's models of "heterogeneity." The coexistence of these notions also references a hybridity, with

---

26. Among Nuevomexicanos, "güero" tends to mean someone with light or blond hair, regardless of ethnicity. Manuel's use of "güero" seems to be synonymous with the Mexicano partner use of "gringo" and "americano."

27. See Nieto-Phillips, *Language of Blood*.

all its internal asymmetries.[28] Yet, Rosalinda and Milagros do not embrace these meanings (or the term). Both daughters identify as "Mexican American." Milagros asserts, "Yeah, 'cause I think if you say Hispanic, uh, people are, it's not really saying who you are, and you could be from, um, like Colombian-American and you're considered Hispanic or you can be from any other Spanish-speaking country and you're a Hispanic, and if I say Mexican American it's saying a little more of who I am." With the term "Mexican American," Milagros and Rosalinda seem to desire more specificity. When asked how she would identify her father, Milagros explains, "Hispanic, I guess 'cause, um, I think, uh, his blood's kind of a little bit died down through, there's not much Mexican in it anymore or any other thing, so he's just a Hispanic." It is noteworthy that Nicolás Navarro conceptualizes "Hispanic" as the most accurate identification due to the word's utility in encompassing the coexistence of multiple identities. However, Milagros views this same multiplicity as a sort of "watering down" of Mexican identity. Her phrase, "just Hispanic" communicates a sense of lacking. For Milagros and Rosalinda, the reference point for their identity circulates within the connotations of "Mexican."

Notably, when the daughters clarify the meaning of "American" in "Mexican American," Rosalinda expresses that she is not referring to "rednecks" with the term "American." Rosalinda and Milagros agree that using the term "American" denotes citizenship, much like Pancho's conceptualization of the term. Milagros explains, "When I use 'American' it means, yes, I have that freedom to do all those things you can do." Rather than an embracing of a homogenous "American culture," the Navarro girls' use of "American" functions as a contestatory response. In effect, the use of "Mexican American" talks back to a dominant American society that they perceive "thinks we are just wetbacks." The Navarro daughters' use of "Mexican American" inserts their presence into a vision of America from which they often feel excluded, and, as Aparicio theorizes, they are "re-writing the concept of 'American.'"[29] However, this rewriting of their cultural identities still diverges from the vision of their Nuevomexicano father.

By unpacking the intersection of linguistic practices and cultural identity within the discourses of the Navarro family interview, I explore this divergence a little deeper. Below, I reproduce a relatively long excerpt from the family's group plática to better explore this intersection and its concomitant divergences. These moments from the conversation begin with Nicolás reiterating his ideas about Spanglish:

---

28. See Aparicio, *Negotiating Latinidad*.
29. Aparicio, "Intimate (Trans)Nationals," 282.

NICOLÁS: Like I said before, I think our language over here is Spanglish. I see Spanglish being the future language of our Hispanic culture from coast to coast. Es la ventaja que tenemos nosotros de aquí. . . . With Spanglish we can jump from one language to the other without even having to stop. I believe that's what our future language is going to be.

MILAGROS: It's just like a couple of words. It seems like I hear more English in the speaking of Spanglish than what I hear Spanish. I'd say it's like 80 percent English, 20 percent Spanish.

NICOLÁS: Yeah, but that's what I'm talking about—that I see the future of our Hispanic culture with such a blend. It may be 80/20, but you're still going to have a mixture.

MILAGROS: Either way the English kind of overrides it.

NICOLÁS: And that's because that's what we use the most because now we deal with more people who use English than Spanish.

ROSALINDA: But that was back then. But think about it now. Now it's great to know Spanish.

NICOLÁS: I guess that maybe it's my generation. That maybe we carry our Spanglish a little more fluent and to us mixing is like no big deal. Because they're trying to be more fluent in one or the other.

Nicolás uses Spanglish to describe not only a linguistic practice but also a cultural identity. In his individual interview he refers to "the Spanglish lives we live." Spanglish embodies Nicolás's idea of Hispanic. Nicolás's theorizations underscore the interconnectedness between language and identity. He emphasizes a cultural mix and a linguistic mix that continuously inform each other. Yet, Rosalinda and Milagros clearly state that they do not speak Spanglish and that they do not subscribe to their father's identity vision. Milagros focuses on the absorption of Spanish by English within the Spanglish practices that her father references. This focus on the dominance of English seems to erase the empowerment that Nicolás derives from what Mignolo terms "bilanguaging love" or "love for being between languages."[30] Whereas Nicolás finds victory and pride within translanguaging practices,[31] even if the amount of Spanish is less than English, Milagros and Rosalinda view Spanglish as always already culturally absorbed by English dominance.

---

30. Mignolo, *Local Histories/Global Designs*, 274.
31. García, *Bilingual Education*, 45, defines translanguaging as "multiple discursive practices in which bilinguals engage in order to make sense of their bilingual worlds. Translanguaging therefore goes beyond what has been termed code-switching . . . although it includes it, as well as other kinds of bilingual language use and bilingual contact."

These divergences can, perhaps, be best described through Stuart Hall's use of "coupling." Hall explains the logic of coupling as a tool of empowerment in which one can be "black and British, not only because that is a necessary position to take . . . but because even those two terms . . . do not exhaust all of our identities."[32] Hall's strategy of coupling makes possible the existence of multiple differences at the same moment within one's identity rather than binary oppositions. This coexistence does not necessarily erase the asymmetrical power relations attributed to these differences from both within and outside of the Mexicano-Nuevomexicano families (i.e., Lowe's multiplicity and heterogeneity), and because of this we can view the logic of coupling as congruent with the logic of relational identities, horizontal hierarchies, and hybridity. For Nicolás, he can use Spanish and English together, and this does not diminish his Hispanic identity. On the contrary, it affirms it. For Nicolás, English can be just as Hispanic as Spanish. However, Milagros and Rosalinda affirm their cultural identities by keeping the languages separate, ascribing to the ideology of double monolingualism and "by trying to be more fluent in one or the other." For these Mexicana-Nuevomexicanas, the presence of English is equivalent to cultural erasure and homogenization.

Interestingly, the cultural "identity flows" that travel between Nicolás and his daughters are not so different. It is not necessarily that the Navarro girls are operating outside of a system of Latinidad, cultural hybridity, or "feeling brown" in favor of binaries and cultural essentializations. It is simply that the Navarro daughters' reality of these concepts looks different from that of their father due to divergent language experiences. The apparent tensions, disjunctures, and multiplicities[33] between the Navarro daughters and their father reveal distinct strategies to negotiate hybridity from different localities. Pennycook suggests the concept of "transcultural flows," in which language and cultural identities collide in a "reorganization of the local."[34] I suggest that both Nicolás and his daughters are involved in "transcultural flows" of hybridity that "reorganiz[e] the local." However, Nicolás's notion of "local" and Rosalinda and Milagros's notion of "local" originate from different "angles of vision."[35] Carmen Fought's words illuminate these different positionalities. She explains,

> There are, then, multiple cultural groups available within which (and against which) Latino speakers can define and enact their identities, including: a)

---

32. Hall, "What Is the 'Black'?," 29.
33. Used here according to Lowe's definition.
34. Pennycook, *Global Englishes and Transcultural Flows*, 6–7.
35. Appadurai, *Modernity at Large*.

the heritage culture of other countries (e.g., Mexico), b) the immigrant Latino culture in the USA, c) the second-generation (and later) Latino culture in the USA, and d) other US cultural groups, including the dominant European-American culture and the cultures of other ethnic minority groups such as African-Americans.[36]

Whereas Nicolás's generation is more fluent in the translanguaging practice of Spanglish, Rosalinda and Milagros do not recognize this practice as relevant or useful. Their concept of "local" involves separateness. Perhaps this is due to the fact that Nicolás operates in a system that recognizes "the second-generation (and later) Latino culture in the USA," while Rosalinda and Milagros seem to be operating in a system in which they define and enact their identities in comparison with monolingual Mexican Spanish speakers.

The Navarro sisters' identity flows exist in direct opposition to Sánchez and García's conceptualization of translanguaging "as a transformative endeavor which reframes solidified ideologies of double monolingualism and linguistic hierarchies that posit the language practices of white monolingual middle-class speakers as better than those of others."[37] In contrast to this translanguaging stance, the Navarro daughters speak Spanish to their Mexicana mother and to their Mexicano/a/x family members in Mexico. Blending the languages would not make communicative sense in the context of monolingual Spanish-speaking family members, and, as Rosalinda states, "It's just confusing." Additionally, as reported in chapter 2, Rosalinda and Milagros tend to speak English with Nuevomexicano/a/x family members. Therefore, they do not view the mixing of Spanish and English as natural or necessary. Rosalinda and Milagros negotiate this linguistic separateness in response to the reality of what "local" is to them. In explaining this reality, Milagros reflects, "Like, I'm not really a part of one solid thing. . . . I don't want to say I don't belong here, but this is not my group. But over there is not my group." Rosalinda then adds, "Even sometimes when we go over there a lot of people—there's occasionally people who think we are just snotty Americans. And there are times when we're here and we meet redneck people, and they think we are just wetbacks." It seems that Rosalinda and Milagros are operating in a local system that reacts to imposed binaries between "here" and "there," (i.e., snotty American vs. wetback). Milagros and Rosalinda's rejection of Spanglish practices, and of their father's vision of identity, illustrates that their positionalities involve reacting to Mexican family members and dominant Anglo

---

36. Fought, *Language and Ethnicity,* 71–72.
37. Sánchez and García, "Introducción," 2.

society. Their "Latina/o matrix of intelligibility"[38] does not include or recognize their father's sense of Nuevomexicano/Hispanic identity.

THE LOCATION OF LANGUAGE IN CULTURAL IDENTITIES

The linguistic and cultural intersections revealed in the preceding discussion of Spanglish provide a useful entryway into thinking through the ways that language experiences inform the Mexicano-Nuevomexicano conversations about cultural identity. Language ideologies linking Spanish proficiency to identity surface as a salient discourse within the Mexicano-Nuevomexicano narratives. Bonnie Urciuoli refers to this connection as the "lamination of culture and language"[39] or the assumption that culture and language always co-occur. For example, Alicia defines the term "Hispanic" as based in locality and language. She explains, "For me, personally, it just means being from New Mexico and being a Spanish speaker." Similarly, when Verónica defines the term "Chicano," she invokes place and linguistic ability: "Chicana, to me, is someone who was born and raised here and learned Spanish here and kind of just absorbed the culture—Hispanic culture from here." Edna also defines "Hispanic" as distinctly New Mexican with Spanish language ability. She states, "Hispanic to me means born in New Mexico speaking Spanish." Olivia further specifies that being Hispanic means that "I was raised northern New Mexican and I can speak Spanish and my parents are Hispanic." Olivia's description emphasizes the "New Mexicanness" in identifying as Hispanic while also equating this localness with an ability to speak Spanish.

Another dimension to the "lamination of culture and language" described above occurs in Antonio's disassociation with the term "Mexican." When I asked him if he would ever use the term "Mexican" to describe himself, he responds, "Maybe once I'm older and I would then know how to actually speak the language. Because I mean I really don't want to claim that I'm Mexican, when I don't even know how to speak Spanish. So maybe once I'm older and I know how to speak it, then yeah." Antonio seems to view himself as in the process of "becoming Mexican." He states that he prefers to identify as "Hispanic." Yet, he clarifies, "but I have like strong Mexican blood in me since my dad is from Mexico." The co-occurrence of language and culture in Antonio's definition of "Mexican" precludes him from being able to presently claim a Mexican identity. He views an "authentically" Mexican identity as dependent

---

38. See Cárdenas, *Constituting Central American-Americans,* for a discussion around the "Latina/o matrix of intelligibility" (113, 117).

39. Urciuoli, "Whose Spanish?"

on his own increased linguistic ability. Yet, when I asked Antonio if Spanish was necessary to identify as "Hispanic," he clearly responded that it was not necessary.

Antonio's thoughts are very similar to Ana's opinions about the cultural identity of her Mexicano-Nuevomexicano son, Rolando. She explains,

> And I think we always tell our kids, you know, don't be embarrassed of your culture or your heritage. And you know, you're Mexican, you better, darn better speak Spanish, you know, because that is who—I mean, that is part of who you are and you need to know the language. . . . I think that they have a higher bar they have to achieve than, than I do. Because, I mean, ah, my family spoke Spanish. Um, and I—you know, I don't know. I guess I don't, I didn't really feel that way for us.

Ana echoes Antonio's conceptualization of "Mexican" as equivalent to a certain level of linguistic ability and linguistic responsibility. Like Antonio, Ana emphasizes that these requirements are not necessary when one identifies as "Hispanic" or, what Ana terms, "us." These manifestations of Urciuoli's "lamination of culture and language" represent Appadurai's "deeply perspectival constructs" of the Mexicano/a/x-Nuevomexicanos/as/xs regarding which identities are linked to linguistic ability. There is not necessarily a consensus to be reached. However, highlighting the (re)productions of these linkages provides insight into the ongoing processes of inclusion and exclusion as the Mexicano/a/x-Nuevomexicanos/as/xs theorize about their cultural identities. For example, linguistic ability is included when defining certain identity terms, which in turn includes and excludes certain individuals. Urciuoli explains further, "Language has a complicated place in processes of identity formation. It occupies a place in the list of things one 'has' when one 'has' a culture. But the link is not a necessary one, it is not always there, and when it is there, it may or may not signify belonging."[40]

Milagros Navarro grapples with this idea of "having a language" as equivalent to "having a culture" when she speaks about those who have Hispanic last names, but do not speak Spanish. She comments,

> People who have a Hispanic last name but who don't speak Spanish? I just, I don't know. I don't know what to consider them. I guess I'd consider them Hispanic but like when I think about it a lot more, I just think well, they're

---

40. Urciuoli, "Whose Spanish?," 264. Valdés, "Ethnolinguistic Identity," focuses on the link between language and identity formation among two G3 preadolescent young girls and is relevant to Urciuoli's ideas about "having" a culture.

kind of lost. They're just like they're not Hispanic. They're not white. They're not anything. They're just, it kind of seems like they're just this invisible people who doesn't have a name for themselves, and that's kind of how I view them. Like anyone around here who has that Spanish last name and who speaks Spanish, that's Hispanic. But anyone who just has that name has just, and doesn't have that language, has completely lost who they are or what kind of made them into who they are. That's just kind of how I view it. . . . It's a loss of identity. A whole big group of people who are part of a lost generation.

Milagros, at first, attributes the designation of "Hispanic" to those who do not "have" the language. Yet, as her thoughts continue to flow, the designation shifts. Those with a Spanish last name who do not speak Spanish are then removed from the identity category of "Hispanic" into a group that seems to be identity-less. Milagros's words enforce a certain policing of identity boundaries around linguistic ability. Suzanne Romaine comments on these ethnolinguistic boundaries:

When the link between language and culture is intact, boundaries and identities may be taken for granted. However, because identities emerge in response to economic, cultural and political forces, perceptions realign themselves to changing situations. In some groups there may be debate about which particular aspect of their culture is of prime significance, or whether someone can be a 'real' member of the cultural group without speaking the associated language.[41]

Clearly, Milagros's words express a boundary of exclusion that judges authentic group membership in terms of Spanish ability. Alexa Guzmán expresses a similar opinion. She states, "Well, like people say that they're Hispanic. Like the people—like—I don't know. I think if they're Hispanic, they should know like some Spanish. Like I know a lot of Hispanics that don't know like nothing in Spanish." Alexa's use of the phrase "say that they're Hispanic" calls into question this identity because of the lack of linguistic ability in Spanish. This comment aligns with Aparicio's observation that "because of their 'lack' of competence in Spanish, most English-dominant Latinos/Latinas have been excluded from consideration as truly Mexican or Hispanic."[42] Interestingly, whereas Milagros removes the designation of "Hispanic" and labels them as

---
41. Romaine, "Identity and Multilingualism," 11.
42. Aparicio, "Of Spanish Dispossessed," 268.

"invisible," Alexa continues to use the term as an identifier. The fact that Alexa affirms that she knows "a lot of Hispanics" who do not have this linguistic ability adds an element of simultaneous recognition and rejection regarding these individuals.

Although the preceding Mexicano/a/x-Nuevomexicano/a/x accounts affirm an inextricable connection between linguistic ability and cultural identity, Alexa's words acknowledge that Hispanics without this ability do, in fact, exist. Verónica concurs. She states, "I mean to me if they are Martínez, they are Hispanic. They have to have Hispanic somewhere; whether or not they speak Spanish or not." This "having Hispanic somewhere" fits with Fought's words regarding linguistic ability and ethnicity. She explains,

> It is also important to note that the linguistic expression of identity for Latinos and Latinas in the USA is not only or even primarily signaled by an ability to speak Spanish. A large number of the speakers born here, especially from the third generation and later, are completely monolingual in English . . . so they must mark their ethnicity with resources other than the use of Spanish.[43]

Nicolás Navarro refers to this marking in the form of "cultural awareness." Nicolás comments on Hispanics in the area who do not speak Spanish. He explains, "I feel that there's less Spanish spoken, but by the same token I see, um, the younger kids are more aware of their culture and more proud to be a Hispanic. . . . They'll still say a few words. Maybe they're not, um, able to have a complete conversation in Spanish. . . . At the same time, their awareness of their culture is still alive." Nicolás and Verónica reference a cultural marking that goes beyond linguistic marking. Even in terms of linguistic ability, there is a certain validation of the linguistic "pieces" that these Hispanics may still possess. This is consistent with Lowe's notion of hybridity as the formation of cultural practices that mark "the history of survival within relationships of unequal power and domination."[44] These remaining pieces of Spanish, and even Nicolás's practice of Spanglish, reference a linguistic and cultural survival. Even if Spanish proficiency is absent, its absence is still referenced at some level in discussions about cultural identity.

Despite this validation of the linguistic "pieces" by Nicolás and Verónica, it is notable that more than half of the Mexicano/a/x-Nuevomexicano/a/x subjects continue to cite Spanish language ability as a criterion for identity. Given

---

43. Fought, *Language and Ethnicity*, 70.
44. Lowe, *Immigrant Acts*, 67.

the sociolinguistic context of New Mexico, in which such a large population of Nuevomexicanos/as/xs have experienced language shift,[45] it might be expected that these younger generations of Mexicano/a/x-Nuevomexicanos/as/xs would not hold such rigid connections between cultural identities and linguistic proficiency. Yet, as noted in chapter 2, all of the Mexicano/a/x-Nuevomexicanos/as/xs have a regular exposure to Spanish that diverges from their Nuevomexicano/a/x peers. I return to the conversation in the Navarro living room to provide some insight. Previously, I referenced Rosalinda challenging her father's viewpoint regarding Spanglish and the dominance of English in this practice. Rosalinda creates a distinction between generational viewpoints of bilingualism. She states, "But that was back then. But think about it now. Now it's great to know Spanish." The contrast between "then" and "now" may shed some light on the policing of linguistic borders in the realm of cultural identities. Nicolás's language experience, along with many other Nuevomexicano/a/xs' language experiences, does belong to another historical and cultural moment. He acknowledges this when he responds, "I guess maybe it's my generation." The historical memory of language oppression and dispossession[46] still exists in the family histories of those of Nicolás's generation. Rosalinda and Milagros feel that Spanish is now valued. Their Mexicano/a/x-Nuevomexicano/a/x language experience has never been without this "value" of Spanish, and they have never been without Spanish linguistic ability. In Aparicio's words, they have not been "of Spanish dispossessed."[47] Perhaps the lamination of culture and language is so strong among several Mexicano/a/x-Nuevomexicanos/as/xs because of this difference in language experience, generation, and reference point. Rosalinda and Milagros have not been victims of an intergenerational linguistic terrorism[48] or suffered from language oppression in New Mexico.

However, as I mentioned in chapter 2, we do see a certain lamenting among all Navarro family members regarding the lack of Spanish ability in the eight-year-old youngest Navarro daughter. It will be the topic of a future study to explore the ways in which new identities emerge and perceptions about "Hispanic" realign in the Navarro family in response to her potential dispossession from Spanish. The future of the youngest Navarro daughter, like the Spanglish reality of her father, has the potential to shed light on the role

---

45. Bills and Vigil, *Spanish Language of New Mexico*; and Gonzales-Berry, "Which Language?"
46. MacGregor-Mendoza, "Aquí no se habla español"; and Aparicio, "Of Spanish Dispossessed."
47. Aparicio, "Of Spanish Dispossessed."
48. Anzaldúa, *Borderlands/La Frontera*.

that English plays in the construction of Mexicano/a/x-Nuevomexicano/a/x identity. I contend that English can also be theorized as a crucial element of US Latino/a/x identity and particularly Mexicano/a/x-Nuevomexicano/a/x identity. Rosa explores English language practices as potential indexes of US Latino/a/x panethnicity and explains that "it becomes possible to investigate processes of being/doing Latinx in Spanish *and* English."[49] Therefore, rather than viewing English as an intrusion or inauthentic presence in Spanish, I argue that English also functions as an index of Latinidad.

ETHNIC LABELS, MEXICANO-NUEVOMEXICANO LIVES

I use the subheading above to reference Suzanne Oboler's seminal 1995 study *Ethnic Labels, Latino Lives*, which interrogates the homogenization of Latinos/as/xs in the US through the use of ethnic labels. In this section, I am interested in tracing the ways in which these labels flow within the narratives of the Mexicano-Nuevomexicano families, how they contest concomitant processes of homogenization, and how they engage with notions of specificity and locality. I highlight the ways in which the Mexicano/a/x-Nuevomexicanos/as/xs struggle with and expand upon existing identity categories to describe their unique positionalities. Oboler notes that, "while the homogenizing nature of ethnic labels is perhaps inevitable, the lack of historical memory that often accompanies their use means that there is often very little understanding of the conditions under which each label was created and through which its meanings and social value have been shaped and change over time."[50] The exploration of Mexicano/a/x-Nuevomexicano/a/x cultural identities in this section illustrates the interplay between historical meanings and resemantifications in order to unpack the identity terms that possess cultural currency for the Mexicano/a/x-Nuevomexicanos/as/xs.

Regarding labels, when asked their terms of preference, the Mexicano/a/x-Nuevomexicano/a/x subjects offered several different responses. Of the fifteen Mexicano/a/x-Nuevomexicano/a/x subjects, two identify as "Mexicano/Mexicana," four identify as "Mexican American," one identifies as "Mexicana Hispana," and one identifies as "Chicana." The remaining seven individuals identify as "Hispanic." Clearly, the Mexicano/a/x-Nuevomexicanos/as/xs do not all conceptualize their cultural identities in the same way, because they

---

49. Rosa, *Looking like a Language*, 22.
50. Oboler, *Ethnic Labels, Latino Lives*, xvi.

deploy five different terms. Absent from these identifications is the designation of "Latino/a/x." Not a single participant (Mexicano/a/x, Nuevomexicano/a/x, or Mexicano/a/x-Nuevomexicano/a/x) spoke of identifying with the term "Latino/a/x." Only within the context of filling out applications did the Mexicano/a/x-Nuevomexicanos/as/xs reference any association with the term. Alicia explains, "When I think of Latino/Latina I think of—I don't know, someone either, like, from middle America or South America—even Mexico, I think they can call themselves Latino or Latina." Olivia simply states, "We don't use that word here." The consensus among most of the participants is that "Latino/a/x" refers to someone from Latin America and is not a relevant term in their everyday lives. In contrast, the term "Hispanic" is uttered frequently and circulates widely within the Mexicano/a/x-Nuevomexicano/a/x narratives. Because nearly half of the Mexicano/a/x-Nuevomexicanos/as/xs identified as "Hispanic,"[51] most of my analysis centers on the multiple layers of meaning associated with this term, as well as the process of semantic inversion[52] that occurs around it. However, Mexicano/a/x-Nuevomexicanos/as/xs' theorizations around the terms "Mexican" and "Mexican American" are also notable, and so I explore them briefly as well.

Alejandro, Angélica, Milagros, and Rosalinda all identify with the term "Mexican American." I previously highlighted Milagros and Rosalinda's associations with "American" and the term "Mexican American" when discussing the identity disjunctures in their family unit. Similarly, Angélica identifies as "Mexican American" because "My mom is Mexican and my dad is American." Again, the associations with the term "American" seem to be based on nationality and citizenship rather than on whiteness or what Rosalinda terms "rednecks." Additionally, three of these four Mexicana-Nuevomexicanas report having dual citizenship. They report this fact almost immediately after they identify as "Mexican American." The positioning of the topic of dual citizenship in the conversation supports the connotation of "American" as based on notions of nationality rather than ethnicity.

Slightly different from "Mexican American," Edna Santos identifies as "Mexicana," and she is quite straightforward about why she chooses this identification. She explains,

---

51. In a study of approximately one hundred Spanish heritage learners in Albuquerque, Wilson, "Diversity in Definition," found the predominance of the identity label "Hispanic" in his data as well. Over 88 percent of the participants preferred this term, whereas less than 20 percent identified with the term "Mexican" or "Mexican American." Some of these participants identified with multiple terms.

52. See Zentella, "Plenary Address."

I say that I'm Mexicana because of my mom, you know. I mean, if somebody asked me, "Are you Hispanic or Mexican?" I say, "Mexicana." Um, I don't know if it's because I don't—I kind of, like, when we were growing up, like, I used to always remember my dad, like, bad-mouthing Mexicans, you know. And he worked with a lot of them. I will say, you know, my dad's Hispanic. My mom's Mexican. I'm Mexicana and Hispanic, but I'd rather say Mexicana. I don't know why. I guess it's because of my mom and, like, how she doesn't really—she hides it a lot. You know what I mean?

Edna's preference for "Mexicana" serves as a response to the invisibility of her mother's Mexicana identity. She clearly acknowledges the cultural identities of both of her parents and even utilizes the strategy of coupling (Hispanic and Mexicana) to honor both parents. However, she exhibits her own agency in choosing to align her identity with her Mexicana mother as an oppositional response to the discrimination Mexicanos/as/xs have experienced from Hispanics. It is almost as if Edna wishes to compensate for her mother's hesitancy in expressing her own Mexicana cultural identity. Again, as we have seen in previous chapters, issues of gender manifest themselves in the case of the Santos family. However, Edna addresses this male dominance by asserting her own Mexicana identity.

Carolina Santos also affirms her Mexicana identity but does not choose one parent's cultural designation over the other. She produces a new term. Carolina explains, "My dad is Hispano and my mom is Mexicana. I guess I'm Mexicana Hispana. [Not] until I grew up did I realize there was a difference between Mexican and New Mexican. I knew there was a difference in the way he spoke and the way she spoke and the way my grandma and grandpa spoke, but, after a while, it kind of all meshed into one." Carolina highlights her perception of language difference, but this did not necessarily translate into a perception of different cultures in her home. Urciuoli reminds us that "it should thus be clear that bilinguals do not literally 'have' two languages or cultures."[53] Carolina's home did not contain borders that bounded each of her parent's cultural identities into neat packages. She did not literally live two cultures, as in the term "bicultural," but instead lived one culture of difference and hybridity that "kind of all meshed into one."

In the same way that Carolina's use of the term "Mexicana Hispana" indexes cultural hybridity, the remaining seven Mexicano/a/x-Nuevomexicanos/as/xs also activate discourses around hybridity and difference through their use of the term "Hispanic." This is the fundamental distinguishing factor in the

---

53. Urciuoli, "Whose Spanish?," 259.

Mexicano/a/x-Nuevomexicanos/as/xs' use of the term "Hispanic" and its highly contested and critiqued panethnic use within the larger Latino/a/x US. Oboler's work focuses on the increased circulation of the term as a panethnic unifier beginning in the 1970s and the challenges that such a term presents. She explains,

> Like other ethnic labels currently used to identify minority groups in this country, the term Hispanic raises the question of how people are defined and classified in this society and in turn how they define themselves in the United States. It points to the gap between the self-identification of people of Latin American descent and their definition through a label created and used by others. . . . Insofar as the ethnic label Hispanic homogenizes the varied social and political experiences of more than 23 million people of different races, classes, languages, national origins, genders, and religions, it is perhaps not surprising that the meanings and uses of the term have become the subject of confusion and debate in the social sciences, government agencies, and much of the society at large.[54]

Oboler emphasizes homogenization, erasure of difference, and lack of agency when discussing the term. Indeed, the term was not created organically by the people it was supposed to represent, but instead was created by "activists, government officials, and media executives" who "institutionalized the Hispanic category and developed a national movement to popularize the Hispanic identity."[55] Cristina Mora's analysis of the term explores the inherent ambiguity in its use. She states,

> This ambiguity allowed stakeholders to reduce any potential resistance to the idea of panethnicity. By pointing toward a vague cultural definition of panethnicity, stakeholders could position the category as broad and as complementary to, rather than in conflict with, national identity. One did not have to speak Spanish or have a Spanish surname to be Hispanic because panethnicity was predicated on a set of historically based cultural values. More important, stakeholders suggested that one did not have to choose between nationality and panethnicity because one could be both Hispanic and Mexican, or Hispanic and Puerto Rican. . . . As a result, an immigrant with close connections to his or her homeland could claim to be as Hispanic as a fourth-generation individual with little or no connection to Latin America.[56]

---

54. Oboler, *Ethnic Labels, Latino Lives*, 2–3.
55. C. Mora, *Making Hispanics*, 5.
56. C. Mora, *Making Hispanics*, 156.

Like Oboler, Mora historically situates the careful and conscious construction of the term "Hispanic." Yet, the question remains, To what degree do Mexicano/a/x-Nuevomexicanos/as/xs use the term in the panethnic, ambiguous, and homogenizing ways that Oboler and Mora document?

In actuality, the Mexicano/a/x-Nuevomexicanos/as/xs mobilize the term "Hispanic" to denote an attachment to a specific locality, as well as multiplicity, heterogeneity, and hybridity. For example, when describing their Nuevomexicano/a parents, all of the Mexicano/a/x-Nuevomexicanos/as/xs used the term "Hispanic" or "hispano/a" to identify them. Also, Alicia, Edna, Verónica, and Olivia clearly state that being "Hispanic" means being from New Mexico. Olivia goes one step further and specifies that "Hispanic" means being raised in northern New Mexico. Thus, Oboler's concerns that the term "Hispanic" conceals "the specificity of the diverse histories and experiences of the population identified as Latinos in the United States"[57] are not applicable to this particular Mexicano/a/x-Nuevomexicano/a/x use of the term. The Mexicano/a/x-Nuevomexicanos/as/xs infuse the term with a specific regional identity. In essence, their use of the term embodies a transcultural flow that reorganizes the term's locality and resemantifies the term as representing specificity rather than homogeneity.

It is important to note that the Mexicano/a/x-Nuevomexicanos/as/xs often use "hispano/a" and "Hispanic" interchangeably. Nieto-Phillips documents Nuevomexicanos/as/xs' use of the term "hispano" in the late nineteenth and early twentieth centuries as possessing "a particular meaning and rhetorical function in the context of New Mexico's struggle for statehood."[58] Nieto-Phillips explains that the term "hispano" mobilized a Spanish heritage narrative in a particular historical moment that was "the source of collective identification with the land and with a historical discourse of conquest, settlement, and occupation."[59] The historical trajectory of the term "hispano" is much more extensive than that of "Hispanic." However, I suggest that it is due to the close association between the two words that "Hispanic" takes on strong connotations of place and region in New Mexico. The Mexicano/a/x-Nuevomexicano/a/x use of the term, in essence, localizes it and activates a certain "grounded identidad."[60] Alicia highlights this locally "grounded identidad" in her explanation regarding why she claims a Hispanic identity over a Mexican identity. After asking Alicia if she uses the term "Mexican" to describe herself, she responds,

---

57. Oboler, *Ethnic Labels, Latino Lives*, 16.
58. Nieto-Phillips, *Language of Blood*, 81.
59. Nieto-Phillips, *Language of Blood*, 8.
60. See Rúa, *Grounded Identidad*.

No, not really, just because I know I'm Mexican—part Mexican—I just, like—I've never really—I mean I grew somewhat in that culture, but I never really grew up in it. And I never really lived in Mexico, so I—I don't like to call myself Mexican because I'm not—I don't consider myself—like my dad—he's Mexican. But to say that I am—no, I always emphasize just the Hispanic.

Interestingly, Alicia also associates a sense of place and localness with a Mexican identity. This notion of locality precludes Alicia from claiming a "Mexican" identity because she does not locate herself entirely in the place and culture of Mexico. Alicia explains that she is "part Mexican." However, because she considers herself fully a part of New Mexico, she aligns herself with the term "Hispanic."

Mexicana-Nuevomexicana Sylvia's alignment with the term "Hispanic" also conveys an association with northern New Mexico, but she reveals her use of the term as a strategy to avoid discrimination. Sylvia lowers her voice as she speaks to me and explains,

Here, especially since it's more . . . Hispanic based, they always talk about Mexicans and wetbacks and blah, blah, blah, blah. I don't really tell too many people, except, like, my close friends, that I'm half, that my father's from Mexico because I—I'm embarrassed, I guess. I don't wanna be made fun of, 'cause it gets made fun of—thrown around a lot here.

Sylvia was born and lived in Tucumcari, New Mexico, until she was in high school. Sylvia, her sister, and her mother moved to Las Vegas (one hour away from Tucumcari) during her senior year. As a "newcomer" to Las Vegas she already knew she was viewed as an "outsider" because she was not a native Las Vegas Hispanic. Sylvia married a local Las Vegas Nuevomexicano soon after high school, and, because her in-laws were from a well-known West Las Vegas family, she became associated with them. Sylvia continues, "Las Vegas is also very prejudiced in their own way, except now, I'm no longer the minority. I'm part of the majority. They don't know that I'm half-Hispanic—I mean half-Mexican. . . . I guess that's why I don't disclose it very often." The horizontal hierarchies of Latinidad are made visible in Sylvia's description of navigating identity in Las Vegas. Sylvia's narrative illustrates that the term "Hispanic" is not a neutral term, not simply related to pride of place in New Mexico. Sylvia speaks of engaging in Rúa's process of "colando-ing,"[61] in which individuals

---

61. Rúa, "Colao Subjectivities," 122.

emphasize different elements of their identities depending on different circumstances. Often, identities are "aguao" or "cargao" as a reaction to instances of racialization. Sylvia hesitates to disclose her Mexican heritage as a result of this racialization in Las Vegas. The axes of power related to multiplicity and heterogeneity are apparent in the ways in which Sylvia positions herself in relationship to Las Vegas Hispanics and in the ways in which she is positioned by the Las Vegas Hispanic community.

Aside from these complex place-based associations, "Hispanic" also represents cultural hybridity and difference. Consider Antonio's words: "Hispanic to me means half-blooded. You have one parent from Mexico and then the other from here. . . . It means somebody—yeah, who has like half—that has like, either like New Mexican blood and Mexican blood, you know?" Antonio's description of his identification with "Hispanic" actually addresses both place (through his use of "here") and the coexistence of multiple identities. Antonio acknowledges that his identity contains different cultural components, and he asserts that "Hispanic" denotes these distinct pieces. Adrian attributes a similar meaning to "Hispanic." He states, "I would say I'm half Mexican and half Hispanic. My dad's Mexican. I would just say Hispanic." To Adrian, "Hispanic" represents "the half and half." Similarly, Verónica explains, "I'm Hispanic. My mom is Hispanic and my dad is Mexico." Verónica seeks an identity term that captures Mexico and her mother's Hispanic world, and she finds this through the term "Hispanic." For Verónica, the term allows her to embrace both parents' cultures.

Rolando's conceptualization of "Hispanic" also allows him to honor both of his parents' backgrounds. Rolando reflects,

> I usually just say Hispanic. It's the easiest. It's kind of all-encompassing is what I see it as. . . . If they are interested, I'll give them the rundown: New Mexican Hispanic and then Mexican, half and half, and depending on . . . obviously if you are talking to someone from New Mexico they know the difference. . . . I view it as all-encompassing, so it's not like an omission on my part or anything like that.

Rolando's vision of "Hispanic" functions somewhat panethnically in his use of the phrase "all-encompassing." Yet, his idea of all-encompassing is still infused with specificity. He explains that it encompasses both the New Mexican Hispanic and the Mexican. Additionally, Rolando's reference to a New Mexican "knowing the difference" highlights the fluency in inter-Latino/a/x cultural knowledge that Rolando perceives New Mexicans to possess. Like Cárdenas's notion of a "Latina/o matrix of intelligibility," Rolando cites a

Nuevomexicano/a/x matrix of intelligibility referencing "local regimes of recognition regarding Latinidad."[62] He acknowledges New Mexicans' proficiency in reading his cultural difference. Rolando concludes his remarks about his identity by exclaiming, "I'm both! But I'm neither. I couldn't say I'm one." The fact that Rolando resists picking one term over the other illustrates the utility that he attributes to the term "Hispanic." Aparicio finds that a number of her participants choose the term "Latino" for many of the same reasons that my participants choose the term "Hispanic." They view the term as "a true reflection of who they are"[63] without having to choose. For Rolando, "Hispanic" allows him to embrace the tensions and contradictions in being both, neither, in-between, and half and half. The Mexicano/a/x-Nuevomexicano/a/x resemantification of "Hispanic" also rewrites the term and connects it in new and hybrid ways to the unique life experiences of the Mexicano/a/x-Nuevomexicanos/as/xs.

CONCLUDING THOUGHTS: PRODUCTIVE DISJUNCTURES AND IDENTITY (RE)PRODUCTIONS

In a May 23, 2018, episode of the NPR and Futuro Media podcast *Latino USA* titled "Of Bloodlines and Conquistadors," journalist María Hinojosa describes identity in northern New Mexico. She states,

> In northern New Mexico, being Hispanic means something a little different than what we might think of in the rest of the country. In fact, most people here use the term Hispano instead. Hispano is an identity that is specific to northern New Mexico and southern Colorado. It's people who see themselves as descendants of Spanish settlers, basically having a direct lineage to Spain.[64]

Hinojosa attempts to "translate" northern New Mexico Hispanic identity for a national, primarily Latino/a/x, audience. It seems she begins by referencing the panethnic and homogenizing notion of Hispanic as "what we might think of in the rest of the country," although that statement in itself essentializes Latino/a/x identity by assuming "we" all think the same. Next, although her effort acknowledges specificity and place-based identity formations, her explanation erases the historical political meanings around "Hispano" and

---

62. Cárdenas, *Constituting Central American-Americans*, 113.
63. Aparicio, "Intimate (Trans)Nationals," 282.
64. Hinojosa and Freleng, "Of Bloodlines and Conquistadors."

perpetuates static and one-dimensional perceptions of identity in northern New Mexico. Ultimately, there is no flow—no movement—in her description.

The Mexicano-Nuevomexicano families, and specifically the Mexicano/a/x-Nuevomexicano/a/x subjects, challenge notions of fixed identities, binary categories, and neutral identity terms. The familial disjunctures, as well as the semantic inversion of existing identity terms, allow us to see the constant dynamic (re)productions of cultural identities within the Mexicano-Nuevomexicano families. Hinojosa's words do not allude to this complexity, but instead recur to tired narratives about New Mexican Spanish identity that erase our relational language experiences and cultural hybridities. The convergences and divergences between meanings about identity and difference also illustrate the continued activation of Latinidad in the Mexicano-Nuevomexicano families through horizontal hierarchies. Amidst the acceptance and rejection of terms and definitions, the Mexicano-Nuevomexicano family members are actively participating in the co-construction of meaning and the production of inter-Latino/a/x knowledge, even if this knowledge creates a landscape of disjunctures. It is within the disjunctures and the contradictions that we gain significant insight into the processes and language experiences from which the dynamic terms for Mexicano/a/x-Nuevomexicano/a/x cultural identities emerge.

CHAPTER 5

"The Spanglish Lives We Live"

Reframing New Mexican Spanish through Spanglish and Contemplating Ethnolinguistic Futures

> I became trilingual. I was learning the Spanish that my father wanted us to learn, the New Mexican Spanish of my community, and English at school.
> —Mari Luci Jaramillo, *Madam Ambassador*

In a recent *New York Times* article, northern New Mexico garnered the national spotlight. The headline from the April 2023 article reads, "New Mexico Is Losing a Form of Spanish Spoken Nowhere Else on Earth: A dialect from the state's earliest Spanish-speaking settlers has endured for over 400 years in the state's remote mountain villages. But its time may be running out."[1] The author, Simon Romero, profiles the Spanish spoken in northern New Mexico, or Traditional New Mexican Spanish,[2] and contemplates its future. Emphasizing its unlikely survival over the course of several centuries, the article explains,

> For more than 400 years, these mountains have cradled a form of Spanish that today exists nowhere else on earth. Even after the absorption of their lands into the United States in the 19th century, generations of speakers somehow kept the dialect alive, through poetry and song and the everyday exchanges on the streets of Hispanic enclaves scattered throughout the region.[3]

Romero underscores the experience of language shift and makes clear the disassociation between younger generations of Nuevomexicanos/as/xs and the

---

1. Romero, "New Mexico Is Losing."
2. Bills and Vigil, *Spanish Language of New Mexico*.
3. Romero, "New Mexico Is Losing."

traditional dialect. The article concludes with two opinions. First, the article quotes Taos educator and writer Larry Torres. Torres asserts, "The language absolutely will survive. . . . It may not be the same language that our ancestors recognized, but we're using a form of 15th century Spanish with 21st century English."[4] A slightly different opinion about the future of northern New Mexican Spanish is given by linguist Mark Waltermire. He states, "It is hard to see a path forward for the dialect—which does not mean Spanish will disappear from New Mexico. . . . It's just being replaced."[5] Waltermire explains that with the arrival of recent Mexican immigrants, northern New Mexican Spanish is being replaced by Mexican Spanish. After the article's publication, numerous friends, colleagues, and family members shared the article with me and on social media. Nuevomexicano/a/x family and friends in particular expressed a sense of "feeling seen," and articulated pride in the attention our homeland and home language was receiving. Yet, in considering the future of northern New Mexican Spanish, the article elides the dynamic zones of encuentro that inform this future. The article depicts a binary of northern New Mexican Spanish versus Mexican Spanish without accounting for the complex Mexicano/a/x-Nuevomexicano/a/x meeting places. In this chapter, I would like to offer a type of counternarrative to the *New York Times* article by exploring the ideologies around northern New Mexican Spanish and the translanguaging practice of Spanglish in the Mexicano-Nuevomexicano context.

In what follows, I unpack the crucial role of English, and the ideologies that surround it, in constructing discourses about New Mexican Spanish. A fascinating finding that resonates throughout all the interviews is that the majority of the participants describe New Mexican Spanish by invoking the presence of English. This invocation is mostly viewed as negative. Just as Spanish has a long-standing presence in New Mexico, English also has a long-standing presence in New Mexican Spanish.[6] My data suggest that contemporary definitions of New Mexican Spanish based on the Mexicano/a/x-Nuevomexicano/a/x narratives define New Mexican Spanish through the term Spanglish.[7] All participants in one way or another equate the use of English and Spanglish with New Mexican Spanish. These descriptions often reflect

---

4. Romero, "New Mexico Is Losing."
5. Romero, "New Mexico Is Losing."
6. See Bills and Vigil, *Spanish Language of New Mexico*; and Lipski, *Varieties of Spanish*.
7. In a subsequent section in this chapter, I define "Spanglish" more in-depth. However, I would like to call attention to the fact that the term itself is contested. Otheguy and Stern, "On So-Called Spanglish," 85, reject the use of the term because "there is no objective justification for the term, and because it expresses an ideology of exceptionalism and scorn." Yet, Zentella, "Plenary Address," and Urciuoli, "Whose Spanish?," insist that the term "Spanglish" should be respected and captures the lived experiences of US Latinos/as/xs.

Zentella's "Spanglish bashing." The connection between the presence of English in New Mexican Spanish and the ideologies that accompany this influence not only contribute one more dimension to ideologies around authenticity (i.e., New Mexican Spanish isn't real Spanish due to the presence of English) but also reframe definitions of Traditional New Mexican Spanish. This is notable because it speaks to a resemantifying of New Mexican Spanish based on contact with English, rather than popular characterizations of New Mexican Spanish as an archaic and isolated variety. This chapter has two parts. The first examines Mexicano-Nuevomexicano families' characterizations of New Mexican Spanish as analogous to Spanglish. I then explore ideas around the intergenerational transmission of Spanglish within the families. This first part draws on the Mexicano/a/x-Nuevomexicano/a/x participants' responses to questions that ask them to characterize their Spanish, their family members' Spanish, and any differences or similarities that they note between family members' Spanish varieties. The second part of this chapter contemplates Mexicano/a/x-Nuevomexicano/a/x ethnolinguistic futures in terms of New Mexican Spanish and introduces the concept of "linguistic querencias" as a way to think about these futures.

SOME NOTES ABOUT NEW MEXICAN SPANISH, SPANGLISH, AND TRANSLANGUAGING

My purpose in this discussion is not to provide a descriptive analysis of New Mexican Spanish or Spanglish, but instead to map out how the Mexicano-Nuevomexicano families define these terms. Nevertheless, I would like to highlight a few relevant features of both New Mexican Spanish and Spanglish to better understand the implications of equating New Mexican Spanish with Spanglish. I addressed the feature of archaisms in Traditional New Mexican Spanish in the introduction with Vergara Wilson's 2015 overview.[8] Here, I revisit the frequent popular description of New Mexican Spanish as "archaic" and as "Spanish of sixteenth-century Spain."[9] Bills and Vigil address this characterization:

> It merits explicit mention that New Mexican Spanish is, of course, Spanish. It shares with all other varieties of Spanish the overwhelming stock of its lexical, grammatical, and phonological features. These features were passed

---

8. Vergara Wilson, "Panorama of Traditional."
9. Bills and Vigil, *Spanish Language of New Mexico*, 14.

down across many generations from the fifteenth-century inhabitants of the Iberian peninsula. New Mexican Spanish is "archaic" in this sense, just as all Spanish dialects are. However, retentions from earlier periods are typically classified as "archaisms" only when they remain in one variety of the language after they have disappeared in another variety that the classifier accepts as the "correct" or "standard" variety. Because of its history of relative seclusion, New Mexican Spanish is often characterized as highly "archaic" in this restricted sense.[10]

The Mexicano-Nuevomexicano families have already emphasized some of the most common archaisms in the preceding narratives. These include Andrea's mention of the term "calzones" for "pants"; Pía's mention of "silleta" for "chair"; the morphological archaism of "truje" instead of the more common "traje" mentioned by Gabriela and Luis; Verónica's mention of "lonas" for "jeans"; and the stigmatized archaisms of "asina" and "cuasi" mentioned by the Navarros. Interestingly, both "asina" and "cuasi" are documented in other geographic contexts of Mexican American and Mexican Spanish.[11] The phonological feature of the aspiration of /s/ in both of these contexts, represented by the letter "j" in "cuaji" and "ajina," is, however, unique to New Mexico.

Yet, Bills and Vigil make clear that "you'll find in New Mexican Spanish just as many or more 'new' forms as 'archaic' forms."[12] They highlight specific internal innovations or "the independent development of the language by means of internal resources."[13] They state that these innovations generally occurred in response to new concepts and circumstances. They continue, "Connections with the mainstream evolution in Spanish were too weak for the New Mexicans to keep pace with parallel changes, permitting these homegrown linguistic adaptations to take root and thrive."[14] I emphasized some of these adaptations in the lexical elicitation activity, with the variables "bat" and "turkey" and the New Mexican variants of "ratón volador" and "ganso de la tierra." Words like "globo" for "light bulb" and "chopos" for "slippers" are also independent developments within New Mexico.[15] Other "new" forms are those words influenced by Nahuatl. For example, Verónica's reference to her mother's use of "cajete" falls under this category of a Nahuatlalism.

---

10. Bills and Vigil, "Ashes to Ashes," 49.
11. Lipski, *Varieties of Spanish*, 94, 97.
12. Bills and Vigil, *Spanish Language of New Mexico*, 15.
13. Bills and Vigil, *Spanish Language of New Mexico*, 15.
14. Bills and Vigil, *Spanish Language of New Mexico*, 15.
15. Bills and Vigil, *Spanish Language of New Mexico*.

In addition to certain archaisms, internal innovations, and indigenous influence, the nearly two hundred years of contact between Spanish and English in New Mexico contributes to the feature that is the central focus of this section. The influence of English on New Mexican Spanish is almost exclusively limited to "the lexical inventory,"[16] and it is these words that carry the weight of "incorrectness" and "inauthenticity" for the Mexicano/a/x-Nuevomexicano/a/x subjects. We have already heard mention of some of these uses when Pía mentions the loanwords "mopear" and "telefón," in Carolina's critique of her father's use of "Crismes" for "Christmas," in Edna's mention of the semantic extension "línea," and in Edna and Milagros's mention of the loanwords "troca" and "queque" later in this chapter. When referencing the term "Spanglish," all of my participants denote loanwords and/or code-switching between English and Spanish as the most common elements that define the practice. For example, Rose's Nuevomexicano husband, Mike, describes Spanglish as the following: "I'll be having a conversation with you, but I'm saying stuff in English, and then in Spanish, you know? A few words here and there in Spanish, or a few words here and there in English."

I have previously used the phrase "translanguaging practice of Spanglish," and I want to be clear that I am categorizing "Spanglish" under the larger umbrella of translanguaging. I draw from Ofelia García in defining translanguaging as "multiple discursive practices in which bilinguals engage in order to make sense of their bilingual worlds. Translanguaging therefore goes beyond what has been termed code-switching . . . although it includes it, as well as other kinds of bilingual language use."[17] Translanguaging encourages a perspective that begins with "the meaning-making of racialized bilingual communities"[18] rather than a code-centric view of language. Despite these theoretical considerations around translanguaging, it is important to note that often my participants do utilize the term "code-switching" and subscribe to views of their linguistic practices that are rigidly categorized as belonging to either Spanish or English. These viewpoints reflect ideologies of "double monolingualism" and Lippi-Green's standard language ideology. García and Sánchez explain that language scholars also often focus on linguistic features first, rather than on the larger discursive context of the Latino/a/x bilingual speaker: "Traditionally, bilingual language use has been studied from the perspective of the language itself, and not of its speakers, leading scholars to characterize bilingual speech as reflecting language contact." [19]Although I do

---

16. Bills and Vigil, "Ashes to Ashes," 54.
17. García, *Bilingual Education*, 45.
18. N. Flores, "Foreword," xix.
19. García and Sánchez, "Making of the Language," 31.

not subscribe to privileging linguistic features or notions of language contact over the broader ethnolinguistic realities of the speaker, in my analysis I honor the ways in which my participants characterize their linguistic behaviors and those of their families. These characterizations often include notions of language contact and/or code-centric views of this behavior. When discussing Spanglish in the context of New Mexican Spanish and English influence, I do believe it is helpful to describe the contact-induced speech phenomena that occur in the contact situation between English and Spanish in New Mexico. Thus, I do describe this contact phenomena as components of Spanglish language practices, but I do not engage in an isolated analysis of these phenomena that is decontextualized from the broader Mexicano-Nuevomexicano ethnolinguistic context.

These contact phenomena are not unique to the New Mexico context. Lipski outlines these phenomena as lexical borrowings, translated idiomatic expressions (or calques), and code-switching. Semantic loans or semantic calques are also included among these phenomena.[20] Otheguy and García elaborate on the use of neologisms and add an additional layer to the consideration of loanwords as a necessary phenomenon due to new cultural concepts.[21] Lipski explains that "in the context of English-Spanish bilingualism, all three phenomena have at times been referred to as Spanglish, although each is found in some form or another in every bilingual community in the world, past and present."[22] Bills and Vigil refer to these phenomena in the New Mexican context as "anglicisms."[23] The New Mexico Colorado Spanish Survey focuses attention most centrally on code-switching and lexical borrowings. These are also the features that the Mexicano-Nuevomexicano families commonly connect to New Mexican Spanish. However, code-switching most definitely dominates their discourses about Spanglish in New Mexico. This is significant because code-switching has often been associated with negative language ideologies.

Returning to the disparaging opinions about Spanglish highlighted previously by Zentella, she states that "second-generation Latin@s are accused of not knowing Spanish or English and of corrupting both."[24] She cites accusations of bilingual behavior signifying semilingualism and alingualism[25] and narrow views of bilinguals as "ideal" or "balanced."[26] However, over forty

---

20. See Haugen, "Analysis of Linguistic Borrowing," 214, 219.
21. Otheguy and García, "Convergent Conceptualizations."
22. Lipski, *Varieties of Spanish*, 224.
23. Bills and Vigil, *Spanish Language of New Mexico*, chapter 10.
24. Zentella, "Latin@ Languages and Identities," 328.
25. Skutnabb-Kangas, *Bilingualism or Not?*
26. Weinreich, *Languages in Contact.*

years of sociolinguistic research has affirmed that the abilities to code-switch, both intersententially and intrasententially, demonstrate tremendous skill and ability in both languages without violating grammatical rules in either language.[27] Although these studies offer definitive linguistic proof of the cognitive abilities of bilinguals in both languages, dominant language ideologies both outside and inside of US Latino/a/x communities are often still overridden with negative perceptions of Spanglish and code-switching in particular.

With a clearer understanding of what constitutes New Mexican Spanish and the translanguaging practice of Spanglish, we can better understand the implications of equating New Mexican Spanish with Spanglish. As we have seen, the narratives of the Mexicano/a/x-Nuevomexicano/a/x subjects invoke the English influence in New Mexican Spanish (and examples of it) more than any other feature of New Mexican Spanish mentioned above. Although certain archaic and uniquely innovative features of New Mexican Spanish were mentioned by Mexicano/a partners, often it was only after several follow-up questions, usually regarding their Nuevomexicano/a partners' grandparents, aunts, uncles, or parents. For example, when I asked Mexicano José Luis about his communication with Nuevomexicanos/as/xs, he explains,

> El español que hablan aquí es como las canciones que cantan, las mexicanas; nomás las arreglan como ellos quieren, pero no, no se parece en nada. Es lo que decimos nosotros, que hablan como dicen ellos, el spanglish que hablas tú, y es muy diferente, o sea casi el 100 por ciento. Nosotros no les entendemos ni el español a muchos . . . porque hablan puras tonterías, hablan puras . . . ahí lo hablan mitad en español y mitad inglés, y lo que hablan ellos es muy diferente a lo que sabemos nosotros.

> [The Spanish they speak here is like the songs they sing, the Mexican songs; they just arrange them however they want, but they don't sound anything like the original. It's what we say about how they speak, the Spanglish that you speak, and it is very different, like 100 percent different. We don't even understand much of their Spanish . . . because they speak pure nonsense, they speak pure . . . there they speak half in Spanish and half English, and what they speak is very different from what we know.]

---

27. Gumperz and Hernández-Chávez, "Cognitive Aspects of Bilingual Communication"; Valdés, "Social Interaction and Code-Switching Patterns"; Poplack, "Sometimes I'll Start a Sentence"; Poplack and Sankoff, "Code-Switching"; Lipski, "Linguistic Aspects"; Otheguy, García, and Fernández, "Transferring, Switching, and Modeling"; Zentella, *Growing Up Bilingual*; Torres Cacoullos and Travis, *Bilingualism in the Community*; and Bessett and Carvalho, "Structure of US Spanish."

However, a few moments later, I ask about the communication with his in-laws, and he states,

> Con mi suegra y sus hermanos, siempre hablaban ellos hablaban muy bien español, muy bien. Y las dos personas que le estoy hablando que yo trabajé, nunca mixteaban[28] el español y el inglés, nunca; porque ellos crecieron, son nacidos aquí pero ellos crecieron hablando el español, ellos sí sabían. No como las generaciones . . . más jóvenes. Sí, o sea ya estas generaciones de ahorita no saben nada, la mayoría.

> [With my mother-in-law and her brothers and sisters, they always spoke very good Spanish, very good. And the two people I work with that I was telling you about, they never mixed Spanish and English, never; because they grew up, they were born here, but they grew up speaking Spanish, they did know it. Not like the younger generations. Yeah, I mean this generation today doesn't know anything, the majority.]

For the Mexicano/a partners, the first association they tend to make with New Mexican Spanish is an oftentimes incomprehensible mixture with English. Their perceptions perpetuate negative ideologies about mixing Spanish and English. The fact that they identify a "good" Spanish that does not mix Spanish and English only with older generations points to Spanglish as the contemporary indicator of New Mexican Spanish. Indeed, the lexical elicitation activity illustrates that, at least at the time of the activity, less than half of the Mexicano/a/x-Nuevomexicano/a/x subjects produce any of the Nuevomexicano "archaic" variants for the lexical items. This, perhaps, fulfils Bills and Vigil's prediction about the disappearance of Traditional New Mexican Spanish and is most definitely consistent with Waltermire's research and Del Angel Guevara's study.[29] Undoubtedly, the first frame of reference for the Mexicano/a/x-Nuevomexicano/a/x subjects regarding New Mexican Spanish is Spanglish.

CONSTRUCTING AN EQUATION: NEW MEXICAN SPANISH EQUALS SPANGLISH

Verónica describes New Mexican Spanish as "Spanish with a spin to it." Consistently, the Mexicano/a/x-Nuevomexicanos/as/xs define this "spin" as the

---

28. Interestingly, José Luis employs a loanword with "mixtear."
29. See Bills and Vigil, "Ashes to Ashes," as well as Waltermire, "Mexican Immigration," and Del Angel Guevara, "Returning to Northern New Mexico."

influence of English on New Mexican Spanish. This "spin," or the explicit mention of English and Spanish-English contact phenomena in defining New Mexican Spanish, is one way in which the Mexicano/a/x-Nuevomexicanos/as/xs construct parallels between New Mexican Spanish and Spanglish. Mexicano-Nuevomexicano Rolando Quintana from Santa Fe describes New Mexican Spanish below:

> New Mexico Spanish . . . it just doesn't flow as well. . . . A lot of people "speak Spanish," but they don't really speak Spanish. It's just, they know some words, and it's more Spanglish is what it is. . . . Throw in an "o" at the end of a lot of words and pretend it's Spanish! . . . And then there is New Mexico's own dialect too and vocabulary and some things that aren't even words anywhere else or even in the dictionary. . . . They think it sounds right, or they've grown up thinking it sounds right, but it's not even Spanish.

Rolando's perception of New Mexican Spanish is fascinating because, unlike many of the Mexicano-Nuevomexicano couples, he does not engage in a process of distinction between lexical items in order to differentiate New Mexican Spanish from Mexican Spanish. It is the presence of English that defines New Mexican Spanish for Rolando. He questions the validity of "New Mexico's own dialect" because of its lack of standardization and manifests the standard language ideology as well as the belief that New Mexico's Spanish is isolated and irrelevant.

These words, along with his description of "throw[ing] in an 'o,'" create a description of New Mexican Spanish as based in English.[30] He also references loanwords ("an English word with a Spanish ending") in his account. Likewise, Milagros talks of "typical New Mexican Spanish" as "just that mesh with English and Spanish and then, um, uh, I don't know. . . . Over here they have 'troca,' and then it's 'camión' or 'camioneta' or whatever it is there." Milagros again references a mesh or mix of English and Spanish particularly through loanwords like "troca." Edna offers a similar description:

> You know, so like my dad's Spanish is real, like—northern New Mexico is where they put a little bit of English in with their Spanish. Like, um, when they say "línea" or "queque" for "cake" you know, and stuff like that. And I used to talk like that, you know. I'm not going to, you know, say anything bad about it, but I used to talk like that and people used to look at me like, "What are you saying?"

---

30. These associations are consistent with Rodríguez-Ordóñez, McCrocklin, and Tiburcio's 2023 research, "Spanglish and Tex-Mex," on the ways in which Tex-Mex is being defined by Spanglish in the Rio Grande Valley in Texas.

It is interesting that Edna emphasizes that "she used to talk like that." When she refers to "people," she clarifies that she is talking about Mexicanos/as/xs. Edna's perceptions about her previous Spanish use, as well as Milagros's use of "here" and "there," allude to a notion of progress towards Mexican Spanish that, again, activates the ideologies of correctness and authenticity.

Antonio discusses the role of English in New Mexican Spanish in terms of direct translations. He explains,

> With like the Mexican, like they know what everything like translates to. Like they know how to translate things properly. But with the New Mexican Spanish, they just like, they put the literal meaning from English to Spanish . . . but with like Mexican . . . they know what to say properly. But with the New Mexican, they just put it the way they see it in English, that's the way they put it in Spanish.

Antonio equates New Mexican Spanish with a series of "improper" literal translations or calques.[31] The presence of English activates the ideology of correctness and, in this case, renders New Mexican Spanish as improper. Rolando, Milagros, Edna, and Antonio's descriptions all reveal the central role of English in defining New Mexican Spanish and the ways in which English activates the language ideologies that have been at the heart of this book.

In addition to referencing English directly and providing examples of contact features such as loanwords and calques, New Mexican Spanish and Spanglish are also connected through a specific set of descriptors. Angélica's father, Francisco, invokes these descriptors: "We got the lazy Spanish," explains Francisco. I repeat in an interrogatory tone, "The lazy Spanish?" He replies, "Yeah, everything is like the short word. . . . Like when you say, ah, . . . to say 'a chair' for them es 'una silla' y nosotros decimos 'sieta' . . . the lazy way." Francisco's description of New Mexican Spanish as "lazy" and "short" when compared to "them" or Mexicanos/as/xs is also consistent with notions of slowness attributed to New Mexican Spanish by the Mexicano/a/x-Nuevomexicanos/as/xs. All fifteen Mexicano/a/x-Nuevomexicanos/as/xs describe New Mexican Spanish as slower in comparison to Mexican Spanish. For example, Alicia states, "They speak it slower. . . . Yeah, like, I notice hearing my dad or my dad's family. They speak it fast, like, blah, blah, blah." Alejandro states something similar: "Mexican people usually speak faster and a lot more clear and fluent." Rolando also explains, "Someone who grew up in Mexico speaks Spanish

---

31. Literal translations from English to Spanish. See Otheguy, García, and Fernández, "Transferring, Switching, and Modeling"; Otheguy and García, "Convergent Conceptualizations"; and Lipski, *Varieties of Spanish*.

faster and turns it to more of a stream." Lastly, when Carolina recalls her Mexicana mother speaking with her paternal Nuevomexicana grandmother, she describes how she always spoke "a little bit faster still, but trying to let them catch up. Yeah, because hers is such a rapid pace that it's just, she was trying to let them catch up. She would speak and let them soak it in to see what she was saying. Then she would continue speaking."

I would like to bring together these ideas of New Mexican Spanish as lazy and slow with another descriptor: random. Recall Angélica's comparison between the Spanishes spoken by her two sides of the family. She states that New Mexicans "just put whatever words they had and made a new word." She elaborates a few minutes later with an image of mixing the languages up "like scrambled eggs." In a similar vein, Rolando explains New Mexican Spanish as "Throw in an 'o' at the end of a lot of words and pretend it's Spanish!"[32] Verónica explains the New Mexican Spanish of her maternal grandparents: "They would just put random words together." Lazy, slow, random. Not real Spanish. Just made up. All of these descriptions are consistent with ideologies regarding Spanglish. Consider these phrases: "lazy, sloppy, cognitively confused"; "a linguistic mish-mash"; "a deficient code spoken by deficient speakers." The preceding phrases are reported by Zentella in her exploration of "Spanglish bashing" as ways in which Spanglish and its speakers have been pejoratively characterized.[33] Although these parallel descriptions do not at any time utilize the term "English" or examples of contact phenomena between English and Spanish, they contribute to the construction of the synonymous relationship between Spanglish and New Mexican Spanish through underscoring analogous perceptions of these overlapping varieties.

SPANGLISH: THE LANGUAGE OF THE FUTURE?

One of the most fascinating implications of equating Spanglish with New Mexican Spanish is that it provides a reframing of the notions of "old" and "new." Generally, Spanglish is popularly viewed as a "new" phenomenon associated with young, US-born, second-generation Latinos/as/xs. Ilan Stavans's problematic monograph about Spanglish is entitled *Spanglish: The Making of a New American Language*. HBO Latino's 2008 series *Habla Ya* features multiple young Latinos/as/xs speaking about Spanglish. Even Zentella's seminal 1997 study of el bloque[34] highlights code-switching practices among the US-born

---

32. Here Rolando seems to be referencing Hill's notion of mock Spanish.
33. Zentella, "Latin@ Languages and Identities."
34. Zentella, *Growing Up Bilingual*.

Puerto Rican children in this New York neighborhood. From these and many other associations of Spanglish in popular culture, code-switching and other contact features are conceptualized as a "young" practice. Yet, consider the ways in which the Mexicano/a/x-Nuevomexicano/a/x subjects describe Spanglish in terms of "old" and "new." Upon my asking Mexicana-Nuevomexicana Angélica Loredo if she mixed Spanish and English, she responds that she does not mix the languages. When I asked her who in her life does this, she states, "Uh, my grandparents, mostly. You know and just older people." Interestingly, Angélica does not associate her own linguistic practices with this mixing, but instead associates these practices with older generations, namely, her paternal grandparents and their peers. Recall Verónica's words about "the old timers" using New Mexican Spanish: "My grandma and grandpa spoke what I call New Mexican Spanish, which is Spanglish." Again, a Mexicana-Nuevomexicana subject associates Spanglish practices with her grandparents. Alicia also attributes Spanglish/New Mexican Spanish use to her Nuevomexicano/a grandparents. When I asked her about the ways that different members of her family speak, she explains about her grandparents: "The difference is they use a lot of the English words, like the Spanglish, I guess. My grandpa—I heard him say 'elque' for elk." Alicia does not identify with these practices, but attributes them to an older generation.

Additionally, when she talks about New Mexican Spanish, she highlights her lack of familiarity with the "older" Traditional New Mexican Spanish. She explains,

> Because some of their Spanish I don't know because of the New Mexican Spanish, so some of the words I'm, like, what?—and then when they give me the other word then I'm, like, oh, ok. . . . And then my grandma—for "pants," says "calzones." So the first time she said that I'm, like, what? So it's just different ways like that, like I've heard them say. It's—now I hear it more and, like, I can pick it out. But it's still kind of, like, huh?

Notably, we see that what has long been considered an "old" archaic Spanish variety in New Mexico is actually new for Alicia, whereas Spanglish is something with which she is familiar and associates with older Nuevomexicanos/as/xs. Thus, we have an interesting reversal: Spanglish is old and familiar, while older, "archaic," noncontact features of Traditional New Mexican Spanish are new and unfamiliar. The Mexicano/a/x-Nuevomexicano/a/x subjects' perceptions of New Mexican Spanish and Spanglish challenge a popular belief system about fixed generational categories and ages associated with Spanglish practices.

With this "oldness" of Spanglish in mind, I address the implications of intergenerational transmission of Spanglish in New Mexico. The preceding narratives give us some indication that both the Mexicano/a/x-Nuevomexicanos/as/xs' Nuevomexicano/a grandparents and parents speak Spanglish. This calls attention to an intergenerational presence and persistence of Spanglish practices. Nicolás Navarro emphasizes this presence:

> Nosotros tenemos nuestra lengua aquí y lo llamamos Spanglish. Y podemos hablar español, le digo yo a mi esposa y at the same moment jump into English and jump back into Spanish y seguirle hablando en las dos idiomas como que si nada. Es nomás así es la cultura de nosotros acá y se dice uno munchas palabras totalmente son en inglés pero le ponemos el sonido del español.
>
> [We have our language here and we call it Spanglish. And we can speak Spanish, I tell my wife, and at the same moment jump into English and jump back into Spanish and continue speaking the two languages like nothing. It's just that that is how our culture is here and one says many words completely in English, but with a Spanish sound.]

Nicolás's use of the phrase "nuestra lengua" and of the deictic adverbs "aquí" and "acá" identify Spanglish with New Mexico and his community. He also references that his mother grew up linguistically the way he did, with both English and Spanish. For Nicolás, Spanglish is a source of language pride. He continues, "I call that a new language, I tell my wife either way no matter how you think about it, I tell her Spanglish is the new language of the future. . . . And they'll be seeing that a lot more I think in the future. Um, people are not going to be ashamed of, um, speaking Spanglish. . . . Our language reflects the Spanglish lives that we live." Nicolás establishes Spanglish as a long-standing linguistic code in his community and Nuevomexicano family. However, in his narrative above he also infuses the term with "newness" and predicts Spanglish as the language of the future. Yet, Nicolás's attitudes about Spanglish are not echoed by his daughter. Milagros explains, "No, I don't speak Spanglish. I just speak Spanish. . . . Spanish is an official language, not Spanglish." Nicolás's daughter does not include herself in her father's vision of "the Spanglish lives we live." In fact, Nicolás's daughter shuts down any notion of Spanglish being part of her linguistic future. Thus, intergenerational transmission of Spanglish seems to stop with Nicolás's daughters. Is this the case with all of the Mexicano/a/x-Nuevomexicanos/as/xs?

I ask the Mexicano/a/x-Nuevomexicanos/as/xs two questions that can, perhaps, illuminate the future of Spanglish and New Mexican Spanish in these families. The first question is if the Mexicano/a/x-Nuevomexicanos/as/xs characterize their Spanish as more Mexican or New Mexican. The overwhelming majority (86 percent) of the Mexicano/a/x-Nuevomexicanos/as/xs describe their Spanish as more Mexican. This finding, as well as the finding mentioned previously that the Mexicano/a/x-Nuevomexicanos/as/xs do not report knowing any New Mexican Spanish variants for the variables in the lexical elicitation activity, is consistent with Bills and Vigil's findings about the future of New Mexican Spanish and Waltermire's 2015 research.[35] Bills and Vigil explain, "The features in decline across the generations are frequently those that are particularly characteristic of Traditional Spanish. . . . These distinctive features are being replaced under the pressure of two forces: English on one side, and Mexican Spanish and Standard Spanish on the other."[36] According to the Mexicano/a/x-Nuevomexicanos/as/xs' responses, if we continue to equate Spanglish with New Mexican Spanish, not only are the more unique features being lost, but the New Mexican Spanish that is infused with contact features is also not being transmitted. Additionally, I ask the Mexicano/a/x-Nuevomexicanos/as/xs if they use Spanglish. The responses are rarely clear-cut "yes" or "no" answers. Angélica and Milagros do, however, respond with an emphatic "no" and voice negative perceptions about Spanglish. Rolando and Antonio also report that they do not use Spanglish, but they are both clear that they do not have any negative opinions about it. Edna does not report currently using Spanglish; however, she states that she "used to talk that way." Although Spanglish was part of her past, she does not consider Spanglish as part of her current linguistic repertoire.

The remaining nine Mexicano/a/x-Nuevomexicanos/as/xs report using Spanglish, but only under certain circumstances, and they often attribute notions of "incorrectness" to its use. For example, when I asked Alicia if she speaks Spanish to older people in her community, she responds, "More of, like, the Spanglish because—again, my bad habit comes out of where, like, they'll speak to me in Spanish and there I go, speaking in English." Alicia characterizes her mixing of languages[37] as a "bad habit." She uses Spanglish out of necessity, but it seems to be a practice she wishes she could correct. Similarly, Alejandro reports using Spanglish "not very often." He explains, "If we were having a conversation, whatever language we stuck to, was what we stuck to. And then with—I mean if we started talking about something else, then we'd switch it." Alejandro describes his language use as keeping English and Span-

---

35. Bills and Vigil, *Spanish Language of New Mexico*; and Waltermire, "Mexican Immigration."

36. Bills and Vigil, *Spanish Language of New Mexico*, 217–18.

37. Bürki, "El español en las películas," refers to this practice as asymmetrical bilingual discourse.

ish separate. Similarly, siblings Olivia and Adrian both characterize Spanglish as something used to joke around with family members. Olivia states that Spanglish is "just funny"; "it's not serious at all"; and, lastly, she states, "it's incorrect." Both Rosalinda and Alexa report using Spanglish in situations of lexical gaps. Rosalinda explains that she uses Spanglish "when I don't know a word." Alexa states, "Sometimes, like whenever I forget what to say in Spanish, I'll say it in English." None of these accounts exhibits the language pride that Nicolás Navarro demonstrates towards Spanglish. Carolina explains that she uses Spanglish among family and friends, but she clarifies, "I think it would be negative if I was talking to a Mexican." In this instance, Carolina's description of her Spanglish use disassociates Mexicanos/as/xs from Spanglish and, again, equates Spanglish with Nuevomexicano/a/x linguistic practices. Rose's description of her use of Spanglish departs from other Mexicano/a/x-Nuevomexicano/a/x accounts in that she emphasizes the normalcy and frequency of Spanglish practices in her home. However, her account does not necessarily display pride, because she ends her reflection with the evaluation that Spanglish is still "incorrect." Rose states, "We use it always—every time. All the day. All the time.... Actually, I think it—I don't think of it as so much a positive. I—but I don't see it as negative. I just don't think it's correct." The fact that Spanglish is "normal" and frequent in her home does not necessarily ensure that it is a practice that inspires pride.

INTERGENERATIONAL TRANSMISSION OF SPANGLISHES

Verónica also emphasizes the normalcy of Spanglish both in her childhood and in her present home with her children and husband. However, unlike Rose, she embraces Spanglish as "our language." The exchange below between myself, Verónica, and her Nuevomexicana mother illustrates this:

VERÓNICA: Spanglish—Spanglish—my—my grandma and grandpa used to speak, you know, "Emilia, ve afuera y agarra the can," you know? I mean it was just that whole mix of the Spanish and English. I—so I—that, to me, was normal.... So I didn't—that's all I got from—growing up, Spanglish, to me, was normal. I didn't know that it even was Spanglish. That's just—that's how they talked. That's how we grew up with. Spanglish is our language.
LG: Even your dad?
VERÓNICA: Oh, yeah, my dad does it all the time, I mean we all do, even my husband. We do the whole Spanglish thing. That's our language. That's our culture now.

JUANITA: That's why a lot of people don't know that Luis is Mexican.
VERÓNICA: Yeah, because he is able to do that so easily.

Verónica's account of her childhood affirms the intergenerational presence of Spanglish in her home. She also recognizes the reality of translanguaging and does not artificially divide languages into prescribed codes. This is consistent with García's concept of translanguaging:

> Our concept of translanguaging shifts the lens from cross-linguistic influence, proposing that what bilinguals do is to intermingle linguistic features that have hereto been administratively or linguistically assigned to a particular language or language variety. Translanguaging is thus the communicative norm of bilingual communities and cannot be compared to a prescribed monolingual use.[38]

Verónica's Mexicano father is even able to pass for Nuevomexicano because of his Spanglish abilities and the realities of his transculturation. The current strength of Spanglish in her home is also affirmed by her mentioning that her first-generation Mexicano husband also speaks Spanglish. It seems that Verónica and her family do, indeed, embody a vibrant present and future for Spanglish.

Yet, Verónica makes an important distinction between the Spanglish her Nuevomexicano/a grandparents spoke and the Spanglish she currently speaks in her home. She explains, "Because the Spanish that my grandma and grandpa had was very—it was already Spanglish, but it was like English words with Mexican mixed in it . . . but it really does come from an English root. . . . There were some words that were like only unique to here that we never heard them in Mexico." Verónica distinguishes her grandparents' Spanglish from the Spanglish she speaks with her husband and children. It is significant that Verónica invokes the existence of multiple Spanglishes. From a linguistic standpoint, it seems that she is associating the Spanglish of her Nuevomexicano/a grandparents with a form of code-switching that has English as its matrix language, whereas the Spanglish she identifies with has Spanish as its matrix language.[39] This distinction is important because it allows us to see the lack of an intergenerational transmission of the Spanglish of her grandparents and the manifestation of a different Spanglish that has more Spanish. Verónica's theorization contributes to the understanding of Spanglish

---

38. García, *Bilingual Education*, 51.
39. Muysken, "Code-Switching and Grammatical Theory."

as multiple. It highlights the understudied diversity of Spanglish within distinct US Latino/a/x communities. Zentella calls attention to the fact that some loanwords are more distributed than others throughout the country.[40] Escobar and Potowski also document the different distributions and uses of Spanish loanwords throughout the United States.[41] This work acknowledges that contact phenomena look different among different groups of US Latinos/as/xs. Additionally, Rodríguez-Ordóñez, McCrocklin, and Tiburcio find that Spanglish serves as an important bilingual practice in the Rio Grande Valley of Texas, yet "interpretations of Spanglish are dependent on interpretations of the relative values of English, Spanish, and (if different) Tex-Mex."[42] Interestingly, many of the participants in this study make a distinction between Tex-Mex and Spanglish and "deem Spanglish as a superior form of mixing languages. 'Tex-Mex' in contrast, was shown to be linked to a localized style of Spanglish and connected to a more informal way of speaking."[43] In the Rio Grande Valley, it seems that Latino/a/x perceptions of Tex-Mex are similar to those of New Mexican Spanish and New Mexican Spanglish. The conceptualization of Tex-Mex as a different form of Spanglish also contributes to the study of Spanglish diversity in the Latino/a/x US.

I propose that the distinction between Spanglishes speaks to the different language experiences in which they are embedded. We see that Verónica perceives code-switching to sound and feel different between older Nuevomexicanos/as/xs and her code-switching with her G1 husband. Therefore, the Spanglish of Verónica's second-contact generation Nuevomexicano/a grandparents is different from the Spanglish of a Mexicana-Nuevomexicana who identifies her Spanish strongly with Mexico and has married a first-generation Mexicano. Certainly, we cannot homogenize Spanglish. Zentella states that "Spanglish cannot be reduced to static dictionary entries; it is a creative and rule-governed way of speaking bilingually that is generated by and reflects living in two cultures."[44] Through Verónica's family we see that homogenous binaries between English and Spanish do not work in characterizing Nuevomexicano/a/x and Mexicano/a/x-Nuevomexicano/a/x Spanglish. Regardless of the Spanglish variety in the Mexicano/a/x-Nuevomexicano/a/x families, the translanguaging practice of Spanglish has been transmitted to Verónica and continues to be affirmed in her current household. Therefore, Spanglish is and is not a part of Verónica's future. The more English-based

---

40. Zentella, "Lexical Leveling."
41. Escobar and Potowski, *El español de los Estados Unidos*.
42. Rodríguez-Ordóñez, McCrocklin, and Tiburcio, "Spanglish and Tex-Mex," 69.
43. Rodríguez-Ordóñez, McCrocklin, and Tiburcio, "Spanglish and Tex-Mex," 69.
44. Zentella, "Dime con quién hablas," 33.

Spanglish of her Nuevomexicano/a grandparents is not part of her future linguistic repertoire. However, the more Spanish-based Spanglish of her parents, and of her current household, is the language of Verónica's future. Clearly, Spanglish is nuanced, with regional and generational differences. Rosa illustrates one example of more recent innovative work on multiple Spanglishes in his theorization around what he terms "inverted Spanglish" among US Latinos/as/xs of Mexican and Puerto Rican backgrounds in Chicago.[45] Examining the multiple Spanglishes among US Latinos/as/xs is an understudied area of research, and the Mexicano-Nuevomexicano family units can play an important role in advancing future work.

NEW ETHNOLINGUISTIC FUTURES

The attitudes expressed by Mexicano/a/x-Nuevomexicanos/as/xs about New Mexican Spanish and the fact that they mostly characterize their own Spanish as "Mexican" seems to suggest that the Mexicano/a/x-Nuevomexicano/a/x subjects may not be steering northern New Mexican Spanish into the future. This would seem to affirm the predictions made in the *New York Times* article and those made by Bills and Vigil, Travis and Villa, Waltermire, and Del Angel Guevara, among others.[46] However, in the spirit of the acts of agency, recovery, and maintenance from chapter 2, I propose a different vision that takes the Mexicano-Nuevomexicano zones of encuentro into account. Two recent interviews with Nuevomexicana Penélope of Española and Mexicana Pía of Las Vegas reveal a potential alternative trajectory.

Ten years after our initial pláticas, I met with Penélope in Española to reconnect and catch up. Initially, our conversation focused on the recent passing of her father; however, several minutes into the conversation, Penélope revealed new linguistic strategies she was implementing. She began by asking, "Do you know when you, when you came and you did your meeting with us and talking about words?" I nodded my head, and she continued, "I realized that we did give up a lot of our language so that they would understand what we're talking about. So I'm raising my grandson with old Spanish." Penélope references the influence that her Mexicano/a/x ex-husband and ex-suegros had on her Spanish use. Now that she is raising her grandson full-time,

---

45. Rosa, *Looking like a Language*.
46. Bills and Vigil, *Spanish Language of New Mexico*; Travis and Villa, "Language Policy and Language Contact"; Waltermire, "Mexican Immigration"; and Del Angel Guevara, "Returning to Northern New Mexico."

Penélope decides she wants to change course and recover the New Mexican Spanish that she feels she has lost. She explains further:

> I'm teaching him our words for things because I don't want him growing up with the Mexican ones. If he's gonna learn that somewhere, he's gonna learn it not from me.... And so I talk to him in half English, half Spanish, ... the way I grew up.... And I'm teaching Mexicans our words.... 'Cause my contractors are Mexican.... And I tell them if they ... wanna laugh at the word that you're saying, I tell them, "Mi palabra es propio," I'm telling you. And I take out my little dictionary and I tell 'em, you know, don't make fun of the language that we have because it's, it's true language.... It's very old Spanish.

Penélope's agency in determining a different linguistic future for herself and her grandson is deeply grounded in maintaining New Mexican Spanish. She also seems to be inverting a previous hierarchy regarding the hegemonic Mexican lexical items in her household, perhaps due to their dominance in her life with her ex-husband's family. Penélope takes on the role of advocate for revitalizing New Mexican Spanish in her life, as well as in that of her grandson, and even promotes it among Mexicanos/as/xs in her community. Her realization that she had "given up" a lot of her language precipitates an urgency to recover it.[47] This recovery process would not have been possible without the zones of encuentro created by her partnership with her Mexicano ex-husband. Penélope's actions work to combat the replacement of New Mexican Spanish by Mexican Spanish that Waltermire mentions in the *New York Times* article. Replacement is not a foregone conclusion.

Likewise, Mexicana Pía Loredo tells me of a shift in her language practices and language beliefs. Although we had maintained contact over social media, Pía and I had also not met in-person to catch up since 2013. When we met in her living room in Las Vegas, she was eager to share with me some new pedagogical strategies she was implementing in her classroom. Pía continues to work at the same elementary school; however, the school itself has relinquished its dual-language immersion status. Yet, Pía earned her state bilingual certification and was now able to have her own Spanish classroom, in which she provided the students with forty-five minutes of daily Spanish exposure. After sharing her experience taking courses about New Mexican Spanish in preparation for the New Mexico bilingual certification exam (La Prueba), Pía excitedly reveals,

---

47. This urgency mirrors that expressed in Arnold and Martínez-García, "Traditional New Mexican Spanish."

> Yo quedé enamorada del español de Nuevo México. Antes decía, "Qué mal hablan." Ahora digo, "Wow, ¡qué joya, qué emoción!" Yo estoy apasionada. . . . Yo no sé, es algo personal, es algo personal porque digo es parte de la cultura y yo lo vivo muy de cerca con mi suegro porque él habla así. Mi suegro tiene 90 años y aprendí yo las palabras.
>
> [I have fallen in love with New Mexican Spanish. Before, I would say, "They speak so badly here." But now I say, "Wow, what a treasure! How exciting!" I am so passionate. . . . I don't know, it's something personal, it's something personal because I say it's part of the culture and it's very close to me because my father-in-law speaks like this. My father-in-law is ninety years old, and I have learned his words.]

Pía conveys a complete transformation from her previous position on New Mexican Spanish. Whereas ten years prior she would worry about falling into bad habits or "esas cositas" with New Mexican Spanish and the ways in which she and her daughter could suffer ridicule in Mexico, Pía has now become a champion for New Mexican Spanish. She continues,

> Entonces yo lo que trato de hacer con mis estudiantes es meterle un poco en la cultura de sus abuelos, el idioma de ellos. Me compré el diccionario de Rubén Cobos y yo lo leo y digo cuántas palabras, mi mamá en México, mi mamá usaba ciertas palabras y yo estoy, no sé cómo expresarlo. Francisco me dice, "Tú estás apasionada con esto" y le digo "Francisco, ¿tú has escuchado esta palabra?"
>
> [What I try to do is expose my students to the culture of their grandparents, their language. I bought myself the Rubén Cobos dictionary and I read it and I say how so many words, my mom in Mexico, she used some of these words and I'm just, I don't know how to express it. Francisco says to me, "You are so passionate about this," and then I ask him, "Francisco, have you heard this word before?"]

Pía now counts on her Nuevomexicano husband as a linguistic resource. In our plática ten years prior, Pía remarks to Francisco that she has seen a difference in his Spanish in the time they have been together: "Quitaste muchas palabras de tu vocabuario que tenías antes y adoptó las que nosotros usamos. Yo sí he visto el crecimiento de él en un español yo creo un poco más pulido." [You've eliminated a lot of the vocabulary that you had before and he replaced it with words that we use. I have seen his Spanish grow and develop into a more polished Spanish.] Pía has now reversed her perspective on New Mexican Spanish. She takes the initiative to educate herself with the *Dictionary of New Mexico and Southern Colorado Spanish* by Rubén Cobos. Pía appears to have achieved a new "conocimiento."

Anzaldúa defines "conocimiento" as a "deep awareness"[48] and as "the aspect of consciousness urging you to act on knowledge gained."[49] Pía most surely acts on this knowledge in her classroom. She shares, "Yo estoy haciendo con mis estudiantes de segundo año un diccionario nuevomexicano para ellos, y yo veo que los niños se emocionan porque dicen, 'Sí mi abuelito usa esa palabra.'" [I'm having my second-year students make New Mexican Spanish dictionaries, and I see that the kids get really excited because they say, "My grandpa uses that word."'] Pía then shows me examples of these dictionaries and the drawings that she has the students make to accompany the New Mexican Spanish words. Pía expresses joy in what she terms "rescatar esto de ellos" [recover what is theirs]. She is acting to preserve a local treasure and has taken on this task amidst a sense of urgency gained from her "conocimiento." She explains that the curriculum provided to the Spanish teachers has nothing about Nuevomexicano/a/x culture, and she states, "Yo le pongo de mi cosecha" [I give it my own touch]. Pía takes the extra time to gain inter-Latino/a/x linguistic knowledge to prepare her own curriculum. She also tells of her Mexicana-Nuevomexicana daughter gaining a new appreciation for New Mexican Spanish as she has become closer with her Nuevomexicano grandfather and has a job that requires her to assist many Las Vegas ancianos.

Pía's path to conocimiento would not have opened up if not for the Mexicano-Nuevomexicano spaces of encuentro in her life. These zones of encuentro also make possible both Pía's and Penélope's transformations. Their ongoing work to break down linguistic hierarchies can be viewed as a type of "translanguaging pedagogy." García explains,

> Used as pedagogy, translanguaging has the potential to release ways of speaking of Latinos that have been constrained by national languages and ideologies of the modern/colonial world system in which both the United States and Spain participate. In so doing, translanguaging as pedagogy can redress the power of "English" and "Spanish," as constructed by the United States, Spain, and Latin America.[50]

---

48. Anzaldúa, "(Un)Natural Bridges, (Un)Safe Spaces," 5.
49. Anzaldúa, "Now Let Us Shift . . . ," 577.
50. García, "US Spanish and Education," 74.

Pía and Penélope are both enacting pedagogical strategies that break down dominant language ideologies around standard language, correctness, and the hierarchies between a sense of "real" Mexican Spanish and New Mexican Spanish. Mexicana Pía and Nuevomexicana Penélope construct parallel paths towards creating a liberatory space for New Mexican Spanish. I propose that these spaces are also zones of encuentro and that they provide an alternative vision for the future of New Mexican Spanish. I am not proposing that Pía and Penélope's efforts will completely ensure the survival of New Mexican Spanish in their families and communities, but their actions do shed light on the construction of spaces of recovery that infuse daily lived experiences with New Mexican Spanish and translanguaging practices.

CONCLUDING THOUGHTS: TRADITION AND LINGUISTIC QUERENCIAS

Larry Torres declares in the *New York Times* article that New Mexican Spanish will "absolutely survive," but also clarifies that it will be different and, perhaps, unrecognizable to our ancestors because it is "15th century Spanish with 21st century English."[51] Torres's remarks highlight the translanguaging element that New Mexican Spanish has always had. Subscribing to the myth that New Mexican Spanish has remained the same for four hundred years perpetuates a notion of "tradition" that reinforces what AlSayaad terms a "temporally situated concept" and a "static authoritative legacy."[52] Because of New Mexico's colonial and postcolonial histories, New Mexican Spanish has always marked "the history of survival within relationships of unequal power and domination"[53] through its hybridity. The Mexicano/a/x-Nuevomexicano/a/x equation of New Mexican Spanish with Spanglish is actually a more accurate representation of New Mexican Spanish's linguistic and sociopolitical history than notions of geographic isolation and an untouched archaic variety. Penélope and Pía provide us with new ways to keep New Mexican Spanish present, even amidst an increased Mexicano/a/x presence. These innovative approaches lead us away from reductive thinking that limits Nuevomexicanos/as/xs as the only speakers and caretakers of New Mexican Spanish. AlSayaad explains that "tradition does not come to an end when a highly circumscribed utopia ceases to exist; tradition is what we make and sustain everyday and everywhere."[54]

---

51. Romero, "New Mexico Is Losing."
52. AlSayaad, "End of Tradition," 23.
53. Lowe, *Immigrant Acts*, 67.
54. AlSayaad, "End of Tradition," 26.

Problematizing the "traditional" in Traditional New Mexican Spanish allows for reversals in course, acts of recovery, and new conceptualizations of "old" and "new" languaging practices.

When Penélope reflects on her wishes for her grandson, she states, "I want him to have that sense of community. . . . I want him to know this is my valley. This is my place." This desire for her grandson to feel a sense of home and belonging in Española illustrates a desire for querencia. Recall Arellano's notion of "querencia" as a "love of place."[55] By consciously working to expose her grandson to New Mexican Spanish, Penélope also advances a sense of "linguistic querencia." I suggest that linguistic querencia connects linguistic practices, including translanguaging practices, to a sense of place and home. I do not propose that linguistic querencias in New Mexico only consist of a connection to New Mexican Spanish but instead that they embody the shared linguistic homeplaces of diverse languaging practices that include the use of Mexican Spanish, New Mexican Spanish, English, and all the ethnolinguistic crossings that occur within and between these practices. Pía and Penélope in a sense have become the caretakers of these linguistic querencias. Their linguistic "homemaking" provides a vision for the ethnolinguistic futures of Mexicanos/as/xs, Nuevomexicanos/as/xs, and Mexicano-Nuevomexicanos/as/xs. It is important to note that linguistic revitalization and language recovery in New Mexico involves Mexicanos/as/xs, as well as Nuevomexicanos/as/xs. However, Pía's role in linguistic querencias shows us that it is not about Mexicanos/as/xs or Mexican Spanish replacing New Mexican Spanish or Nuevomexicanos/as/xs. Mexicano-Nuevomexicano zones of encuentro illustrate that northern New Mexico ethnolinguistic futures rely on inter-Latino/a/x knowledge production through a linguistic Latinidad.

---

55. Arellano, *Enduring Acequias*, 17.

CONCLUSION

Herencia, Heritage, and Latino/a/x Homes

Karen Roybal coins the term "archive of dispossession" when theorizing about the "herencia" of Mexican American women in post-1848 Southwest territories and the notion that "culture increasingly becomes not only the site of contest and struggle against further Anglo-American incursion and appropriation but also the gendered site of agency and interventions against dispossession."[1] She explains that this dispossession provides a view of colonial structures and the recovery process that "allows us to acknowledge and recognize the processes of displacement that have defined our national history."[2] The encounters, encuentros y desencuentros between Mexicanos/as/xs, Nuevomexicanos/as/xs, and their children allow us to make visible an archive of linguistic displacement and dispossession, but also to move forward with a new idea of herencia. Additionally, Roybal notes how "historical legacies of dispossession and land struggle have been passed down through generations."[3] This framework is helpful for thinking about the ways in which these linguistic legacies of displacement and dispossession have been passed down intergenerationally. These legacies may include intergenerational language shift, but also the intergenerational passing on of "language experience" and a sense of understanding the past to understand the present. Returning to the words

---

1. Roybal, *Archives of Dispossession*.
2. Roybal, *Archives of Dispossession*, 12.
3. Roybal, *Archives of Dispossession*, 12.

of Aída Hurtado, she reminds us that "for Chicana feminists, the recuperation of history happens through the recuperation of language—mainly Spanish. They use the Spanish language as a tie to the past, as a link to the memory of colonization as they cross the border, and as a recuperation of a culture and a self that is not defined by oppression alone."[4] This Chicana feminist perspective ties into the processes at work in the Mexicano-Nuevomexicano zones of encuentro and the notions of recovery they embody.

The important language recovery and language revitalization work that these ethnolinguistic zones of encuentro can accomplish reminds us to expand notions of northern New Mexico herencia/heritage. Consider the events surrounding the statue of Spanish conquistador Don Diego De Vargas removed from Cathedral Park in downtown Santa Fe in June 2020. Following George Floyd's murder and the racial reckonings occurring throughout the nation, Sante Fe Mayor Alan Webber called for the removal of the De Vargas statue (along with two others). Viewed by many locals as a unilateral decision, Webber had the De Vargas statue removed overnight and transported to what the mayor described as "a safe place while we look for its proper home."[5] To this day, the statue's "home" has still not been determined, and many Nuevomexicano/a/x residents have expressed strong disapproval with the decision. A summer 2020 change.org petition entitled "Stop Attacking Our Hispanic Heritage!"[6] sponsored by the "Hispanic People of New Mexico" accumulated over 3,000 signatures in protest of the mayor's actions. Similarly, in September of the same year, the *Santa Fe New Mexican* reported an argument between the president of the Unión Protectiva and the mayor. The organization's president, Virgil Vigil, recounted that he told the mayor, "The feelings are that you don't like our culture, our Hispanic culture, and don't support our Hispanic culture." I suggest that the Mexicano-Nuevomexicano zones of encuentro addressed in this book provide a new vision for heritage. By positioning Mexicano-Nuevomexicano encounters, interactions, and mixed family units at the center of northern New Mexican heritage, we can reframe our past. Villarreal explains that "tradition is a contested and contentious idea that becomes embedded into cultural preservation projects and social movements. . . . Cultural preservation should be defined in terms of continuance, the ability to continue to live and thrive in our homeplaces, to continue producing culture."[7] The Mexicano-Nuevomexicano zones of

---

4. Hurtado, *Intersectional Chicana Feminisms*, 74.
5. Chacón, "Santa Fe Mayor."
6. See Hispanic People of New Mexico, "Stop Attacking Our Hispanic Heritage!" Change.org petition, June 2020, https://www.change.org/p/support-our-hispanic-heritage.
7. Villarreal, "Anthropolocura as Homeplace Ethnography," 213–14.

encuentro have been part of northern New Mexico herencia for more than two hundred years, yet remain absent from discourse regarding heritage and tradition in northern New Mexico. It is my hope that *Zones of Encuentro* complicates these homogeneous notions and demonstrates the ways in which Mexicano-Nuevomexicano families, subjects, and encuentros are living and thriving constitutive elements of home in Nuevo México.

Recently, the gathering of four Santa Fe City Council members on the Santa Fe Plaza in February 2023 to discuss the fate of the destroyed and removed monuments offered a proposal for the monument to be "reconstructed in a way that highlights the fractured lines of breakage and addresses ongoing disparities that stem from the region's complex racial and cultural dynamics."[8] This proposal takes a cue from Villarreal and challenges us to "interrogate what constitutes home not only for ourselves but for our collaborators and seriously confront the more unsettling question of whose homeland is this?"[9] I offer Mexicano-Nuevomexicano zones of encuentro as another site for viewing disparities, but also solidarities, in the northern New Mexico ethnolinguistic heritage.

I highlight one final note regarding the potential implications for this study in future work. Applying the framework of Latinidad in the context of New Mexico forces us to think beyond national origin as the primary point of distinction between Latino/a/x groups, Latino/a/x homes, and heritage. As already established throughout *Zones of Encuentro,* those who identify as Nuevomexicanos/as/xs do not have a recent immigration history and do not identify as Mexican. Locating Nuevomexicanos/as/xs' homeland within the US encourages the consideration of additional US spaces as Latino/a/x homeplaces. It is certainly the case for many Puerto Ricans that home is in fact not the island, but instead el bloque in East Harlem or Humboldt Park in Chicago.[10] Additionally, Zentella demonstrates that home on el bloque can also be defined by linguistic practices such as code-switching.[11] Understanding Nuevomexicanos/as/xs' historical claims to home opens up a line of thinking that is not confined to identifying Latinos/as/xs by country of origin, but instead by US region. It also discourages the dichotomous notion of a bilingual/bicultural individual. The following words from a participant in Pugach's 1999 ethnography in southern New Mexico make this point clear:

---

8. Gilmore, "Four Santa Fe City Councilors."
9. Villarreal, "Anthropolocura as Homeplace Ethnography," 199.
10. See Zentella, *Growing Up Bilingual*; and Pérez, *Near Northwest Side Story.*
11. Zentella, *Growing Up Bilingual,* 114, 134.

Part of my family comes from Mexico and some of my relatives there can't stand to see that I don't honor the Mexican flag. But that's not my flag; that's my ancestors' flag. I don't have an Hispanic culture and I don't have an American culture. I have a culture of where I'm living and I take in everything around me. Because you can't, you can't be totally Hispanic and you can't be totally American. You have to accept something at some point, and when you accept from both I think it's best. I feel more Hispanic when they start talking about race and when you start talking about tradition and culture. But mostly, you're still an American, but you have your Hispanic background. I can't say I'm totally Mexican, totally Hispanic, because I'm not. I live in America, and I'm very much American, but I'm not totally Americanized.[12]

This participant's articulation of a "culture of where I'm living" speaks to a Latino/a/x identity that exists within a US space. It is not an artificial constant border-crossing between two cultures and two languages. It is one US Latino/a/x culture anchored in the place of New Mexico. It is my wish that this book has contributed to the conceptualization of moments of linguistic Latinidad both within the Mexicano-Nuevomexicano families and outside of the families in broader contexts of zones of encuentro in New Mexico and the larger Latino/a/x US. Through the mixed Mexicano-Nuevomexicano family, I provide a model for effectively reframing Latino/a/x homes that illuminates the utility of highlighting language in Latinidad and Latinidad in language.

---

12. Pugach, *On the Border of Opportunity*, 34.

APPENDIX 1

Interview Guide—English Version

I. QUESTIONS FOR THE CHILDREN OF ONE MEXICAN PARENT AND ONE NEW MEXICAN PARENT

A. Background Information

How old are you?
Where were you born?
Where do you live now? (city and zip code)
Do you live alone?
In what other locations have you lived?

B. Family Background

Where were your parents born?
If they were not born in the US, at what age did they arrive to the US?
Where were your parents' parents born?
If they were not born in the US, at what age did they arrive to the US?
What type of jobs have your parents had?
How would you describe your father? What type of person is/was he?

How would you describe your mother? What type of person is/was she?
Do you have brothers or sisters? How old are they?
If they are out of school, what type of jobs do your siblings have?
Do you have a brother or sister with whom you get along best? Why?
Do you have children? If yes, how old are your children?
Are there special days in which your family gets together? When?
Does your family have special traditions for different times of the year? What are they? (I will ask specifically about Holy Week, Lent, autumn traditions, Matanzas, 4th of July, Mexican Independence Day, town/church festivals, Thanksgiving, Christmas, Easter.)
Is there anyone in your family who uses natural remedies?
    Who? What does he/she use?
    Do you use *remedios*?
    Do you know any *curanderos/curanderas* in your community?
Are there members of your family that live in Mexico?
    Who? When do you see them?
    Do you visit them in Mexico? How often do you visit?
    Do you speak to them on the phone?
    When you speak to them, what language(s) do you use?

C. Neighborhood

What do you like most about where you live?
What do you like least?
Do you feel safe in your neighborhood? Why or why not?
Has your neighborhood or community changed over the last few years?
Are there gangs in your community/neighborhood?
Are there other types of problems/concerns that you have about your neighborhood/community?
What are some positive things that occur in your neighborhood/community?
If you could change something about your neighborhood/community, what would you change?
Are there people in your neighborhood or community that only speak Spanish and do not speak English?
How often do you interact with them? What type of interactions do you have with them?

D. Childhood

What types of games did you play when you were a child?
When you were younger did you fight with other kids or with your siblings? Can you remember a particular fight?
Do you have any particular memories that stand out as your favorites from when you were younger?

E. School

What schools did you attend?
Did you like the schools you attended? Why or why not?
Do you think that any of those schools need improvement? What type of improvements?
Sometimes certain teachers are stricter than others. Did you ever have a very strict or demanding teacher? Who was your favorite teacher? Who was your least favorite teacher?
Were there / are there people in your school that only spoke/speak Spanish and did not / do not speak English?
Did you interact with them? How often did you interact with them? What types of interactions did you / do you have with them?
Did/do you hang out with a particular group of friends in (high) school?
Were there different groups of different groups of students in your school?
- Were there / are there different terms or names used to refer to certain groups of students in school?
- Among the Hispanic/Latino groups were there / are there groups or divisions made?
- Are certain types of music or dress associated with these different groups?

F. Work

Where do you work? How long have you had this job? What are some other jobs that you've had?
What do you like most about your job? What do you like least?
Do you use Spanish at your workplace? With whom?

Are there people at your work that only speak Spanish and speak no English? Who? Do you interact with them? What type of interactions do you have with them?

G. Friendships

Who are your best friends?
What do you think is necessary to have a good friendship?
What types of things cause problems between friends?
Have you ever lost a good friend? What happened?
Do you have any friends who only speak Spanish and do not speak English? Who?
How often do you interact with them? What types of interactions do you have with them? How did you meet?

H. Romantic Relationships

Do you have a romantic partner? How did you meet?
What do you think are some of the reasons why couples fight? (If the person is married) What was your wedding like?

I. Identity

Some people use terms like "hispano," "latino," "hispanic," and "Spanish" to identify themselves. What term(s) do you use to identify yourself? What do these terms mean for you?
What different ethnic/cultural groups live in your neighborhood/community?
Are there any conflicts between these groups?
Are there any differences/similarities between these groups? What are they?
Are there any problems between Hispanic and Anglo groups?

J. Language

When you were growing up, what languages were spoken in your house? By whom?
What language(s) did you speak and with whom?
How and with whom did you learn Spanish? English?

Did your parents ever speak or emphasize anything about the importance of Spanish or English? What did they say?
Have you ever had difficulties with a language? Please elaborate.
Have your parents ever had difficulty with a language? Please elaborate.
When, where, and with whom do you use Spanish?
In a typical week, how much Spanish and English do you use? (e.g., 40% English, 60% Spanish)
What language(s) do you plan to teach to your children? How will you accomplish this?
Do you like speaking Spanish? Why or why not?
Describe to me how you speak. If you could rate your Spanish on a scale of 1 to 10, how would you rate it? Why?
(Ask them to also rate their skills in writing, reading, and comprehension.)
(If this has not been mentioned yet) What do you understand by the word *spanglish*?
Do you think that one group speaks Spanish better than others (Mexicans, Puerto Ricans, New Mexicans)?
Can you describe how Mexicans speak Spanish? How do New Mexicans speak Spanish?
Do you know anything about the English Only debate? What do you think about it?
Have you heard anything about the immigration laws in Arizona? What do you know about them? What do you think about them? Should New Mexico pass similar laws?
Have you heard anything about the debate about driver's licenses in New Mexico? What do you know about this debate? What is your opinion about this?
What do you think about bilingual education?
Who has the responsibility of teaching Spanish to Hispanics in New Mexico?
Have you taken Spanish classes in school? What were they like? What did you like about them? What didn't you like about them?

K. Cultural Influences

How did your parents meet?
Do you know about the reactions of their families to their relationship?
What type of cultural influences were there in your home? Specifically, what Mexican influences were there and what New Mexican influences were there? Please elaborate.
What types of foods were cooked in your house? Who prepared the food?

Do you know how to cook? What do you like to make?
What type of music do you listen to?
In a typical week, what is the percentage of Spanish music to English music that you listen to?
How do you listen to music? Radio stations?
Do you go to dances or clubs or bars? Which ones? What type of music do they play there?
Have you ever been in a situation in which someone questioned whether or not you were Mexican or New Mexican? What happened? How did you react?
Have you ever felt the need to emphasize one heritage or culture over another?
Have you ever felt the need to de-emphasize or hide one heritage or culture? Why? How did you do this?
Do you think that your Spanish sounds more Mexican or New Mexican? Why?
What have others told you about your Spanish?
Are you able to change the way your Spanish sounds according to different situations or the people that are around you? Please elaborate.

II. QUESTIONS FOR THE MEMBERS OF MEXICAN AND NEW MEXICAN COUPLES

A. Background Information

How old are you?
Where were you born?
Where do you live now? (city and zip code)
Who do you live with?
In what other locations have you lived?

B. Family Background

Where were your parents born?
If they were not born in the US, at what age did they arrive to the US?
Where were your parents' parents born?
If they were not born in the US, at what age did they arrive to the US?
What type of jobs have your parents had?
How would you describe your father? What type of person is/was he?
How would you describe your mother? What type of person is/was she?
Do you have brothers or sisters? How old are they?
If they are out of school, what type of jobs do your siblings have?

Do you have a brother or sister with whom you get along best? Why?
Do you have children? If yes, how old are your children?
Are there special days in which your family gets together? When?
Does your family have special traditions for different times of the year? What are they? (I will ask specifically about Holy Week, Lent, autumn traditions, Matanzas, 4th of July, Mexican Independence Day, town/church festivals, Thanksgiving, Christmas, Easter.)
Is there anyone in your family who uses natural remedies?
    Who? What does he/she use?
    Do you use *remedios*?
    Do you know any *curanderos/curanderas* in your community?
Are there members of your family that live in Mexico?
    Who? When do you see them?
    Do you visit them in Mexico? How often do you visit?
    Do you speak to them on the phone?
    When you speak to them, what language(s) do you use?

C. Neighborhood

What do you like most about where you live?
What do you like least?
Do you feel safe in your neighborhood? Why or why not?
Has your neighborhood or community changed over the last few years?
Are there gangs in your community/neighborhood?
Are there other types of problems/concerns that you have about your neighborhood/community?
What are some positive things that occur in your neighborhood/community?
If you could change something about your neighborhood/community, what would you change?
Are there people in your neighborhood or community that only speak Spanish and do not speak English?
How often do you interact with them? What type of interactions do you have with them?

D. Childhood

What types of games did you play when you were a child?
When you were younger did you fight with other kids or with your siblings?
    Can you remember a particular fight?

Do you have any particular memories that stand out as your favorites from when you were younger?

E. School

What schools did you attend?
Did you like the schools you attended? Why or why not?
Do you think that any of those schools need improvement? What type of improvements?
Sometimes certain teachers are stricter than others. Did you ever have a very strict or demanding teacher? Who was your favorite teacher? Who was your least favorite teacher?
Were there / are there people in your school that only spoke/speak Spanish and did not / do not speak English?
Did you interact with them? How often did you interact with them? What types of interactions did you / do you have with them?
Did/do you hang out with a particular group of friends in (high) school?
Were there different groups of different groups of students in your school?
- Were there / are there different terms or names used to refer to certain groups of students in school?
- Among the Hispanic/Latino groups were there / are there groups or divisions made?
- Are certain types of music or dress associated with these different groups?

F. Work

Where do you work? How long have you had this job? What are some other jobs that you've had?
What do you like most about your job? What do you like least?
Do you use Spanish at your workplace? With whom?
Are there people at your work that only speak Spanish and speak no English? Who? Do you interact with them? What type of interactions do you have with them?

G. Friendships

Who are your best friends?
What do you think is necessary to have a good friendship?

What types of things cause problems between friends?
Have you ever lost a good friend? What happened?
Do you have any friends who only speak Spanish and do not speak English? Who?
How often do you interact with them? What types of interactions do you have with them? How did you meet?

H. Identity

Some people use terms like "hispano," "latino," "hispanic," and "Spanish" to identify themselves. What term(s) do you use to identify yourself? What do these terms mean for you?
What different ethnic/cultural groups live in your neighborhood/community?
Are there any conflicts between these groups?
Are there any differences/similarities between these groups? What are they?
Are there any problems between Hispanic and Anglo groups?

I. Language

When you were growing up, what languages were spoken in your house? By whom?
What language(s) did you speak and with whom?
How and with whom did you learn Spanish? English?
Did your parents ever speak or emphasize anything about the importance of Spanish or English? What did they say?
Have you ever had difficulties with a language? Please elaborate.
Have your parents ever had difficulty with a language? Please elaborate.
When, where, and with whom do you use Spanish?
In a typical week, how much Spanish and English do you use? (e.g., 40% English, 60% Spanish)
What language(s) do you plan to teach to your children? How will you accomplish this?
Do you like speaking Spanish? Why or why not?
Describe to me how you speak. If you could rate your Spanish on a scale of 1 to 10, how would you rate it? Why?
(Ask them to also rate their skills in writing, reading, and comprehension.)
(If this has not been mentioned yet) What do you understand by the word *spanglish*?
Do you think that one group speaks Spanish better than others (Mexicans, Puerto Ricans, New Mexicans)?

Can you describe how Mexicans speak Spanish? How do New Mexicans speak Spanish?

Do you know anything about the English Only debate? What do you think about it?

Have you heard anything about the immigration laws in Arizona? What do you know about them? What do you think about them? Should New Mexico pass similar laws?

Have you heard anything about the debate about driver's licenses in New Mexico? What do you know about this debate? What is your opinion about this?

What do you think about bilingual education?

Who has the responsibility of teaching Spanish to Hispanics in New Mexico?

Have you taken Spanish classes in school? What were they like? What did you like about them? What didn't you like about them?

J. Romantic Relationship

How did you meet your partner?

Did your family have a positive or negative reaction to your relationship? Please elaborate. Do you know if his/her family had any positive or negative reactions to your relationship? What were they? What were the reactions of his/her family?

What is your relationship like with your in-laws? What is your partner's relationship like with your family?

(If the couple is married) What was your wedding like?

Did you have any particular misunderstandings or difficulties when you started seeing each other?

Did you have any particular misunderstandings or difficulties when you began living together and/or got married?

Do you remember any particular funny experiences?

What do you think are some of the reasons why couples fight? What were/are some of the reasons why you and your partner fight/fought?

In your relationship have you noticed cultural differences? Please elaborate.

Did you have any difficulties communicating? Please elaborate.

What do you tell/teach your children about their culture? What types of traditions do you emphasize in your home?

What language(s) do you use in your home?

What language(s) do you use with your partner?

What language(s) do you use with your children?

What language(s) do you use with your extended family?

Do you feel that your partner or your partner's family has influenced your English or Spanish use? In what way?

Do you notice any differences between your family's Spanish and the Spanish of your partner and his/her family?

What type of foods are served or prepared in your home? What do you like to make?

What type of music do you listen to? What specific radio stations do you listen to?

Do you attend dances or go out to bars/clubs in your town? What type of music is played there?

APPENDIX 2

Interview Guide—Spanish Version

A. PREGUNTAS PARA LOS HIJOS (MX-NMX)

Datos generales

¿Cuántos años tienes?
¿Dónde naciste?
¿Dónde vives ahora?
¿Vives solo/a? ¿Cuál es tu código postal?
¿En qué otros lugares has vivido?

La familia

¿Dónde nacieron tu mamá y papá?
Si no nacieron en E.U., ¿a qué edad llegaron a los USA?
Y ¿dónde nacieron los papás de ellos?
Si no nacieron en E.U., ¿a qué edad llegaron a los USA?
¿Qué tipos de trabajos han tenido tus padres?
¿Qué tipo de persona era/es tu papá?
¿Qué tipo de persona era/es tu mamá?
¿Tienes hermanos? ¿Cuántos años tienen y a qué se dedican?

¿Tienes un hermano/una hermana con quien te llevas mejor que con los demás? ¿Por qué?
¿Tienen hijos? ¿Cuántos años tienen?
Toda mi familia se reúne en Navidad. ¿Hay un día especial en que toda la familia se reúne?
¿Tienen tradiciones específicas para diferentes épocas del año? ¿Cuáles son?
- Semana santa/cuaresma
- Thanksgiving
- Tradiciones de otoño (piñon, chicos, la cosecha)
- Matanzas
- Cuatro de julio
- 16 de September
- Fiestas de la iglesia or town fiestas

¿Hay alguien en tu familia que usa remedios naturales?
¿Quién?
¿Qué usa?
¿Conoces a un curandero en tu comunidad?
¿Hay miembros de tu familia que viven en México?
¿Quiénes? ¿Cuándo los ves?
¿Los visitas en México? ¿Con qué frecuencia?
¿Los hablas por teléfono?
Cuando hablas con ellos, ¿qué idioma usas?

El vecindario

¿Qué es lo que más te gusta sobre donde vives?
¿Qué es lo que menos te gusta?
¿Te sientes segura/o en tu vecindario? ¿Por qué?
¿Ha cambiado tu vecindario en los últimos años?
¿Hay pandillas en tu vecindario?
¿Qué tipos de problemas hay?
¿Qué cosas buenas ocurren en tu vecindario?
Si pudieras hacer algo para mejorar tu vecindario, ¿qué harías?

La niñez

¿Qué jugabas cuando eras niño/a? ¿Cómo se juega? ¿Cuáles son las reglas del juego?

Cuando eras niño/a, ¿peleabas con otros niños o con tus hermanos? ¿Puedes recordarte de una pelea en particular?

¿Puedes contarme una memoria muy linda de cuando eras niño/a o adolescente?

¿Hay personas en tu vecindario o comunidad que solo hablan español y no hablan inglés? ¿Quiénes? ¿Interactúas con ellos?

¿Con qué frecuencia interactúas con ellos? ¿Qué tipo de interacciones tienes con ellos?

La escuela

¿A qué escuelas fuiste?

¿Era(n) escuela(s) buena(s) o mala(s)? ¿Por qué?

¿Qué piensas que se podría hacer para mejorar las escuelas?

¿Cómo era/es la escuela donde estudiaba?

¿Estaba lejos de casa?

A mí me dicen que a veces los maestros o maestras pueden ser fuertes.
    ¿Tuviste maestras fuertes o exigentes? ¿Quién era la maestra que más te gustaba? ¿Quién era la maestra que más odiabas?

¿Había muchas peleas en la escuela? ¿Cuál fue la mejor pelea que vio?

¿Hay personas en tu escuela que solo hablan español y no hablan inglés? ¿Quiénes?

¿Interactúas con ellos? ¿Con qué frecuencia interactúas con ellos? ¿Qué tipo de interacciones tienes con ellos?

¿Cómo era tu grupo de amigos?

¿Había diferentes grupos en la escuela? Por ejemplo,
    ¿Utilizaban diferentes términos/nombres para hablar de ciertos grupos de estudiantes?
    Entre los hispanos/latinos en la escuela, ¿había diferentes grupos?
    ¿Se asociaba una cierta forma de vestir o un cierto tipo de música con los diferentes grupos?

El trabajo

¿Dónde trabajas? ¿Siempre has tenido ese trabajo? Si no, ¿qué otros trabajos has tenido?

¿Usas el español en tu trabajo?

¿Qué te gusta más de tu trabajo? ¿Qué es lo que te gusta menos?

¿Hay personas en tu trabajo que solo hablan español y no hablan inglés? ¿Quiénes? ¿Interactúas con ellos? ¿Con qué frecuencia interactúas con ellos? ¿Qué tipo de interacciones tienes con ellos?

Las amistades

¿Quiénes son tus mejores amigos?
¿Qué es necesario para tener una buena amistad?
¿Qué cosas causan problemas entre las amistades?
¿Has perdido un buen amigo? ¿Qué pasó?
¿Tienes amigos que solo hablan español y no hablan inglés? ¿Quiénes? ¿Interactúas con ellos? ¿Con qué frecuencia interactúas con ellos? ¿Qué tipo de interacciones tienes con ellos?

Las relaciones amorosas

¿Tienes pareja? ¿Dónde conociste a tu pareja?
¿Cuáles son algunas causas de las peleas entre una pareja? (Si la persona está casada) ¿Cómo fue el casorio?
¿Por qué crees que tanta gente se divorcia hoy en día?

Otros temas

¿Qué harías si te ganaras un millón de dólares?
¿Ha habido un momento en tu vida que pensaste que te ibas a morir?
¿Puedes recordar un sueño bonito que has tenido? ¿Y una pesadilla?

La identidad

Hay gente que se identifica como hispano o latino o hispanic o Spanish. ¿Cómo te identificas tú? ¿Qué significan estos términos para ti?
¿Qué grupos étnicos viven en tu vecindario?
¿Cómo se llevan los diferentes grupos? ¿Hay problemas entre los grupos?
¿Qué diferencias hay entre los diferentes grupos hispanos? (Nuevomexicanos y mexicanos)
¿Hay problemas entre los hispanos y los anglos/gringos?

El idioma

Cuando eras niña/o, ¿qué idiomas se hablaban en tu casa?
¿Qué idiomas hablabas tú y con quiénes?
¿Cómo y con quién aprendiste el español? ¿Inglés?
¿Decían tus padres algo acerca de la importancia de algún idioma? ¿Qué decían?
¿Has tenido algunas dificultades por el lenguaje?
¿Y qué tal tus padres?
Hoy en día, ¿cuándo y dónde usas español? ¿Usas español con tus amigos?
¿Qué idioma(s) le(s) vas a enseñar a tu(s) hijo(s)? ¿Cómo vas a lograr esto?
¿Te gusta hablar español?
Descríbeme el español que hablas. Es decir, en una escala de uno a diez, ¿dónde lo ubicas?
¿Por qué dices que tu español es así?
(Ask them to also rate their skills in writing, reading, and comprehension.)
En una semana normal, si lo podrías cuantificar, ¿cuánto español hablas y cuánto inglés? (ej.: 40% español y 60% inglés)
(Si no lo han mencionado todavía) ¿Qué entiendes por el espanglish?
¿Crees que un grupo nacional (mexicanos, puertorriqueños, etc.) habla el español mejor que otro grupo?
¿Puedes describir cómo hablan los mexicanos? ¿Los nuevomexicanos?
¿Sabes algo del debate sobre English Only? ¿Qué piensas de esto?
¿Sabes algo sobre los debates sobre la inmigración en Arizona? ¿Qué piensas de esto? ¿Piensas que Nuevo México debe aprobar un proyecto de ley parecido?
¿Qué piensas de la educación bilingüe?
¿Quién tiene la responsabilidad de enseñarles español a los hispanos de Nuevo México?
¿Has tomado clases de español? ¿Cómo eran? ¿Qué te gustó más? ¿Qué no te gustó?

Influencias culturales

¿Cómo se conocieron tus papás?
¿Sabes cómo reaccionaron sus familias?
¿Qué influencias culturales había en tu casa? Específicamente, ¿qué influencias mexicanas y qué influencias nuevomexicanas? ¿Puedes describirlas?
¿Qué tipo de comida había en la casa? ¿Quién la preparaba?

¿Sabes cocinar? ¿Qué te gusta preparar?
¿Qué tipo de música escuchas? ¿artistas? ¿estaciones de radio? ¿bailes?
¿Alguna vez has estado en una situación en que alguien cuestionaba que eres MX o NMX? ¿Qué pasó? ¿Cómo reaccionaste?
¿Alguna vez has sentido la necesidad de enfatizar uno o el otro?
O al revés, ¿has sentido la necesidad de ocultar o deenfatizar uno o el otro? ¿Por qué? ¿De qué manera lo hiciste?
¿Crees que tu español suena más MX o NMX?
¿Qué te han dicho otras personas acerca de tu español?
En algunas ocasiones, ¿cambias tu español de uno a otro?

B. PREGUNTAS PARA LAS PAREJAS

Datos generales

¿Cuántos años tienes?
¿Dónde naciste?
¿Dónde vives ahora?
¿Vives solo/a? ¿Cuál es tu código postal?
¿En qué otros lugares has vivido?

La familia

¿Dónde nacieron tu mamá y papá?
Si no nacieron en E.U., ¿a qué edad llegaron a los USA?
Y ¿dónde nacieron los papás de ellos?
Si no nacieron en E.U., ¿a qué edad llegaron a los USA?
¿Qué tipos de trabajos han tenido tus padres?
¿Qué tipo de persona era/es tu papá?
¿Qué tipo de persona era/es tu mamá?
¿Tienes hermanos? ¿Cuántos años tienen y a qué se dedican?
¿Tienes un hermano/una hermana con quien te llevas mejor que con los demás? ¿Por qué?
¿Tienen hijos? ¿Cuántos años tienen?
Toda mi familia se reúne en Navidad. ¿Hay un día especial en que toda la familia se reúne?
¿Tienen tradiciones específicas para diferentes épocas del año? ¿Cuáles son?

Ask about:
- Semana santa/cuaresma
- Thanksgiving
- Tradiciones del otoño (piñon, chicos, la cosecha)
- Matanzas
- Cuatro de julio
- 16 de septiembre
- Fiestas de la iglesia or town fiestas

¿Hay alguien en tu familia que usa remedios naturales?
   ¿Quién?
   ¿Qué usa?
   ¿Conoces a un curandero en tu comunidad?
¿Hay miembros de tu familia que viven en México?
   ¿Quiénes? ¿Cuándo los ves?
   ¿Los visitas en México? ¿Con qué frecuencia?
   ¿Los hablas por teléfono?
   Cuando hablas con ellos, ¿siempre los hablas en español?

El vecindario

¿Qué es lo que más te gusta sobre donde vives?
¿Qué es lo que menos te gusta?
¿Te sientes segura/o en tu vecindario? ¿Por qué?
¿Ha cambiado tu vecindario en los últimos años?
¿Hay pandillas en tu vecindario?
¿Qué tipos de problemas hay?
¿Qué cosas buenas ocurren en tu vecindario?
Si pudieras hacer algo para mejorar tu vecindario, ¿qué harías?

La niñez

¿Qué jugabas cuando eras niño/a? ¿Cómo se juega? ¿Cuáles son las reglas del juego?
Cuando eras niño/a, ¿peleabas con otros niños o con tus hermanos? ¿Puedes recordarte de una pelea en particular?
¿Puedes contarme una memoria muy linda de cuando eras niño/a o adolescente?
¿Hay personas en tu vecindario o comunidad que solo hablan español y no hablan inglés?

¿Quiénes? ¿Interactúas con ellos? ¿Con qué frecuencia interactúas con ellos? ¿Qué tipo de interacciones tienes con ellos?

La escuela

¿A qué escuelas fuiste?
¿Era(n) escuela(s) buena(s) o mala(s)? ¿Por qué?
¿Qué piensas que se podría hacer para mejorar las escuelas?
¿Cómo era/es la escuela donde estudiaba?
¿Estaba lejos de casa?
A mí me dicen que a veces los maestros o maestras pueden ser fuertes.
    ¿Tuviste maestras fuertes o exigentes? ¿Quién era la maestra que más le gustaba? ¿Quién era la maestra que más odiaba?
¿Había muchas peleas en la escuela? ¿Cuál fue la mejor pelea que vio?
¿Había personas en tu escuela que solo hablan español y no hablan inglés?
    ¿Quiénes?
¿Interactúas con ellos? ¿Con qué frecuencia interactúas con ellos? ¿Qué tipo de interacciones tienes con ellos?
¿Qué piensas de la educación bilingüe?
¿Quién tiene la responsabilidad de enseñarles español a los hispanos de Nuevo México? ¿Has tomado clases de español? ¿Cómo eran? ¿Qué te gustó más? ¿Qué no te gustó?
¿Cómo era tu grupo de amigos?
¿Había diferentes grupos en la escuela? Por ejemplo,
    ¿Utilizaban diferentes términos/nombres para hablar de ciertos grupos de estudiantes?
    Entre los hispanos/latinos en la escuela, ¿había diferentes grupos?
    ¿Se asociaba una cierta forma de vestir o un cierto tipo de música con los diferentes grupos?

El trabajo

¿Dónde trabajas? ¿Siempre has tenido ese trabajo? Si no, ¿qué otros trabajos has tenido?
¿Usas el español en tu trabajo?
¿Qué te gusta más de tu trabajo? ¿Qué es lo que te gusta menos?
¿Hay personas en tu trabajo que solo hablan español y no hablan inglés?
    ¿Quiénes? ¿Interactúas con ellos? ¿Con qué frecuencia interactúas con ellos? ¿Qué tipo de interacciones tienes con ellos?

Las amistades

¿Quiénes son tus mejores amigos?
¿Qué es necesario para tener una buena amistad?
¿Qué cosas causan problemas entre las amistades?
¿Has perdido un buen amigo? ¿Qué pasó?
¿Tienes amigos que solo hablan español y no hablan inglés? ¿Quiénes?
¿Interactúas con ellos? ¿Con qué frecuencia interactúas con ellos? ¿Qué tipo de interacciones tienes con ellos?

Otros temas

¿Qué harías si te ganaras un millón de dólares?
¿Ha habido un momento en tu vida que pensaste que te ibas a morir?
¿Puedes recordar un sueño bonito que has tenido? ¿Y una pesadilla?

La identidad

Hay gente que se identifica como hispano o latino o hispanic o Spanish.
    ¿Cómo te identificas tú? ¿Qué significan estos términos para ti?
¿Qué grupos étnicos viven en tu vecindario?
¿Cómo se llevan los diferentes grupos? ¿Hay problemas entre los grupos?
¿Qué diferencias hay entre los diferentes grupos hispanos? (Nuevomexicanos y mexicanos)
¿Hay problemas entre los hispanos y los anglos/gringos?

El idioma

Cuando eras niña/o, ¿qué idiomas se hablaban en tu casa?
¿Qué idiomas hablabas tú y con quiénes?
¿Cómo y con quién aprendiste el español? ¿Inglés?
¿Decían tus padres algo acerca de la importancia de algún idioma? ¿Qué decían?
¿Has tenido algunas dificultades por el lenguaje?
¿Y qué tal tus padres?
Hoy en día, ¿cuándo y dónde usas español? ¿Usas español con tus amigos?
¿Qué idioma(s) le(s) vas a enseñar a tu(s) hijo(s)? ¿Cómo vas a lograr esto?
¿Te gusta hablar español?

Descríbeme el español que hablas. Es decir, en una escala de uno a diez, ¿dónde lo ubicas? ¿Por qué dices que tu español es así?
(Ask them to also rate their skills in writing, reading, and comprehension.)
En una semana normal, si lo podrías cuantificar, ¿cuánto español hablas y cuánto inglés? (ej.: 40% español y 60% inglés)
(Si no lo han mencionado todavía) ¿Qué entiendes por el espanglish?
¿Crees que un grupo nacional (mexicanos, puertorriqueños, etc.) habla el español mejor que otro grupo?
¿Puedes describir cómo hablan los mexicanos? ¿Los nuevomexicanos?
¿Sabes algo del debate sobre English Only? ¿Qué piensas de esto?
¿Sabes algo sobre los debates sobre la inmigración en Arizona? ¿Qué piensas de esto? ¿Piensas que Nuevo México debe aprobar un proyecto de ley parecido?

Preguntas para las parejas

¿Cómo conociste a tu pareja?
¿Cómo reaccionó tu familia? ¿Sabes cómo reaccionó la familia de tu pareja?
Si está casado/a, ¿cómo fue el casorio?
¿Tenían mal entendidos o dificultades cuando se acaban de casar o cuando empezaron a vivir juntos? ¿Te acuerdas de una experiencia cómica?
¿Cuáles son algunas causas de las peleas entre una pareja? ¿Entre ustedes específicamente?
¿Notaron diferencias culturales?
¿Tenían dificultades con la comunicación?
¿Cómo te llevas con tus suegros y la familia de tu pareja? ¿Cómo se lleva tu pareja con tu familia?
¿Qué les dices a tus hijos sobre su cultura? ¿Cuáles son las tradiciones que enfatizas en la casa?
¿Qué idioma usas en la casa?
¿Con tu pareja?
¿Con tus hijos?
¿Con las familias extendidas?
¿Piensas que tu pareja o su familia ha influenciado tu uso del español o el inglés?
¿Notas diferencias entre el español de tu familia y el español de tu familia?
¿Qué tipo de comida preparas en la casa?
¿Qué tipo de música escuchan en la casa? ¿estaciones de radio?
¿Asisten a bailes?

BIBLIOGRAPHY

AlSayyad, Nezar. "The End of Tradition or the Tradition of Endings?" In *The End of Tradition?*, edited by Nezar AlSayyad, 1–28. London: Routledge, 2004.

Álvarez, Sonia E., Elisabeth Jay Friedman, Ericka Beckman, Maylei Blackwell, Norma Stoltz Chinchilla, Nathalie Lebon, Marysa Navarro, and Marcela Ríos Tobar. "Encountering Latin American and Caribbean Feminisms." *Signs: Journal of Women in Culture and Society* 28, no. 2 (2002): 537–79.

American Immigration Council. "Immigrants in New Mexico." August 6, 2020. https://www.americanimmigrationcouncil.org/research/immigrants-in-new-mexico.

Anaya, Rudolfo. Foreword to *Querencia: Reflections on the New Mexico Homeland,* edited by Vanessa Fonseca Chávez, Levi Romero, and Spencer Herrera, xiii–xxii. Albuquerque: University of New Mexico Press, 2020.

Anzaldúa, Gloria. *Borderlands/La Frontera: The New Mestiza*. San Francisco: Aunt Lute Books, 1987.

———. "Now Let Us Shift . . . the Path of Conocimiento . . . Inner Work, Public Acts." In *This Bridge We Call Home: Radical Visions for Transformation,* edited by Gloria Anzaldúa and Analouis Keating, 540–78. London: Routledge, 2013.

———. "(Un)Natural Bridges, (Un)Safe Spaces." In *This Bridge We Call Home: Radical Visions for Transformation,* edited by Gloria Anzaldúa and Analouis Keating, 1–5. London: Routledge, 2013.

Aparicio, Ana, Andrea Bolivar, Alex E. Chávez, Sherina Feliciano-Santos, Santiago Ivan Guerra, Gina M. Pérez, Jonathan Rosa, Gilberto Rosas, Aimee Villarreal, and Patricia Zavella. Introduction to *Ethnographic Refusals, Unruly Latinidades,* edited by Alex E. Chávez and Gina M. Pérez, xiii–xxxv. Santa Fe: School for Advanced Research Press, 2022.

Aparicio, Frances R. "Chicago Latinidad: The MexiRican and Other IntraLatino/a Subjects." Paper presented at the XXIX International Congress of the Latin American Studies Association, Toronto, Canada, October 2010.

———. "Cultural Twins and National Others: Allegories of Intralatino Subjectivities in U.S. Latino/a Literature." *Identities: Global Studies in Culture and Power* 16 (2009): 622–41.

———. "Intimate (Trans)Nationals." In *The Latina/o Midwest Reader*, edited by Omar Valerio-Jiménez, Santiago Vaquera-Vásquez, and Claire Fox, 271–86. Urbana: University of Illinois Press, 2017.

———. "Jennifer as Selena: Rethinking Latinidad in Media and Popular Culture." *Latino Studies* 1, no. 1 (2003): 90–105.

———. "Latinx Studies: Notes from an Emerita." The Latinx Project at NYU, February 5, 2021. https://www.latinxproject.nyu.edu/intervenxions/latinx-studies-notes-from-an-emerita.

———. *Negotiating Latinidad: Intralatina/o Lives in Chicago*. Urbana: University of Illinois Press, 2019.

———. "Of Spanish Dispossessed." In *Language Ideologies: Critical Perspectives on the Official English Movement, Volume 1*, edited by Roseann Dueñas Gonzalez and Ildikó Melis, 248–75. Mahwah, NJ: Lawrence Erlbaum Associates, 2000.

———. "Reading the 'Latino' in Latino Studies: Towards Reimagining our Academic Location." *Discourse* 21, no. 3 (1999): 3–18.

———. "Whose Spanish, Whose Language, Whose Power?" *Indiana Journal of Hispanic Literatures* 12 (Spring 1998): 5–25.

Aparicio, Frances R., and Susana Chávez-Silverman. Introduction to *Tropicalizations: Transcultural Representations of Latinidad,* edited by Frances R. Aparicio and Suana Chávez-Silverman, 1–17. Hanover, NH: University Press of New England, 1997.

Appadurai, Arjun. *Modernity at Large: Cultural Dimensions of Globalization*. Minneapolis: University of Minnesota Press, 1996.

Arellano, Juan Estevan. *Enduring Acequias: Wisdom of the Land, Knowledge of the Water*. Albuquerque: University of New Mexico Press, 2014.

Arnold, Patricia, and María Teresa Martínez-García. "Traditional New Mexican Spanish: The Past, Present, and Future." In *Contact, Community, and Connections: Current Approaches to Spanish in Multilingual Populations,* edited by Scott M. Alvord and Gregory L. Thompson, 175–202. Delaware: Vernon Press, 2019.

Bernal-Enríquez, Ysaura. "Factores socio-históricos en la pérdida del español del Suroeste en los Estados Unidos y sus implicaciones para la revitalización." In *Research on Spanish in the United States: Linguistic Issues and Challenges,* edited by Ana Roca, 121–36. Somerville, MA: Cascadilla Press, 2000.

Bessett, Ryan M., and Ana M. Carvalho. "The Structure of US Spanish." In *Heritage Language Teaching: Critical Language Awareness Perspectives for Research and Pedagogy,* edited by Serigo Loza and Sara M. Beaudrie, 44–62. New York: Routledge, 2021.

Bhabha, Homi. *The Location of Culture*. London and New York: Routledge Press, 1994.

Bills, Garland D. "New Mexican Spanish: Demise of the Earliest European Variety in the United States." *American Speech* 72 (1997): 154–71.

Bills, Garland D., and Neddy A. Vigil. "Ashes to Ashes: The Historical Basis for Dialect Variation in New Mexican Spanish." *Romance Philology* 53 (1999): 43–66.

———. *The Spanish Language of New Mexico and Southern Colorado: A Linguistic Atlas*. Albuquerque: University of New Mexico Press, 2008.

Bills, Garland, Eduardo Hernández-Chávez, and Alan Hudson. "The Geography of Language Shift: Distance from the Mexican Border and Spanish Language Claiming in the Southwestern U.S." *International Journal of the Sociology of Language* 114 (1995): 9–27.

Bills, Garland, Alan Hudson, and Eduardo Hernández-Chávez. "Spanish Home Language Use and English Proficiency as Differential Measures of Language Maintenance and Shift." *Southwest Journal of Linguistics* 19 (2000): 11–27.

Bucholtz, Mary. "Sociolinguistic Nostalgia and the Authentication of Identity." *Journal of Sociolinguistics* 7, no. 3 (2003): 398–416.

Bucholtz, Mary, and Kira Hall. "Identity and Interaction: A Sociocultural Linguistic Approach." *Discourse Studies* 7 (2005): 585–614.

Bürki, Yvette. "El español en las películas estadounidenses: Aproximación discursiva." *Círculo de Lingüística Aplicada* 36 (2008): 3–25.

Cárdenas, Maritza E. *Constituting Central American-Americans: Transnational Identities and the Politics of Dislocation.* New Brunswick, NJ: Rutgers University Press, 2018.

Carrillo-Rowe, Aimee. "Be Longing: Toward a Feminist Politics of Relation." *NWSA Journal* 17, no. 2 (2005): 5–46.

Chacón, Daniel. "Santa Fe Mayor Gets into Public Spat over De Vargas Statue with Spanish Cultural Group Leader." *Santa Fe New Mexican,* September 16, 2020, A-1.

Cisneros, René, and Elizabeth Leone. "Mexican American Language Communities in the Twin Cities: An Example of Contact and Recontact." In *Spanish in the US Setting: Beyond the Southwest,* edited by Lucia Elias-Olivares, 181–210. Rosslyn, VA: National Clearinghouse for Bilingual Education, 1983.

Clary-Lemon, Jennifer. "'We're Not Ethnic, We're Irish!': Oral Histories and the Discursive Construction of Immigrant Identity." *Discourse and Society* 21 (2010): 5–25.

Cobos, Rubén. *A Dictionary of New Mexico and Southern Colorado Spanish.* Santa Fe: Museum of New Mexico Press, 2003.

Constable, Ann. "Our Lady, Almost Home: 12-Foot Statue Should Arrive Today." *Santa Fe New Mexican,* July 22, 2008, A-1.

Contreras, Russel. "Spanish Colonial Monuments Fuel Race Strife in US Southwest." The Associated Press, June 27, 2020. https://apnews.com/article/california-new-mexico-hispanics-us-news-ap-top-news-ea5516d25f301833a5709e8e455333eb.

Creese, Angela, and Fiona Copland. *Linguistic Ethnography: Collecting, Analyzing, and Presenting Data.* London: Sage Publications, 2015.

Daiute, Colette, and Cynthia Lightfoot, eds. *Narrative Analysis: Studying the Development of Individuals in Society.* Thousand Oaks, CA: Sage Publications, 2004.

Dávila, Arlene. *Latinx Art: Artists, Markets, and Politics.* Durham, NC: Duke University Press, 2020.

De Genova, Nicholas, and Ana Y. Ramos-Zayas. *Latino Crossings: Mexicans, Puerto Ricans, and the Politics of Race and Citizenship.* New York: Routledge, 2003.

De Houwer, Annick. *Bilingual First Language Acquisition.* Bristol, UK: Multilingual Matters, 2009.

De Onís, Catalina (Kathleen) M. "What's in an 'X'?: An Exchange about the Politics of 'Latinx.'" *Chiricù Journal: Latina/o Literature, Art, and Culture* 1, no. 2 (2017): 78–91.

Del Angel Guevara, Mario Esteban. "Returning to Northern New Mexico: A Study of the Nuevomexicano Lexicon." PhD diss., University of New Mexico, 2023.

Delgado Bernal, Dolores. "Using a Chicana Feminist Epistemology in Educational Research." *Harvard Educational Review* 68, no. 4 (1998): 555–82.

Dorian, Nancy C. *Language Death: The Life Cycle of a Scottish Gaelic Dialect.* Philadelphia: University of Pennsylvania Press, 1981.

Dowling, Julie. "'I'm Not Mexican . . . pero soy mexicano': Linguistic Context of Labeling among Mexican Americans in Texas." *Journal of Southwest Linguistics* 24 (2005): 53–63.

——. *Mexican Americans and the Question of Race*. Austin: University of Texas Press, 2014.

Durán, Crisitina. "Panaderias, peluquerias, y carnicerias: Re-Mexicanizing the Urban Landscapes of a Southwest City." PhD diss., University of New Mexico, 2007.

Eagleton, Terry. *Ideology: An Introduction*. London: Verso, 1991.

Errington, Joseph. "Ideology." *Journal of Linguistic Anthropology* 9, no. 1–2 (1999): 115–17.

Escobar, Ana María, and Kim Potowski. *El español de los Estados Unidos*. Cambridge: Cambridge University Press, 2015.

Fierros, Cindy O., and Dolores Delgado-Bernal. "Vamos a platicar: The Contours of Pláticas as Chicana/Latina Feminist Methodology." *Chicana/Latina Studies* 15, no. 2 (Spring 2016): 98–121.

Fishman, Joshua. "Language Maintenance and Language Shift as Fields of Inquiry." *Linguistics* 9 (1964): 32–70.

——. "The Rise and Fall of the 'Ethnic Revival' in the USA." *Journal of Intercultural Studies* 4, no. 3 (1983): 5–46.

——. "Who Speaks What Language to Whom and When?" In *The Bilingualism Reader*, edited by Li Wei, 55–70. London: Routledge, 2000.

Flores, Juan. "The Latino Imaginary: Dimensions of Community and Identity." In *Tropicalizations: Transcultural Representations of Latinidad*, edited by Frances R. Aparicio and Susana Chávez-Silverman, 183–93. Hanover, NH: University Press of New England, 1997.

Flores, Nelson. "Foreword: The Transformative Possibilities of Translanguaging." In *Transformative Translanguaging Espacios: Latinx Students and Their Teachers Rompiendo Fronteras sin Miedo*, edited by Maite T. Sánchez and Ofelia García, xix–xxi. Bristol, UK: Multilingual Matters, 2022.

Fonseca-Chávez, Vanessa. "Contested Querencia in *The Last Conquistador* (2008) by John J. Valadez and Cristina Ibarra." In *Querencia: Reflections on the New Mexico Homeland*, edited by Vanessa Fonseca-Chávez, Levi Romero, and Spencer Herrera, 79–97. Albuquerque: University of New Mexico Press, 2020.

Fonseca-Chávez, Vanessa, Levi Romero, and Spencer Herrera, eds. *Querencia: Reflections on the New Mexico Homeland*. Albuquerque: University of New Mexico Press, 2020.

Fought, Carmen. *Language and Ethnicity*. Cambridge: Cambridge University Press, 2006.

Galindo, D. Letticia. "Language Attitudes towards Spanish and English Varieties: A Chicano Perspective." *Hispanic Journal on Behavioral Sciences* 17 (1995): 77–99.

García, Lorena, and Mérida Rúa. "Processing Latinidad: Mapping Latino Urban Landscapes through Chicago Ethnic Festivals." *Latino Studies* 5, no. 3 (2007): 317–39.

García, Ofelia. *Bilingual Education in the 21st Century: A Global Perspective*. Hoboken, NJ: Wiley Blackwell, 2009.

——. "US Spanish and Education: Global and Local Intersections." *Review of Research in Education* 38, no. 1 (2014): 58–80.

García, Ofelia, and Ricardo Otheguy. "The Language Situation of Cuban Americans." In *Language Diversity, Problem or Resource?: A Social and Educational Perspective on Language Minorities in the United States*, edited by Sandra McKay and Sau-ling Cynthia Wong, 166–92. Cambridge, MA: Newbury House, 1988.

García, Ofelia, and Maite T. Sánchez. "The Making of the Language of US Latinxs: Translanguaging Tejidos." In *Transformative Translanguaging Espacios: Latinx Students and Their Teachers Rompiendo Fronteras sin Miedo*, edited by Maite T. Sánchez and Ofelia García, 19–46. Bristol, UK: Multilingual Matters, 2022.

García Acevedo, María Rosa. "The Forgotten Diaspora: Mexican Immigration to New Mexico." In *The Contested Homeland: A Chicano History of New Mexico*, edited by Erlinda Gonzales-Berry and David R. Maciel, 215–38. Albuquerque: University of New Mexico Press, 2000.

Giles, Howard, and Philip M. Smith. "Accommodation Theory: Optimal Levels of Convergence." In *Language and Social Psychology*, edited by Howard Giles and Robert N. St. Clair, 45–65. Baltimore: Blackwell, 1979.

Gilmore, Nicholas. "Four Santa Fe City Councilors Pitch Proposal to Rebuild Plaza Obelisk." *Santa Fe New Mexican*, February 4, 2023.

Gómez, Laura. *Manifest Destinies: The Making of the Mexican American Race*. New York: New York University Press, 2007.

Gonzales, María Dolores. "Todavía decimos 'Nosotros [los] mexicanos': Construction of Identity Labels among Nuevo Mexicanos." *Journal of Southwest Linguistics* 24 (2005): 65–77.

Gonzales-Berry, Erlinda. "Which Language Will Our Children Speak?: The Spanish Language and Public Education Policy in New Mexico, 1890–1930." In *The Contested Homeland: A Chicano History of New Mexico*, edited by Erlinda Gonzales-Berry and David R. Maciel, 169–90. Albuquerque: University of New Mexico Press, 2000.

Gonzales-Berry, Erlinda, and David Maciel. Introduction to *The Contested Homeland: A Chicano History of New Mexico*, edited by Erlinda Gonzales-Berry and David R. Maciel, 1–22. Albuquerque: University of New Mexico Press, 2000.

Gray, Ann. *Research Practice for Cultural Studies*. London: Sage Publications, 2003.

Griswold del Castillo, Richard. *La Familia: Chicano Families in the Urban Southwest, 1848 to the Present*. South Bend, IN: University of Notre Dame Press, 1984.

Gumperz, John J., and Eduardo Hernández-Chávez. "Cognitive Aspects of Bilingual Communication." In *El lenguaje de los chicanos: Regional and Social Characteristics Used by Mexican Americans*, edited by Eduardo Hernández-Chávez, Andrew D. Cohen, and Anthony F. Beltramo, 154–63. Arlington, VA: Center for Applied Linguistics, 1975.

Gutiérrez, David G. "Globalization, Labor Migration, and the Demographic Revolution: Ethnic Mexicans in the Late Twentieth Century." *The Columbia History of Latinos in the United States since 1960*, edited by David G. Gutiérrez, 1–44. New York: Columbia University Press, 2004.

———. *Walls and Mirrors: Mexican Americans, Mexican Immigrants, and the Politics of Ethnicity*. Berkley: University of California Press, 1995.

Guzmán, Gabriela. "Tensions among Hispanic Groups Erupt in Schools." *Albuquerque Journal*, November 6, 2005, A1.

Hall, Stuart. "Cultural Identity and Diaspora." In *Identity: Community, Culture, Difference*, edited by Jonathan Rutherford, 222–37. London: Lawrence and Wishart, 1990.

———. "The Multicultural Question." In *Stuart Hall Essential Essays, Volume 2: Identity and Diaspora*, edited by David Morley, 95–133. Durham, NC: Duke University Press. 2019.

———. "What Is the 'Black' in Black Popular Culture?" In *Black Popular Culture*, edited by Gina Dent, 20–33. Seattle: Bay Press, 1992.

Haugen, Elinar. "The Analysis of Linguistic Borrowing." *Language* 26, no. 2 (1950): 210–31.

Hernández, José Esteban. "Language, Contact, and the Negotiation of Salvadoran Identities in a Mixed-Latino Community." In *Spanish in the United States: Attitudes and Variation*, edited by Scott M. Alvord and Gregory L. Thompson, 11–30. New York: Routledge, 2020.

Hidalgo, Margarita. "Spanish Language Shift Reversal on the US–Mexico Border and the Extended Third Space." *Language and Intercultural Communication* 1 (2001): 57–73.

Hill, Jane. "Mock Spanish: The Indexical Reproduction of Racism in American English." *Language and Culture* 13, no. 2 (1995): 113–24.

———. "The Racializing Functions of Language Panics." In *Language Ideologies: Critical Perspectives on the Official English Movement, Volume 2*, edited by Roseann Dueñas Gonzalez and Ildikó Melis, 245–67. Mahwah, NJ: Lawrence Erlbaum Associates, 2001.

Hinojosa, María, and Maggie Freleng. "Of Bloodlines and Conquistadors." Produced by Maggie Freleng for NPR and Futuro Media. *Latino USA*, May 23, 2018. Audio podcast. https://www.latinousa.org/2018/05/18/ofbloodlinesanconquistadors/.

Hopper, Paul. *Understanding Cultural Globalization*. Cambridge: Polity Press, 2007.

Hornberger, Nancy. *Bilingual Education and Language Maintenance: A Southern Peruvian Quechua Case*. Dordrecht, Netherlands: Foris Publications Holland, 1988.

Hudson, Alan, and Garland D. Bills. "Intergenerational Language Shift in an Albuquerque Barrio." In *A Festschrift for Jacob Ornstein: Studies in General Linguistics and Sociolinguistics*, edited by Edward L. Blansitt Jr. and Richard V. Teschner, 139–58. Rowley, MA: Newbury House, 1980.

Hurtado, Aída. *Intersectional Chicana Feminisms: Sitios y lenguas*. Tucson: University of Arizona Press, 2020.

Hurtado, Aída, and Luis A. Vega. "Shift Happens: Spanish and English Transmission between Parents and Their Children." *Journal of Social Issues* 60 (2004): 137–55.

Irvine, Judith T., and Susan Gal. "Language Ideology and Linguistic Differentiation." In *Regimes of Language: Ideologies, Polities, and Identities*, edited by Paul V. Kroskrity, 35–83. Santa Fe: School of Advanced Research Press, 2000.

Jaramillo, Cleofas. *Romance of a Little Village Girl*. Albuquerque: University of New Mexico Press, 2000.

Jaramillo, Mari Luci. *Madame Ambassador: The Shoemaker's Daughter*. Tempe, AZ: Bilingual Press/Editorial Bilingüe, 2002.

———. *Sacred Seeds: A Girl, Her Abuelos, and the Heart of Northern New Mexico*. Taos, NM: Barranca Press, 2019.

Jenkins, Devin L. "The Cost of Linguistic Loyalty: Socioeconomic Factors in the Face of Shifting Demographic Trends among Spanish Speakers in the Southwest." *Spanish in Context* 6 (2009): 7–25.

Kroskrity, Paul V. "Regimenting Languages: Language Ideological Perspectives." In *Regimes of Language: Ideologies, Polities, and Identities*, edited by Paul V. Kroskrity, 1–34. Santa Fe: School for Advanced Research Press, 2000.

Labov, William. "The Notion of System in Creole Languages." In *Pidginization and Creolization of Languages*, edited by Dell Hymes, 447–72. Cambridge: Cambridge University Press, 1971.

Lee, Morgan. "At Nearly Half of Population, NM Still Most Latino State." *Albuquerque Journal*, August 12, 2021, A1.

Leeman, Jennifer. "Becoming Hispanic: The Negotiation of Ethnoracial Identity in US Census Interviews." *Latino Studies* 16, no. 4 (2018): 432–60.

———. "Categorizing Latinos in the History of the US Census: The Official Racialization of Spanish." In *A Political History of Spanish: The Making of a Language*, edited by José Del Valle, 305–23. Cambridge: Cambridge University Press, 2013.

Lippi-Green, Rosina. *English with an Accent: Language, Ideology, and Discrimination in the United States*. London: Routledge, 1997.

———. "That's Not My Language: The Struggle to (Re)Define African American English." In *Language Ideologies: Critical Perspectives on the Official English Movement, Volume 1*, edited by Roseann Dueñas Gonzalez and Ildikó Melis, 230–47. Mahwah, NJ: Lawrence Erlbaum Associates, 2000.

Lipski, John. "Linguistic Aspects of Spanish-English Language Switching." Center for Latin American Studies, Arizona State University, 1985.

———. *Varieties of Spanish in the United States*. Washington, DC: Georgetown University Press, 2008.

Lomelí, Francisco A., Victor A. Sorell, and Genaro M. Padilla, eds. *Nuevomexicano Cultural Legacy: Forms, Agencies, and Discourse*. Albuquerque: University of New Mexico Press, 2002.

Lope Blanch, Juan M. "El estudio del español hablado en el suroeste de los Estados Unidos." *Anuario de Letras* 25 (1987): 201–8.

Lowe, Lisa. *Immigrant Acts: On Asian American Cultural Politics*. Durham, NC: Duke University Press, 1996.

Lozano, Rosina. *An American Language: The History of Spanish in the United States*. Oakland: University of California Press, 2019.

Lugones, María. "Decolonial." In *Keywords for Latina/o Studies*, edited by Deb Vargas, Nancy Mirabal, and Lawrence La Fountain-Stokes, 43–47. New York: New York University Press, 2017.

Lynch, Andrew. "Spanish-Speaking Miami in Sociolinguistic Perspective: Bilingualism, Recontact, and Language Maintenance among the Cuban-Origin Population." In *Research on Spanish in the U.S.*, edited by Ana Roca, 271–83. Somerville, MA: Cascadilla Press, 2000.

———. "Toward a Theory of Heritage Language Acquisition: Spanish in the United States." In *Mi Lengua: Spanish as a Heritage Language in the United States, Research and Practice*, edited by Ana Roca and M. Cecilia Colombi, 25-49. Washington, DC: Georgetown University Press, 20003.

MacGregor-Mendoza, Patricia. "Aquí no se habla español: Stories of Linguistic Repression in Southwest Schools." *Bilingual Research Journal* 24, no. 4 (2000): 355–67.

Madrid, Alejandro. *Nor-Tec Rifa! Electronic Dance Music from Tijuana to the World*. Oxford: Oxford University Press, 2008.

———. "Why Music and Performance Studies? Why Now?: An Introduction to the Special Issue." *Revista Transcultural de Música/Transcultural Music Review* 13 (2009).

Martínez, Glenn A. *Mexican Americans and Language: Del dicho al hecho*. Tucson: University of Arizona Press, 2006.

Martínez, Glenn A., and Robert W. Train. *Tension and Contention in Language Education for Latinxs in the United States: Experience and Ethics in Teaching and Learning*. New York: Routledge, 2020.

Martínez, Rebecca Blum, and Mary Jean Habermann López, eds. *The Shoulders We Stand On: A History of Bilingual Education in New Mexico*. Albuquerque: University of New Mexico Press, 2020.

Medina-López, Kelly. "La Llorona as Querencia: Shared Stories and Sense of Place." In *Querencia: Reflections on the New Mexico Homeland*, edited by Vanessa Fonseca-Chávez, Levi Romero, and Spencer Herrera, 273–86. Albuquerque: University of New Mexico Press, 2020.

Meléndez, A. Gabriel. *So All Is Not Lost: The Poetics of Nuevomexicano Communities, 1834–1958*. Albuquerque: University of New Mexico Press, 1997.

Menchaca, Martha. *The Mexican Outsiders: A Community History of Marginalization and Discrimination in California*. Austin: University of Texas Press, 1995.

Mendoza-Denton, Norma. *Homegirls: Language and Cultural Practice among Latina Youth Gangs*. Malden, MA: Blackwell Publishing, 2008.

Mignolo, Walter. *Local Histories/Global Designs: Coloniality, Subaltern Knowledges, and Border Thinking*. Princeton, NJ: Princeton University Press, 2012.

Millán, Amalia. "Viaje por Nuevo México." *La Prensa* (San Antonio, Texas), December 4, 1949. Readex: America's Historical Newspapers.

Milroy, James, and Lesley Milroy. *Authority in Language: Investigating Standard English*. London: Routledge, 1985.

Montes, Verónica. "Mujeres luchadoras: Latina Immigrant Women's Homemaking Practices to Assert Belonging in a Philadelphia Suburb." In *Latinx Belonging: Community Building and Resilience in the United States*, edited by Natalia Deeb-Sossa and Jennifer Bickham Mendez, 95–114. Tucson: University of Arizona Press, 2002.

Montoya, Margaret, and John Nieto-Phillips. "A Conversation about Oñate Statues and Complex Stories." *Albuquerque Journal*, July 8, 2020. NewsBank: Access World News Historical and Current.

Montrul, Silvina. *Incomplete Acquisition in Bilingualism: Re-Examining the Age Factor*. Amsterdam: John Benjamins, 2008.

———. "Second Language Acquisition and First Language Loss in Adult Early Bilinguals: Exploring Some Differences and Similarities." *Second Language Research* 21 (2005): 199–249.

Mora, Anthony. *Border Dilemmas: Racial and National Uncertainties, 1848–1912*. Durham, NC: Duke University Press, 2011.

Mora, Cristina. *Making Hispanics: How Activists, Bureaucrats, and Media Constructed a New American*. Chicago: University of Chicago Press, 2014.

Muñoz, José Esteban. *Disidentifications: Queers of Color and the Performance of Politics*. Minneapolis: University of Minnesota Press, 1999.

———. *The Sense of Brown*. Durham, NC: Duke University Press, 2020.

Muysken, Pieter. "Code-Switching and Grammatical Theory." In *One Speaker, Two Languages*, edited by Lesley Milroy and Pieter Muysken, 177–98. Cambridge: Cambridge University Press, 1995.

Nieto-Phillips, John. *The Language of Blood: The Making of Spanish-American Identity in New Mexico, 1880s–1930s*. Albuquerque: University of New Mexico Press, 2004.

———. "Spanish American Ethnic Identity and New Mexico's Statehood Struggle." In *The Contested Homeland: A Chicano History of New Mexico*, edited by Erlinda Gonzales-Berry and David R. Maciel, 97–142. Albuquerque: University of New Mexico Press, 2000.

Oboler, Suzanne. *Ethnic Labels, Latino Lives*. Minneapolis: University of Minnesota Press, 1995.

Ochoa, Gilda L. *Becoming Neighbors in a Mexican American Community: Power, Conflict, and Solidarity*. Austin: University of Texas Press, 2004.

Oh, Janet, Sun-Ah Jun, Leah M. Knightly, and Terry Kit-fong Au. "Holding on to Childhood Language Memory." *Cognition* 86, no. 3 (2003): B53–64.

Ortiz, Leroy. "A Sociolinguistic Study of Language Maintenance in the Northern New Mexico Community of Arroyo Seco." PhD diss., University of New Mexico, 1975.

Osuna, Steven. "Intra-Latina/Latino Encounters: Salvadoran and Mexican Struggles and Salvadoran–Mexican Subjectivities in Los Angeles." *Ethnicities* 15, no. 2 (2015): 234–54.

Otero, Rosalie C., A. Gabriel Meléndez, and Enrique R. Lamadrid, eds. *Santa Fe Nativa: A Collection of Nuevomexicano Writing*. Albuquerque: University of New Mexico Press, 2009.

Otheguy, Ricardo. "The Linguistic Competence of Second-Generation Bilinguals: A Critique of 'Incomplete Acquisition.'" In *Romance Linguistics 2013: Selected Papers from the 43rd Linguistic Symposium on Romance Languages (LSRL)*, edited by Christina Tortora, Marcel den Dikken, Ignacio L. Montoya, and Teresa O'Neill, 301–19. Amsterdam: John Benjamins, 2016.

Otheguy, Ricardo, Ofelia García, and Mariela Fernández. "Transferring, Switching, and Modeling in West New York Spanish: An Intergenerational Study." *International Journal of the Sociology of Language* 79 (1989): 41–92.

Otheguy, Ricardo, and Ofelia García. "Convergent Conceptualizations as Predictors of Degree of Contact in U.S. Spanish." In *Spanish in the United States: Linguistic Contact and Diversity*, edited by Ana Roca and John Lipski, 135–54. New York: Mouton de Gruyter, 1993.

Otheguy, Ricardo, and Nancy Stern. "On So-Called Spanglish." *International Journal of Bilingualism* 15, no. 1 (2010): 85–100.

Parada, MaryAnn. "Sibling Variation and Family Language Policy: The Role of Birth Order in the Spanish Proficiency and First Names of Second-Generation Latinos." *Journal of Language, Identity and Education* 12 (2013): 299–320.

Paredez, Deborah. *Selenidad: Selena, Latinos, and the Performance of Memory*. Durham, NC: Duke University Press, 2009.

Pelaez López, Alan. "The X in Latinx Is a Wound, Not a Trend." ColorBloq: The Story of Us, September 2018. https://www.colorbloq.org/article/the-x-in-latinx-is-a-wound-not-a-trend.

Pennycook, Alastair. *Critical Applied Linguistics: A Critical Introduction*. London: Routledge, 2001.

———. *Global Englishes and Transcultural Flows*. London: Routledge, 2007.

Pérez, Gina. *The Near Northwest Side Story*. Berkley: University of California Press, 2004.

———. "Puertorriqueñas rencorosas y mejicanas sufridas: Gendered Ethnic Identity Formation in Chicago's Latino Communities." *Journal of Latin American Anthropology* 8, no. 2 (2003): 96–125.

Pew Research Center. "Facts on Latinos in the US." August 16, 2023. https://www.pewresearch.org/hispanic/fact-sheet/latinos-in-the-us-fact-sheet/.

Poplack, Shana. "Sometimes I'll Start a Sentence in Spanish y termino en español: Toward a Typology of Code-Switching." *Linguistics* 18 (1980): 581–616.

Poplack, Shana, and David Sankoff. "Code-Switching." In *Sociolinguistics: An International Handbook of Language and Society*, edited by Ulrick Ammon, Norbert Dittmar, and Klaus J. Mattheier, 1174–80. Berlin: Mouton de Gruyter, 1988.

Potowski, Kim. "Ethnolinguistic Identities and Ideologies among Mexicans, Puerto Ricans, and 'MexiRicans' in Chicago." In *A Sociolinguistics of Diaspora: Latino Practices, Identities and Ideologies*, edited by Rosina Márquez-Reiter and Luisa Martín Rojo, 13–30. London: Routledge, 2015.

———. "'I Was Raised Talking like My Mom': The Influence of Mothers in the Development of Mexiricans' Phonological and Lexical Features." In *Bilingualism and Identity: Spanish at the Crossroads with Other Languages*, edited by Mercedes Niño-Murcia and Jason Rothman, 201–20. New York: John Benjamins, 2008.

———. "Intrafamilial Dialect Contact." In *Handbook of Hispanic Sociolinguistics*, edited by Manuel Díaz-Campos, 579–97. Hoboken, NJ: Wiley-Blackwell, 2010.

———. *IntraLatino Language and Identity: MexiRican Spanish*. Amsterdam: John Benjamins, 2020.

———. "Spanish Language Shift in Chicago." *Southwest Journal of Linguistics* 23 (2004): 87–116.

Potowski, Kim, and Janine Matts. "Interethnic Language and Identity: MexiRicans in Chicago." *Journal of Language, Identity and Education* 6, no. 3 (2008): 137–60.

Potowski, Kim, and Lourdes Torres. *Spanish in Chicago*. Oxford: Oxford University Press, 2023.

Pratt, Mary Louise. *Imperial Eyes: Travel Writing and Transculturation*. New York: Routledge, 1992.

———. *Planetary Longings*. Durham, NC: Duke University Press, 2022.

Pugach, Marleen. *On the Border of Opportunity: Education, Community, and Language at the U.S.–Mexico Line*. Mahwah, NJ: Lawrence Erlbaum Associates, 1998.

Quijano, Anibal. "Coloniality of Power, Ethnocentrism, and Latin America." *NEPANTLA* 1, no. 3 (2000): 533–80.

Ramírez, Catherine S. *Assimilation: An Alternative History.* Berkeley: University of California Press, 2020.

Rivera-Mills, Susana. "Intraethnic Attitudes among Hispanics in a Northern California Community." In *Research on Spanish in the United States: Linguistic Issues and Challenges*, edited by Ana Roca, 377–89. Somerville, MA: Cascadilla Press, 2000.

Roberts, Shelly. *Remaining and Becoming: Cultural Crosscurrents in an Hispano School.* Mahwah, NJ: Lawrence Erlbaum Associates, 2001.

Rodríguez-Ordóñez, Itxaso, Shannon McCrocklin, and Alejandra Tiburcio. "Spanglish and Tex-Mex in the Rio Grande Valley of South Texas: Bilinguals' Perceptions and Valorizations of Speech Styles." *Spanish in Context* 20, no. 1 (2023): 50–75.

Romaine, Suzanne. "Identity and Multilingualism." In *Bilingual Youth: Spanish in English-Speaking Societies*, edited by Kim Potowski and Jason Rothman, 7–31. Amsterdam: Benjamins Publishing, 2011.

Romero, Simon. "New Mexico Is Losing a Form of Spanish Spoken Nowhere Else on Earth." *New York Times*, April 9, 2023. https://www.nytimes.com/2023/04/09/us/new-mexico-spanish.html.

Rosa, Jonathan. *Looking like a Language, Sounding like a Race.* Oxford: Oxford University Press, 2019.

Rosaldo, Renato. *Culture and Truth: The Remaking of Social Analysis.* Boston: Beacon Press, 1989.

Roybal, Karen R. *Archives of Dispossession: Recovering the Testimonios of Mexican American Herederas, 1848–1960.* Chapel Hill: University of North Carolina Press, 2017.

Rúa, Mérida. "Colao Subjectivities: PortoMex and MexiRican Perspectives on Language and Identity." *Centro Journal* 13, no. 2 (2001): 117–33.

———. *A Grounded Identidad: Making New Lives in Chicago's Puerto Rican Neighborhoods.* Oxford: Oxford University Press, 2012.

Rúa, Mérida, and Ana Y. Ramos-Zayas. "Introduction to *Critical Dialogues in Latinx Studies: A Reader*," edited by Ana Y. Ramos-Zayas and Mérida Rúa, 1–10. New York: New York University Press, 2021.

Rubin, Herbert J., and Irene S. Rubin. *Qualitative Interviewing: The Art of Hearing Data.* London: Sage Publications, 2011.

Saavedra, Cynthia M., and J. Joy Esquierdo. "Pláticas on Disrupting Language Ideologies in the Borderlands." In *Disrupting and Countering Deficits in Early Childhood Education*, edited by Fikile Nxumalo and Christopher P. Brown, 37–52. London: Routledge, 2019.

Salgado, Casandra D. "Mexican American Identity: Regional Differentiation in New Mexico." *Sociology of Race and Ethnicity* 6, no. 2 (2020): 179–94.

Sánchez, Maite T., and Ofelia García. "Introducción: Transforming Educational Espacios: Translanguaging sin Miedo." In *Transformative Translanguaging Espacios: Latinx Students and Their Teachers Rompiendo Fronteras sin Miedo*, edited by Maite T. Sánchez and Ofelia García, 1–18. Bristol, UK: Multilingual Matters, 2022.

Sandoval-Sánchez, Alberto. *José, Can You See?* Madison: University of Wisconsin Press, 1999.

Sanz, Israel, and Daniel J. Villa. "The Genesis of Traditional New Mexican Spanish: The Emergence of a Unique Dialect in the Americas." *Studies in Hispanic and Lusophone Linguistics* 4, no. 2 (2011): 417–42.

Schecter, Sandra, and Robert Bayley. *Language as Cultural Practice: Mexicanos en el Norte.* Mahwah, NJ: Lawrence Erlbaum Associates, 2002.

Silva-Corvalán, Carmen. *Language Contact and Change: Spanish in Los Angeles*. New York: Oxford University Press, 1994.

———. "Narrating in English and Spanish: Story Telling in the Words of a 5-Year-Old Bilingual." *Revista Internacional de Lingüística Iberoamericana* 1, no. 2 (2003): 35–58.

Silverstein, Michael. "Language Structure and Linguistic Ideology." In *The Elements: A Parasession on Linguistic Units and Levels*, edited by Paul R. Clyne, William F. Hanks, and Carol L. Hofbauer, 193–247. Chicago: Chicago Linguistic Society, 1979.

———. "The Whens and Wheres—as Well as Hows—of Ethnolinguistic Recognition." *Public Culture* 15, no. 3 (2003): 531–57.

Skutnabb-Kangas, Tove. *Bilingualism or Not? The Education of Minorities*. Clevedon, UK: Multilingual Matters, 1981.

Somos un Pueblo Unido. "Somos Primos PSA." 2009. YouTube video. https://www.youtube.com/watch?v=2SvMRk7Clds&t=13s.

Stavans, Ilan. *Spanglish: The Making of a New American Language*. New York: Harper Collins, 2003.

Tatum, Charles. "On the Border: From the Abstract to the Specific." *Arizona Journal of Hispanic Cultural Studies* 4 (2000): 93–103.

Taylor, Diana. "Transculturating Transculturation." *Performing Arts Journal* 13 (1991): 90–104.

Telles, Edward, and Christina A. Sue. *Durable Ethnicity: Mexican Americans and the Ethnic Core*. Oxford: Oxford University Press, 2019.

Torres Cacoullos, Rena, and Catherine Travis. *Bilingualism in the Community*. Cambridge: Cambridge University Press, 2018.

Train, Robert. "'Real Spanish': Historical Perspectives on the Ideological Construction of a (Foreign) Language." *Critical Inquiry in Language Studies* 4 (2007): 207–35.

Travis, Catherine E., and Daniel J. Villa. "Language Policy and Language Contact in New Mexico: The Case of Spanish." In *Uniformity and Diversity in Language Policy: Global Perspectives*, edited by Catrin Norrby and John Hajek, 126–40. Bristol, UK: Multilingual Matters, 2011.

Travis, Catherine, and Rena Torres Cacoullos. "Making Voices Count: Corpus Compilation in Bilingual Communities." *Australian Journal of Linguistics* 33 no. 2 (2013): 170–94.

Trudgill, Peter. *Dialects in Contact*. Oxford: Basil Blackwell, 1986.

Trujillo, Michael L. *Land of Disenchantment: Latina/o Identities and Transformations in Northern New Mexico*. Albuquerque: University of New Mexico Press, 2010.

Urciuoli, Bonnie. *Exposing Prejudice: Puerto Rican Experiences of Language, Race, and Class*. Boulder, CO: Westview Press, 1996.

———. "Whose Spanish? The Tension between Linguistic Correctness and Cultural Identity." In *Bilingualism and Identity: Spanish at the Crossroads with Other Languages*, edited by Mercedes Niño-Murcia and Jason Rothman, 257–78. New York: John Benjamins, 2008.

Valdés, Guadalupe. "Afterword—No quiero que me la vayan a hacer burla: Issues to Ponder and Consider in the Context of Translanguaging." In *Transformative Translanguaging Espacios: Latinx Students and Their Teachers Rompiendo Fronteras sin Miedo*, edited by Maite T. Sánchez and Ofelia García, 292–301. Bristol, UK: Multilingual Matters, 2022.

———. *Con Respeto, Bridging the Distance between Culturally Diverse Families and Schools: An Ethnographic Portrait*. New York: Teacher's College Press, 1996.

———. "Ethnolinguistic Identity: The Challenge of Maintaining Spanish–English Bilingualism in American Schools." In *Bilingual Youth: Spanish in English-Speaking Societies*, edited by Kim Potowski and Jason Rothman, 113–46. Amsterdam: John Benjamins Publishing, 2011.

———. "Heritage Language Students: Profiles and Possibilities." In *Heritage Languages in America: Preserving a National Resource*, edited by Joy Kreeft Peyton, Donald A. Ranard, and Scott McGinnis, 37–80. Arlington, VA: Center for Applied Linguistics, 2001.

———. "Social Interaction and Code-Switching Patterns: A Case Study of Spanish–English Alternation." In *Bilingualism in the Bicentennial and Beyond*, edited by Gary D. Keller, Richard V. Teschner, and Silvia Viera, 53–85. Tempe, AZ: Bilingual Press/Editorial Bilingüe, 1976.

Valdez, Elena V. "Chicana/o Literature and the Folkloric Difference." PhD diss., Rice University, 2019.

———. "Ownership and Order in the Fiesta de Santa Fe." *Chiricú Journal: Latina/o Literature, Art, and Culture* 3, no. 1 (2018): 120–38.

Valenzuela, Norma A. "Mestiza Consciousness a la MeXicana in Ultima and Agueda Martínez: Bridging and Legitimizing Querencia in the Borderlands." In *Querencia: Reflections on the New Mexico Homeland*, edited by Vanessa Fonseca-Chávez, Levi Romero, and Spencer Herrera, 179–95. Albuquerque: University of New Mexico Press, 2020.

Vázquez, Jessica. *Mexican Americans across Generations*. New York: New York University Press, 2011.

Veltman, Calvin. *Language Shift in the United States*. Berlin: Mouton, 1983.

Vergara Wilson, Damián. "Panorama of Traditional New Mexican Spanish." *Informes del Observatorio / Observatorio Reports* (2015). Faculty of Arts and Sciences of Harvard University: Instituto Cervantes.

Vigil, Neddy, and Garland Bills. "New Mexico and Colorado Spanish Survey [dataset]." University of New Mexico Digital Repository, 2011. https://digitalrepository.unm.edu/cgi/viewcontent.cgi?article=1000&context=span_fsp&httpsredir=1&referer=.

Vila, Pablo. *Crossing Borders, Reinforcing Borders: Social Categories, Metaphors and Narrative Identities on the U.S.–Mexico Frontier*. Austin: University of Texas Press, 2000.

———. "The Polysemy of the Label 'Mexican' on the Border." In *Ethnography at the Border*, edited by Pablo Vila, 105–39. Minneapolis: University of Minnesota Press, 2006.

Villa, Daniel, and Susana Rivera-Mills. "An Integrated Multi-Generational Model for Language Maintenance and Shift: The Case of Spanish in the Southwest." *Spanish in Context* 6 (2009): 26–42.

Villa, Daniel J., and Israel Sanz-Sánchez. "U.S. Mexican Spanish: A Historical Perspective on the Development of the Macro-Dialect Spoken in the Western U.S." *International Journal of the Linguistic Association of the Southwest* 34, no. 1–2 (2015): 129–49.

Villa, Daniel J., and Jens H. Clegg. *U.S. Mexican Spanish West of the Mississippi*. London: Routledge, 2023.

Villarreal, Aimee. "Anthropolocura as Homeplace Ethnography." In *Ethnographic Refusals, Unruly Latinidades*, edited by Alex E. Chávez and Gina M. Pérez, 195–218. Santa Fe: School for Advanced Research Press, 2022.

———. "Coming to Terms with Santa Fe's Entrada Pageant." NMPolitics.net, August 30, 2017. https://nmpolitics.net/index/2017/08/coming-to-terms-with-santa-fes-entrada-pageant/.

Walsh, Catherine. *Pedagogy and the Struggle for Voice: Issues of Language, Power, and Schooling for Puerto Ricans*. Toronto: OISE Press, 1991.

Waltermire, Mark. "Mexican Immigration and the Changing Face of Northern New Mexican Spanish." *International Journal of the Linguistic Association of the Southwest* 34, no. 1–2 (2015): 149–65.

Weinreich, Uriel. *Languages in Contact*. The Hague: Mouton, 1953.

Wilson, Damián. "Diversity in Definition: Integrating History and Student Attitudes in Understanding Heritage Learners of Spanish in New Mexico." *Heritage Language Journal* 8 (2011): 115–33.

Woolard, Kathryn A. "Language Ideology as a Field of Inquiry." In *Language Ideologies: Practice and Theory*, edited by Bambi B. Schieffelin, Kathryn A. Woolard, and Paul V. Kroskrity, 3–47. Oxford: Oxford University Press, 1998.

———. *Singular and Plural: Ideologies of Linguistic Authority in 21st Century Catalonia*. Oxford: Oxford University Press, 2016.

Yin, Robert. *Case Study Research: Design and Methods*. Newbury Park, CA: Sage, 2009.

Zentella, Ana Celia. "The 'Chiquitafication' of U.S. Latinos and Their Languages, or Why We Need an Anthropolitical Linguistics." In *SALSA III: The Proceedings of the Symposium about Language and Society at Austin*, edited by Department of Linguistics, University of Texas, 1–18. Austin: University of Texas, 1995. https://files.eric.ed.gov/fulltext/ED416671.pdf.

———. "'Dime con quién hablas y te diré quién eres': Linguistic (In)Security and Latina(o) Unity." In *A Companion to Latina/o Studies*, edited by Juan Flores and Renato Rosaldo, 25–39. Malden, MA: Blackwell, 2007.

———. Foreword to *Language as Cultural Practice: Mexicanos en el Norte*, by Sandra R. Schecter and Robert Bayley, ix–xiv. Mahwah, NJ: Lawrence Erlbaum Associates, 2002.

———. *Growing Up Bilingual*. Oxford: Blackwell, 1997.

———. "Latin@ Languages and Identities." In *Latinos Remaking America*, edited by Marcelo Suárez-Orozco and Mariela M. Páez, 321–38. Berkley: University of California Press, 2002.

———. "Lexical Leveling in Four New York City Spanish Dialects: Linguistic and Social Factors." *Hispania* 73, no. 4 (1990): 1094–105.

———. "Plenary Address: A Debate about Spanglish." Presented at the 22nd Conference on Spanish in the United States and 7th Conference on Spanish in Contact with Other Languages, Florida International University, Coral Gables / Miami, FL, February 20, 2009.

INDEX

agency, 108, 183; acts of, 97–106, 182; ethnic, 9; invisibility of, 89; linguistic, 88, 100

Albuquerque Journal, 1, 2, 3, 29

alingualism, 170

AlSayaad, Nezar, 186

American, term, 147

American Immigration Council, 33

Americanization, 31, 191

analysis, critical approaches to, 39–41

Anaya, Rudolfo, 9

anglicisms, 170

anthropology, 36; linguistic, 29, 30, 50

Anzaldúa, Gloria, 44, 60, 115; on Chicano Spanish, 135; conocimiento and, 185; on oppression, 62

Aparicio, Ana, 26, 40

Aparicio, Frances, 18, 44, 144; "American" and, 147; on exclusion, 153; horizontal hierarchies and, 75; Latinidad and, 25–26; linguistic power differentials and, 74–75; theories of, 30

Appadurai, Arjun, 141, 142, 145, 152

applied linguistics, 23; critical, 30, 36, 50

archaisms, 167–68, 169

Arellano, Juan Estevan: querencia and, 9, 187

Arnold, Patricia, 20–21

assimilation: Mexicano/a/x, 15; rubric of, 75

authentication, 27, 28, 41; authenticity and, 126

authenticity, 17, 28, 133; authentication and, 126; correctness and, 138; cultural, 17; ideology of, 126, 130, 134; linguistic, 138; power and, 129

auto-encuentro zone, 41–45

awareness, 81, 89, 115, 121, 125; cultural, 154; deep, 185

Bayley, Robert, 17, 24, 37, 88, 99, 103, 105; language choice and, 93; on language maintenance/shift, 98; language socialization and, 91, 109; linguistic abilities and, 110; on patterns of variation/choice, 101

belief systems, familial, 115

Bhabha, Homi, 144

bilanguaging love, 148

bilingual certification exam (La Prueba), 36, 183

bilingual communities, 169

bilingualism, 56, 64, 92, 99, 181; critical, 136; Latinx, 44; Spanish-English, 170; viewpoints of, 155
bilinguals, 103, 148n31, 169, 170; cognitive abilities of, 171
Bills, Garland, 18, 19, 21, 21n92, 32, 33, 56, 89, 90, 107, 167, 168, 178, 182; anglicisms and, 170; on recontact/border proximity, 57; TNMS and, 20, 172
binary oppositions, identity and, 149
blame, discourse of, 104, 105, 106
Blanch, Lope, 19
Bucholtz, Mary, 23; adequation and, 125; on authentication, 27, 28; authenticity and, 126; distinction and, 144; social practice and, 27, 126; sociocultural linguistics and, 30

calques, 170, 174
Cárdenas, Maritza E., 162
Carrillo-Rowe, Aimee, 43
Cathedral Park, 189
change.org petition, 189
Chávez-Silverman, Susana, 44
Chicana, 151; term, 7
Chicana feminist epistemology, 42, 44, 50
Chicana feminist studies, 30, 36, 41–45, 50
Chicana feminists, 189
Chicana/Latina feminist theory, 38
Chicanidad, 12
Chicano, 43; term, 7, 139–40, 151
Chicano Spanish, 135
Chicano/a/x studies, 12
Chihuahua Cathedral, 14–15
chiquitafication, 66–67, 67n34, 74, 75, 83, 117, 138
Cisneros, René, 50, 51, 55; recontact and, 54, 74
citizenship, 8, 140, 147; dual, 157
Clary-Lemon, Jennifer, 142
Cobos, Rubén, 21, 33, 184, 185
code-switching, 56, 82, 84n70, 99, 138, 170, 171, 175; translanguaging and, 169
colando-ing, 161
colonial legacy, 25, 80, 81
colonialism, 24, 32, 42

communication, 101, 103, 106, 121, 171, 172; day-to-day, 110; familial, 109; reality of, 69
constructs, ideological/slippery, 118–22
contact, 74; dialectical, 21, 105; language, 169–70; Spanish-English, 173
contact generation, 61; framework for, 59, 60, 62; notion of, 58, 59
contact zones, 23–31, 35, 105; chaos of, 25; conditions of, 75; language experiences within, 25
Contested Homeland, The (Gonzales-Berry and Maciel), 9
correction, 122, 138; authenticating practice of, 126–37; practice of, 126, 129, 134; as symbolic practice, 133; validation and, 118
correctness, authenticity and, 138
coupling, 149, 158
cultural processes, 39, 41
cultural studies, 36, 50, 51; ethnographic mode of, 39; Latino/a/x, 28, 29–30, 31, 35
culture, 18, 23, 80, 141, 154, 158, 161, 189; American, 147, 191; Anglo-American, 67, 75, 146; changes and, 82; dominant, 117; heritage and, 152; Hispanic, 148, 151, 191; lamination of, 151; language and, 110, 111, 152, 153, 155; Latino, 150; Mexican, 7, 17; minor, 74, 75, 81; Nuevomexicano/a/x, 15; popular, 176; Spanish, 146; territory and, 80

Daiute, Colette, 40
data analysis, 33, 40–41, 50
Dávila, Arlene, 29
De Houwer, Annick, 63
De Vargas, Don Diego, 189
Del Angel Guevara, Mario Esteban, 22, 23, 55, 57, 76, 172, 182
Delgado-Bernal, Dolores, 38, 40, 42
demography, 2, 31, 34
denaturalization, 126, 127, 130
deterritorialization, 80–81, 82, 85
Dictionary of New Mexico and Southern Colorado Spanish, A (Cobos), 21, 185
difference: cultural, 158, 162; cultural identity and, 143; dialect, 77; familial, 144–51; heterogeneity and, 143; hybridity and, 143,

144; linguistic, 124, 126; sameness and, 141; social, 116
directionality, notions of, 94, 95, 96, 101, 102, 104
discrimination, 105, 158
disjunctures, familial, 144–51
displacement, 81; linguistic, 80, 188
dispossession, 10, 81, 136; linguistic, 67, 80, 155, 188
dissonance, 113, 120, 121, 123
distinction, 125, 144; linguistic, 131
divergences, familial, 144–51
diversity, 26, 59, 62, 96, 97, 98, 143, 181; dialectical, 77; linguistic, 134; religious, 125
dominance, 17, 44, 76, 78, 85, 97, 183; cultural, 146; English, 101, 109, 148, 155; male, 158; Spanish, 102
Dorian, Nancy C., 104
Dowling, Julie, 11
dual-language immersion, 36, 102
Durán, Cristina, 4, 11
dynamics, 91, 93, 109; cultural, 190; family, 114; power, 29, 129, 132

Eagleton, Terry, 116
education, 15, 26, 89, 143; bilingual, 31, 197, 202
embarrassment, 62, 63, 132, 152, 161; shame and, 131
"Enchanting Trip, An" (Jaramillo), 14
encuentros, 43, 187; contact zone to, 24–25
English, 120, 135; being/doing Latinx in, 156; dominance/patterns of, 109; identity and, 156; learning, 61; New Mexican Spanish and, 167, 169, 170, 172, 173, 174; Spanglish and, 166; Spanish and, 156, 169; speaking, 99, 105, 108, 110, 171, 172; term, 175; value of, 181
equality, 121; ideologies of, 120; linguistic, 119, 120, 122, 123, 125, 126
erasure, 27, 63, 78, 116, 145, 159; cultural, 146, 149; moments of, 67
Errington, Joseph, 114
Escobar, Ana María, 181
Esquierdo, J. Joy, 39
ethnic labels, 156–63
Ethnic Labels, Latino Lives (Oboler), 156

ethnicity, 140, 146n26, 150, 157; linguistic ability and, 154
ethnography, linguistic, 6, 29, 30, 36, 187
ethnolinguistic futures, 182–87
ethnolinguistic history, 41, 42, 43, 190
exceptionalism, 10, 166n7
experiences: diaspora, 143; identity and, 40; immigrant, 11; language, 5, 6, 25, 30, 31, 42, 62, 97, 151, 155, 164, 188; theorizing, 39–40

family names/demographics, 49 table 2
family portraits, Mexicano-Nuevomexicano, 45–50
Farias, Georgina, 3
Feast of Our Lady of Guadalupe, 4
feeling brown, 142, 143
Fierro, Juanita, 46, 61, 62, 64, 69, 73, 76, 80, 82; on English/Spanish speaking, 108; mistaken identity of, 84; New Mexican Spanish and, 78; Spanish proficiency of, 66, 79
Fierro, Luis, 46, 66, 125, 133, 180; on culture/changes, 82; Mexican/Spanish and, 121; recontact and, 84; sense of self and, 85
Fierro, Verónica, 46, 84, 104, 160, 162, 182; archaisms and, 168; Chicano and, 151; code-switching, 181; cultural marking and, 154; on Hispanics, 154; language use of, 100; linguistic abilities and, 132–33; on New Mexican Spanish, 172–73, 175, 176; Spanglish and, 179, 180, 181; Spanish speaking and, 87, 96, 107–8
Fishman, Joshua, 58, 98, 110
Flores, Juan, 26
Floyd, George, 189
Fought, Carmen, 149–50
fractal recursivity, 131
Futuro Media, 163

Gal, Susan, 116, 131
Galindo, D. Letticia, 16, 55, 56
García, Lorena, 26
García, Ofelia, 44, 92, 159, 169, 170, 180; translanguaging and, 150, 185
García Acevedo, María Rosa, 11, 12
gender, 129, 143, 158; dominance, 78n54
generation, 88; reframing, 57–64

232 • INDEX

Gómez, Laura, 10
Gonzales, Maria Dolores, 10, 11
Gonzales-Berry, Erlinda, 9, 44
Gorman, Richard, 3
Gorman, Robert, Sr., 43
grammatical rules, 21, 171
Gray, Ann, 30, 39–40
Griswold del Castillo, Richard, 7, 8, 13
Gutiérrez, David, 7–8
Guzmán, Alejandro, 46, 93–94, 97, 106; "Mexican American" and, 157; Spanglish and, 178–79; Spanish and, 102, 104
Guzmán, Alexa, 46, 93–94, 97, 106, 153; Hispanics and, 154; Spanglish and, 179; Spanish and, 110
Guzmán, Andrea, 45, 46, 64, 69, 70, 71, 76, 80, 81, 132; communication by, 54; on lexical choices, 118; marriage of, 118; New Mexican Spanish and, 78; receptive skills of, 63; relationship with, 56; Spanish of, 53–54, 62, 63
Guzmán, Manuel, 45, 56, 146, 146n26; communication by, 54; on lexical choices, 118; linguistic policing by, 119; marriage of, 118; Mexicanness of, 53

Habla Ya (series), 175
Hall, Kira, 23
Hall, Stuart: coupling and, 149; on cultural identity, 141; diaspora experience and, 143; hybridity and, 144; sociolinguistics and, 30
herencia, 188, 189, 190
Hernández-Chávez, Eduardo, 89
heterogeneity, 141, 143, 146, 160
Hidalgo, Margarita, 55, 56
hierarchies, 124; horizontal, 75, 142, 143, 149; linguistic, 113, 150
Hill, Jane, 117, 175n32
Hinojosa, Maria, 163, 164
Hispanic: resemantification of, 163; term, 52, 144, 151, 152, 153, 157, 158–59, 160, 161, 162, 163
Hispanics, 154; Mexican tension with, 1; native, 2, 9n29
hispano/a, 7; term, 10, 160, 163–64
home, 52; bicultural, 1; Latino/a/x, 190; migration and, 5

homeplaces, shared cultural/linguistic, 3–7
homogenization, 145, 149, 156, 160
Hopper, Paul, 81, 82
Hornberger, Nancy, 98–99
"How to Tame a Wild Tongue" (Anzaldúa), 44
Hudson, Alan, 89, 90, 107
Humboldt Park, 190
Hurtado, Aida, 41, 42, 43, 55, 87, 189
hybridity, 141, 146, 149, 154, 160, 163; cultural, 158, 162, 164; difference and, 143, 144; identity and, 144

identity, 41, 126, 135, 139, 141–44, 162; American, 146; americana, 144; americano, 146, 146n26; Asian American, 141; binary oppositions and, 149; Chicana, 12; choice of, 110–11; collective, 142, 143; contradictory/complementary, 144; cultural, 6, 9, 17, 52, 90, 110, 140, 141, 143, 147, 149, 151–56, 158, 164; enacting, 16, 149–50; English and, 156; ethnic, 44, 136; ethnolinguistic, 6, 7, 15, 21, 24, 25, 30, 39, 41; flows, 140, 144, 149; gringa, 65, 144–45, 146, 146n26; Hispanic, 146, 149, 151, 153, 159, 163; hybridity and, 144; language and, 52, 148, 152, 152n40, 154–55; Latino/a/x, 17, 27, 157, 163, 191; Mexican, 9, 10, 18, 151–52, 160, 161; Mexicana, 158; Mexicano/a/x-Nuevomexicano/a/x, 138, 144; mistaken, 84; national, 28, 29; New Mexican, 7, 8, 12; Nuevomexicano/a/x, 13–14, 84, 151; Puerto Rican, 18; racial, 136; regional, 10, 29, 140; relational, 142, 149; (re)productions, 163–64; social, 44; Spanish, 164; terms, 140, 153, 164
ideologies, 133–34; constructs of, 118–22; definitions of, 114, 116–17; hegemonic, 135; language, 113, 116–17, 117–18, 121, 123n32, 124, 125–26, 131, 151; overlapping/intersecting/divergings, 114. *See also* language ideologies; standard language ideology
immigrants, Mexican, 8, 11, 16, 112, 127–28, 166
immigration, 18, 146; context of, 58; generational histories and, 57; waves of, 8
incorrectness, 169, 178
interactions, 25; inter-Latino/a/x, 17; inter-Mexican, 16
interconnections, cultural/linguistic, 6, 82
Irvine, Judith, 116, 131

Jaramillo, Cleofas, 14–15
Jaramillo, Mari Luci, 2, 5, 15, 23, 122; memoir of, 4, 51; on Mexican words, 123; quote of, 1, 86, 112, 165
Jenkins, Devin, 89
Jurado, Armando, 48, 86, 88
Jurado, Diana, 48, 69, 75, 86, 88, 105; on perception, 83
Jurado, Rose, 4n11, 48, 83, 86, 89, 94, 108, 133, 169; difference and, 124; English and, 156; language use patterns and, 105; proficiency of, 87; Spanglish and, 179; Spanish use by, 104–5

knowledge: cultural, 39; lack of, 55; organizing, 40; social, 44
knowledge production, 164; community, 40; inter-Latino/a/x, 16, 187; power dynamics of, 29
Kroskrity, Paul V., 114, 115, 116

La Llorona, legend of, 38
la plebe, term, 7
La Sociedad Folklórica, 14
Labov, William, 98
language: allocation, 104; attitudes about, 17, 120; bilingual, 169; claims about, 120; culture and, 110, 111, 152, 152n40, 153, 155; family, 17, 51; heritage, 56; home, 166; identity and, 52, 148, 152; immigrant, 58; lamination of, 151; Mexicano-Nuevomexicano, 21, 25; minority, 99, 105; power and, 113, 116, 128, 129; Pueblo Indian, 135; real/correct, 122
language ability, 109, 151; identity and, 154–55
language behavior, 93, 98, 99
language history, recovery of, 42, 43
language ideologies, 39, 41, 113, 114–18; awareness of, 115; dominant, 171; language structure and, 114
language loss, 59, 60, 64; pattern of, 89
language maintenance, 41, 51, 62, 74, 87, 97, 98, 109–11; intergenerational, 88; in New Mexico, 88–91; second-generation, 60; third-generation, 60, 64
language panics, 117, 122, 124, 131
language practices, 41, 88, 91, 183, 187
language pride, 116, 122, 124
language recovery, 42, 88, 187, 189

language retention, 98; socioeconomic status and, 89
language shaping, 51, 88, 97–106
language shift, 31, 41, 51, 55, 59, 60, 64, 74, 89, 102, 103, 109, 155, 183; experience of, 165–66; intergenerational, 87; reframing of, 88; three-generation model for, 58, 87
language socialization, 88, 109; patterns, 24, 102; practices, 91–97
language transmission, intergenerational, 86, 89, 104, 106, 113, 122–26, 167, 177, 179–82
language use: portraits, 91–97; shaping, 104
language use patterns, 17, 39, 72, 93, 109, 110; changes in, 99, 105; directionality in, 94 fig. 2, 95 fig. 3, 95 fig. 4, 96 fig. 5; family, 90, 97
Latina/o, term, 7
Latinidad, 23–31, 38, 39, 50, 51, 66, 67, 75, 80, 91, 122, 130, 136, 141–44, 149, 156, 163; activation of, 164; agency/self-determination and, 26; different faces of, 114; framework of, 27, 75, 117, 118, 190; horizontal hierarchies of, 161; linguistic, 27, 31, 187; in New Mexico, 28–29; place-making and, 28–29; power dynamics and, 28; recontact and, 56; theories of, 27, 29; zones of, 25–28
"Latino Imaginary," 26
Latino USA, 163
Latino/a/x: being, 29; groups, 19, 24, 43; language experiences of, 42; population, 2
Latinos/as/xs, 26; categorization of, 33; critical studies of, 29–30
Latinx: mixed, 18; term, 2n6, 29
Leone, Elizabeth, 50, 51, 55; recontact and, 54, 74
lexical elicitation, 36, 99, 123, 127, 178
lexicon, 21; differences in, 118–19
Lightfoot, Cynthia, 40
linguistic abilities, 15, 67, 110, 132–33; cultural identity and, 154; ethnicity and, 154
linguistic behaviors, 109, 170
linguistic correctness, 127, 131; ideologies of, 120, 125–26; notions of, 123, 124
linguistic hierarchies, 135–36; intergenerational transmission of, 122–26; patriarchal, 129
linguistic history, 67, 136
linguistic policing, 119, 129, 130

linguistic power plays, 126–37; denaturalization and, 127

linguistic profiles, 54, 57–64, 67

linguistic skills, 67, 137

linguistic tendencies, 62, 68

linguistic validation, 113, 121

Lippi-Green, Rosina, 134, 135, 169; SLI and, 125; social context and, 115

Lipski, John, 22, 64, 129n50, 170

loanwords, 169, 170, 174, 181

Loredo, Angélica, 47, 95, 108, 110, 120–21, 123–24, 133, 135; comparisons by, 175; connection and, 132; "Mexican American" and, 157; Spanglish and, 178; Spanish and, 111; Spanish/English mixing and, 176

Loredo, Francisco, 47, 60, 62, 67, 69, 70, 79, 108; agency of, 61; archaisms and, 168; culture of, 80; lazy Spanish and, 174; Spanish of, 184–85; Spanish proficiency of, 66

Loredo, Pía, 46–47, 69, 79, 120, 122, 123, 132, 169, 182, 187; archaisms and, 168; language maintenance and, 73; language practices / language beliefs of, 183; linguistic connection and, 80; linguistic discovery of, 82; linguistic resources for, 184–85; New Mexican Spanish and, 183–84, 186

Lowe, Lisa, 143, 149; hegemonic positionalities and, 141–42; heterogeneity and, 146; hybridity and, 154; multiplicity and, 142

Lozano, Rosina, 8, 31

Lucero, Jesús María, 14

Lynch, Andrew, 55

Maciel, David, 9

Madame Ambassador (Jaramillo), 1, 15, 86, 112

Madrid, Alejandro, 41, 84

Maestas, Sylvia, 50, 161, 162; language experience of, 99

maintenance, 59, 108; acts of, 97–106

Martinez, Glenn, 5, 6, 115; on language ideologies, 116, 118; language panics and, 117

Martínez-García, María Teresa, 20–21

matrix of intelligibility, 162–63

McCrocklin, Shannon, 181

meaning-making process, 39, 40

Medina, Adrian, 49, 94, 106, 110; Spanglish and, 179

Medina, José, 49, 50; on speaking Spanish, 92–93

Medina, Olivia, 49, 106, 151, 160; on identity, 157; Spanglish and, 179

Medina, Penélope, 49, 50, 69, 75n48, 76, 80, 185, 187; agency of, 183; New Mexican Spanish and, 182–83, 186

Medina-López, Kelly, 38

Menchaca, Martha, 16

Mendoza-Denton, Norma, 16, 55

Mexican, 157n51; becoming, 151; conceptualization of, 152; identifying as, 10; term, 7, 10, 11, 151, 157

Mexican American, 8, 117, 157n51; term, 147, 157

Mexican American Spanish, 168

Mexican Spanish, 66, 117, 120, 178; belief in, 119, 121; comparison to, 174; contemporary, 135; correctness/authenticity and, 173; elevation of, 123; geographic contexts of, 168; New Mexican Spanish and, 22, 76–77, 78–80, 114, 122, 136, 166, 183; predominance of, 76; present and, 76; prettiness of, 123; realness/correctness of, 124; speaking, 75, 77, 122–23; as standard language, 129; superiority of, 124

Mexicana, identifying as, 157–58

Mexicana Hispana, term, 158

Mexicanidad, 78; claiming, 7–12; Nuevomexicanidad and, 83

Mexicanisms, 22, 23

Mexicanization, standardization of, 56

Mexicano, term, 7, 10, 11

Mexicano-Nuevomexicano (MX-NMX) families, 13, 20, 21, 22, 33, 37, 50, 69, 71, 82, 182, 191; archaisms and, 168; described, 35; exploring, 6–7; fixed identities and, 164; knowledge production and, 164; language experiences of, 6, 23; language maintenance and, 87, 88; language practices and, 88; language shift and, 87; language use patterns and, 90, 91–92; linguistic agency and, 88; linguistic diversity in, 97; linguistic profiles of, 58–59; living/thriving of, 190; metalinguistic sense and, 137; narratives of, 28, 31–32; Spanish use by, 109; trust of / access to, 36; zones of contact and, 35

Mexicano-Nuevomexicanos: archive, 4; context, 18, 29, 30, 51, 57; ethnic labels and, 156–63; ethnolinguistic futures of, 187; language experiences of, 51; portraits, 13–16; solidarity, 3; term, 2, 2n5

Mexicano/a/x, 2, 50; identifying as, 10; immigrant, 3; population of, 11; term, 7

mexicanos de aqui, term, 7

Mexicanos/as/xs, 17, 24, 28, 43; ethnolinguistic futures of, 187; home and, 5; knowledge production and, 29; language shift and, 31; Nuevomexicanos/as/xs and, 3, 14, 15, 25, 34; sociohistorical linguistic legacy of, 31

Mexicans, 2, 17; bad mouthing, 158; ethnic, 8; Hispanic tension with, 1; Spanish Americans and, 13

Mignolo, Walter, 81, 148

Millán, Amalia, 13–14

Milroy, James, 120, 123

Milroy, Lesley, 120, 123

Molina, Alicia, 46, 100, 101, 133, 139, 140, 144, 145, 146, 161, 174; English and, 94; "Hispanic" and, 151; identity and, 157, 160; Spanglish and, 176, 178; Spanish and, 104

Molina, Antonio, 94, 100, 101, 102, 140, 144, 145, 146, 162; cultural identity and, 152; on English / New Mexican Spanish, 174; "Hispanic" and, 152; "Mexican" and, 152

Molina, Elizabeth, 46, 62, 63, 64, 69, 71, 72, 72n40, 82, 140, 145; communication with, 68; distinction and, 144; linguistic profile of, 65; recontact and, 67–68; reterritorialization and, 85

Molina, Pancho, 46, 62, 65, 69, 72, 82, 101, 140, 144, 145, 146; "American" and, 147; on "Chicano," 139; communication with, 68; language use by, 100; linguistic oppression and, 81; recontact and, 67–68

monolingualism, 43, 92, 105, 150; double, 149, 169

Montes, Verónica, 5

Montrul, Silvina, 63

Mora, Anthony, 10

Mora, Christina, 159, 160

movement, 141–44

multiplicity, 141, 142, 160

Muñoz, José Esteban, 142, 143

Nahuatl, 22, 135, 168

narratives, 50, 113, 114; concept of, 39; identity, 142; personal, 30

National Hispanic Cultural Center, 21

nationality, 140, 157; Mexican, 7, 8

Navarro, Gabriela, 48, 66, 69, 72, 73, 92, 131; archaisms and, 168; linguistic resources and, 65; linguistic validation and, 121; native Hispanics and, 9n29

Navarro, Milagros, 48, 93, 95–96, 97, 124, 129, 131, 133, 146, 149, 155, 173; "American" and, 147; exclusion and, 153; "Hispanic" and, 153; identity and, 150; on language/culture, 152; loanwords and, 169; "Mexican American" and, 147, 160; Mexican Spanish and, 174; Spanglish and, 148, 178; Spanish proficiency and, 105–6; translanguaging and, 150

Navarro, Nicolás, 48, 61, 62, 64, 69, 72, 112, 113, 131; cultural awareness and, 154; on Hispanic identity, 146; language experience of, 155; linguistic policing and, 129–30; local and, 149; Spanglish and, 147–48, 154, 177, 179; Spanish speaking of, 65–66; translanguaging, 150; usage and, 115

Navarro, Rosalinda, 48, 95–96, 129, 133, 146; identity and, 150; linguistic abilities and, 132; local and, 149; "Mexican American" and, 147, 160; rednecks and, 157; self-policing by, 130, 131; Spanglish and, 148, 166, 179; translanguaging and, 150

neocolonialism, 25, 44, 80

neologisms, 170

New Mexican Spanish, 19, 21, 22, 45, 56, 66, 123, 133, 135, 181; analysis of, 167; appreciation for, 184, 185; archaisms of, 168; attitudes about, 182; characterizations of, 167; chiquitafied, 83; correctness of, 119; described, 166, 172–73, 175; English and, 167, 169, 170, 172, 173, 174; erasure of, 78; future of, 166, 167, 177–78, 182; hybridity of, 167; ideologies of, 167; inferiority of, 124; innovative features of, 171; linguistic/sociopolitical history of, 186; loanwords/calques and, 174; Mexican Spanish and, 22, 76–77, 78–80, 114, 122, 136, 166, 183; notes about, 167–72; pride in, 117; regard for, 119; Spanglish and, 166, 167, 171, 172–75, 176, 177–78, 178–79; speaking, 122–23, 186; varieties in, 19, 22, 178; zone of encuentro for, 166

New Mexico Colorado Spanish Survey (NMCOSS), 18, 37, 38–39, 107, 170

New Mexico Highlands University, 36, 45, 46
"New Mexico Is Losing a Form of Spanish Spoken Nowhere Else on Earth" (Romero), 165
New Mexico Spanish-English Bilingual Corps (NMSEB), 19
New World Spanish (NWS), 18
New York Times, 165, 166, 182, 183, 186
Nieto-Phillips, John, 8, 160
NMCOSS. *See* New Mexico Colorado Spanish Survey
Northern New Mexican Spanish, 22, 23
Northern New Mexico, map of, 32 fig. 1
Nuevo México, recontact inside/outside of, 54–57
Nuevomexicanidad: claiming, 7–12; Mexicanidad and, 83
Nuevomexicano, term, 9, 10
Nuevomexicano/a/x (NMX), 2, 20, 42, 50; population, 31; term, 7
Nuevomexicanos, 21; agency of, 9; land and, 10, 12; Mexicanos and, 4, 12; primos and, 80n60; roots of, 8, 16; Spanish ancestry of, 8, 11
Nuevomexicanos/as/xs, 10, 11, 17, 19, 24, 28, 59; ethnolinguistic futures of, 187; home and, 5; knowledge production and, 29; linguistic deterritorialization of, 84; Mexicanos/as/xs and, 3, 14, 15, 25, 34, 83; sociohistorical linguistic legacy of, 31; Spanish abilities of, 64–65
NWS. *See* New World Spanish

Oboler, Suzanne, 156; "Hispanic" and, 159, 160; homogenization and, 159
Ochoa, Gilda L., 16, 55, 55n7
"Of Bloodlines and Conquistadors" (Hinojosa), 163
oppression, linguistic, 43, 60, 81, 134, 155
Ortiz, Don Gaspar, 14
Ortiz, Leroy, 90, 97, 106, 107
Osuna, Steven, 17
Otheguy, Ricardo, 87n1, 166n7, 170
Our Lady of Guadalupe, 3, 4, 34; homeplaces and, 5
outer sphere, inner sphere and, 137

Parada, MaryAnn, 97

Paredez, Deborah, 82
participants, zone, 35–36
Pelaez López, Alan, 2n6
Pennycook, Alastair, 23; critical applied linguistics and, 30; transcultural flows and, 82, 141, 149; transnational flows and, 110
Pérez, Gina M., 2n6, 17
placemaking, Latinidad and, 28–29
pláticas, 6, 36, 37, 40, 50; Chicana feminist, 39; methodology, 38
positionalities, 143, 156; hegemonic, 141–42
Potowski, Kim, 18, 21, 37, 97, 102, 106, 106n48, 181
power, 141; authenticity and, 129; coloniality of, 138; language and, 113, 116, 128, 129
Pratt, Mary Louise, 24, 25, 56, 105
prescriptivism, 123
proficiency, perceiving, 64–67
Puerto Ricans, 17, 118
Pugach, Marleen, 190–91

Quechua, Spanish and, 98
querencias, 9, 12; linguistic, 43, 52, 167, 186–87
Quijano, Anibal, 138
Quintana, Ana, 4, 4n9, 48, 63, 64, 69, 146; comprehension and, 65; cultural identity and, 152; Spanish use and, 72
Quintana, José Luis, 48, 64–65, 68, 71–72, 146, 171; archaisms and, 168; code-switching and, 84n70
Quintana, Rolando, 48, 92, 93, 94, 106, 162–63, 174, 175n32; cultural identity and, 152; on "Hispanic," 162; language socialization practices and, 91; on New Mexican Spanish, 173, 175; Spanish use and, 102; on speaking Spanish, 174–75

racism, epistemological, 44
Ramirez, Catherine, 15, 75
Ramos-Zaya, Ana Y., 30
raza, term, 7
reacquisition, 71–74, 75, 88
recontact, 54, 55; benefits of, 109; broad interpretation of, 54n2; communal, 71–74; cultural, 51; dynamics of, 56; gauging, 67–71; inside/outside Nuevo México, 54–57; Latinidad and, 56; linguistic, 51; process of, 69, 85, 88; reterritorialization

and, 83–85; study of, 58; transculturative dimension of, 74–82, 83, 84
recovery, 52, 79, 108; acts of, 97–106
resemantification, 156
reterritorialization, 51, 54; recontact and, 83–85
revitalization, 74; idea of, 55; linguistic, 187
Rio Grande Valley, bilingualism in, 181
Rivera-Mills, Susana, 16, 20, 35, 51, 55, 61, 67, 87, 103, 109; "contact generation" model and, 20n86; linguistic profiles and, 58–59; reacquisition generation and, 71, 75
Roberts, Shelly, 9, 90, 91, 97
Rodríguez-Ordóñez, Itzaso, 181
Romaine, Suzanne, 153
Romance of a Little Village Girl (Jaramillo), 14
Romero, Simon, 165
Rosaldo, Renato, 44
Roybal, Karen, 79, 188
Rúa, Mérida, 17, 26, 30, 118; colando-ing and, 161; on data analysis, 40–41
Rubin, Herbert J., 37
Rubin, Irene S., 37

Saavedra, Cynthia M., 39
Sacred Seeds (Jaramillo), 15
Salgado, Casandra, 8
sameness: difference and, 141; horizontal and, 143
Sánchez, Maite C., 92, 150, 169
Sandoval-Sánchez, Alberto, 26, 119
Santa Fe City Council, 190
Santa Fe New Mexican, 3, 189
Santa Fe Plaza, 190
Santos, Carolina, 47–48, 96, 97, 102, 110, 124, 125, 129, 133, 145, 175; on correctness, 127; Hispanic identity and, 146; language shift and, 103; Mexican Spanish and, 128; Mexicana Hispana and, 158; Mexicana identity, 158; Spanglish and, 179; Spanish use and, 103–4
Santos, Edna, 47, 96, 97, 109, 127–28, 129, 133, 160, 173, 174; English use and, 102; "Hispanic" and, 151; on identification, 157–58; language shift and, 103; loanwords and, 169; Mexican Spanish and, 128; Mexicana

and, 158; socialization of, 102; Spanglish and, 178; Spanish use and, 102–3, 104
Santos, Juan, 47, 60, 62, 70, 78n54, 80; agency of, 61; English and, 70n38; Marta and, 128–29; Mexican Spanish and, 77, 78
Santos, Marta, 47, 78n54; English and, 70n38; Juan and, 128–29; Mexican Spanish and, 77, 78; Mexicanidad and, 78; struggle of borders and, 78
Sanz-Sánchez, Israel, 19
Schecter, Sandra R., 17, 24, 37, 88, 99, 103, 105; language choice and, 93; on language maintenance/shift, 98; language socialization and, 91, 109; linguistic abilities and, 110; on patterns of variation/choice, 101
semilingualism, 170
setting, zone, 31–35
shame, 62, 177; embarrassment and, 131
shift/loss category, 59, 60, 64
Silva-Corvalán, Carmen, 35, 58
Silverstein, Michael, 6, 114
SLI. *See* standard language ideology
slippages, 113, 120, 121–22, 124, 137
social distinctions, 116, 131
social practices, 18, 126
socioeconomic status, language retention and, 89
sociolinguistics, 6, 29, 30, 36, 50, 171
solidarity, 2n6, 3, 16, 25, 29, 44, 142; linguistic, 79, 122
Somos Primos, 15, 80n60, 136
Somos un Pueblo Unido, 15, 16
Spanglish, 41, 84n70, 148, 150, 151, 173n30; analysis of, 167; defined, 166n7; disparaging opinions about, 170–71; diversity of, 181; English and, 166; future of, 175–79; intergenerational transmission of, 179–82; loanwords/calques and, 174; maintaining, 73; multiple versions of, 180, 182; New Mexican Spanish and, 166, 167, 171, 172–75, 176, 177–78, 178–79; notes about, 167–72; in popular culture, 176; practice of, 154; reality of, 155; rejection of, 150; Spanish-based, 182; speaking, 154, 171, 178–79; term, 166, 166n7; Tex-Mex and, 173n30, 181; translanguaging practice of, 169, 171
Spanglish (Stavan), 175

Spanglish bashing, 117, 167, 175
Spanish: affirmations, 137–40; archaic, 167; being/doing Latinx in, 156; contextualizing study of, 18–21; dialects, 56, 77; English and, 156, 169; intergenerational persistence of, 61, 67, 73–74, 104, 109; Latina/o identity and, 27; lazy, 174; linguistic value of, 67; multiple versions of, 137; New Mexican changes to, 112–13; Quechua and, 98; revitalizing, 55; speaking, 70, 99, 101, 102–3, 104, 105, 106, 107, 108, 109, 171, 172; term, 7, 10; value of, 181; varieties, 43, 51, 114, 167
Spanish Americans, Mexicans and, 13
standard language ideology (SLI), 125–26, 134
Stavans, Ilan, 175
Stern, Nancy, 166n7
subordination, 44, 121, 125, 143
Sue, Christina A., 16
symbolic associations, 109–11

Taylor, Diana, 74, 75, 79
Telles, Edward, 16
"Tensions among Hispanic Groups Erupt in Schools" (*Albuquerque Journal*), 1
terrorism, linguistic, 60, 137, 155
Tex-Mex, Spanglish and, 173n80, 181
TNMS. *See* Traditional New Mexican Spanish
Torres, Larry, 166, 186
Torres Cacoullos, Rena, 19, 21
Traditional New Mexican Spanish (TNMS), 19, 165, 176, 187; archaisms of, 167; described, 167–68; disappearance of, 20, 172; key features of, 21–23
Traditional Southwest Spanish, 19
Traditional Spanish, 19, 107, 178
Train, Richard, 5, 6
transcultural flows, 82, 110, 141, 149, 160
transculturation, 51, 56, 74, 79, 83, 180
transformation, 80, 141, 143, 144, 184, 185; spaces of, 43
translanguaging, 38, 41, 43, 150, 180, 185; code-switching and, 169; defining, 148n31; notes about, 167–72; practices, 52, 148, 186, 187
Travis, Catherine, 19, 20, 182
tropicalization, 75
Trujillo, Michael, 7

Unión Protectiva, 189
Urciuoli, Bonnie, 137, 151, 152, 152n40, 158
US Census, 2, 33; population figures from, 34 table 1
US Mexican Spanish (USMS), 19

Valdés, Guadalupe, 44, 93, 131–32; bilingual continuum and, 92; minority languages and, 73
Valdez, Elena, 13
Valenzuela, Norma, 12
Vázquez, Jessica, 16
Vega, Luis A., 55, 87
Veltman, Calvin, 58
"Viaje por Nuevo Mexico" (Millán), 13
Vigil, Neddie, 18, 19, 20, 21, 21n92, 32, 33, 56, 107, 167, 168, 178, 182; anglicisms and, 170; TNMS and, 172
Vigil, Virgil, 189
Vila, Pablo, 10, 16, 145
Villa, Daniel, 19, 20, 35, 50, 61, 67, 109, 182; "contact generation" model, 20n86; linguistic profiles and, 58–59; reacquisition generation and, 71, 75
Villarreal, Aimee, 5, 189, 190
Virgen de Guadalupe, 3, 34–35; homecoming of, 4

Walsh, Catherine, 136
Waltermire, Mark, 20, 22, 23, 56, 57, 76, 166, 172, 178, 182, 183; research by, 55
Webber, Alan, 189
Wilson, Vergara Damián, 21, 22, 167
Woolard, Kathryn A., 114, 130

Yin, Robert, 37

Zentella, Ana Celia, 30, 44, 134, 137, 170, 181, 190; anthropological linguistics of, 27; on bilinguals, 103; chiquitafication and, 66–67, 67n34, 74; code-switching and, 175; linguistic portraits and, 138; Spanglish bashing and, 167, 175
zone, term, 24

GLOBAL LATIN/O AMERICAS

FREDERICK LUIS ALDAMA AND LOURDES TORRES, SERIES EDITORS

This series focuses on the Latino experience in its totality as set within a global dimension. The series showcases the variety and vitality of the presence and significant influence of Latinos in the shaping of the culture, history, politics and policies, and language of the Americas—and beyond. It welcomes scholarship regarding the arts, literature, philosophy, popular culture, history, politics, law, history, and language studies, among others.

Zones of Encuentro: Language and Identities in Northern New Mexico
LILLIAN GORMAN

Sanctuary: Exclusion, Violence, and Indigenous Migrants in the East Bay
CRUZ MEDINA

Everyday Dirty Work: Invisibility, Communication, and Immigrant Labor
WILFREDO ALVAREZ

Building Confianza: Empowering Latinos/as Through Transcultural Health Care Communication
DALIA MAGAÑA

Fictions of Migration: Narratives of Displacement in Peru and Bolivia
LORENA CUYA GAVILANO

Baseball as Mediated Latinidad: Race, Masculinity, Nationalism, and Performances of Identity
JENNIFER DOMINO RUDOLPH

False Documents: Inter-American Cultural History, Literature, and the Lost Decade (1975–1992)
FRANS WEISER

Public Negotiations: Gender and Journalism in Contemporary US Latina/o Literature
ARIANA E. VIGIL

Democracy on the Wall: Street Art of the Post-Dictatorship Era in Chile
GUISELA LATORRE

Gothic Geoculture: Nineteenth-Century Representations of Cuba in the Transamerican Imaginary
IVONNE M. GARCÍA

Affective Intellectuals and the Space of Catastrophe in the Americas
JUDITH SIERRA-RIVERA

Spanish Perspectives on Chicano Literature: Literary and Cultural Essays
EDITED BY JESÚS ROSALES AND VANESSA FONSECA

Sponsored Migration: The State and Puerto Rican Postwar Migration to the United States
EDGARDO MELÉNDEZ

La Verdad: An International Dialogue on Hip Hop Latinidades
EDITED BY MELISSA CASTILLO-GARSOW AND JASON NICHOLS